W9-BBX-609

Psychiatric Diagnosis

Psychiatric Diagnosis

Second Edition

DONALD W. GOODWIN, M.D.
Professor and Chairman
Department of Psychiatry
University of Kansas School of Medicine

SAMUEL B. GUZE, M.D.
Spencer T. Olin Professor of Psychiatry
and Head of the Department,
Vice Chancellor for Medical Affairs
Washington University School of Medicine

New York / Oxford
OXFORD UNIVERSITY PRESS
1979

Library of Congress Cataloging in Publication Data

Goodwin, Donald W
Psychiatric diagnosis.
First ed. (1974) by R. A. Woodruff, D. W. Goodwin, and S. B. Guze.
Includes bibliographies and index.
1. Psychology, Pathological–Classification.
2. Mental illness–Diagnosis. I. Guze, Samuel B., joint author. II. Woodruff, Robert A. Psychiatric diagnosis. III. Title. [DNLM: 1. Mental disorders. WM100.3 G656p] RC455.2.C4W67 1979 616.8'9 78-9926
ISBN 0-19-502512-1 ISBN 0-19-502513-X pbk.

Printed in the United States of America

To Eli Robins and the late Robert A. Woodruff, Jr.

Preface to the Second Edition

The first edition of *Psychiatric Diagnosis* was dedicated to our friend and mentor, Eli Robins. The second edition is also dedicated to the late Robert Woodruff. A friend, colleague, and coauthor of the first edition, Doctor Woodruff contributed immeasurably to the book's success. His industry, intelligence, patience, and good humor were sorely missed in preparing the present revision. His untimely death in 1976 made the chore of revision, among other things, a sad one.

Still, revision was necessary. In the five or six years since *Psychiatric Diagnosis* was written, knowledge in psychiatry *has* expanded, despite much gloomy talk about the vicissitudes—fiscal and otherwise—of doing psychiatric research.

Along with updating where updating seemed justified, we have hewed to our original goal: to provide a concise compendium of current knowledge in psychiatry, with abundant citations, not much theory, and as little personal opinion as we could get by with.

A word of apology for the preface to the first edition, which is left intact. The Gertrude Stein quotation has become a dreadful cliché, but after much grappling with it, we could not find a replacement. Another reason to miss Bob Woodruff: assuredly, he would have found one.

Kansas City
January 1979

D.W.G.

Preface to the [illegible] Edition

Preface to the First Edition

A rose is a rose is a rose
GERTRUDE STEIN

Because it remains a rose.

Classification has two functions: communication and prediction. A rose can be defined precisely. It has pinnate leaves, belongs to the rose family, and so forth. When you say "rose" to a person who knows something about the definition, communication results.

A rose also has a predictable life history: it stays a rose. If it changes into a chrysanthemum, it may not have been a rose in the first place. If roses routinely change into chrysanthemums, like caterpillers into butterflies, well and good. Natural history may include metamorphoses but they must be routine to be "natural."

Classification in medicine is called diagnosis, and this book is about diagnosis of psychiatric conditions. Diagnostic categories—diseases, illnesses, syndromes—are included if they have been sufficiently studied to be useful. Like roses, they can be defined explicitly and have a more or less predictable course.

In choosing these categories, the guiding rule was: *diagnosis is prognosis*. There are many diagnostic categories in psychiatry, but few are based on a clinical literature where the conditions are defined by explicit criteria and follow-up studies provide a guide to prognosis. Lacking these features, such categories resemble what sociologists call labeling. Two examples are "passive-aggressive personality" and "emotionally unstable personality," which, like most personality diagnoses, have been inadequately studied for us to know whether they are useful or not.

Not every patient can be diagnosed by using the categories in this book. For them, "undiagnosed" is, we feel, more appropriate than a label incorrectly implying more knowledge than exists.

Terms like "functional" and "psychogenic" and "situational reaction" are sometimes invoked by physicians to explain the unexplained. They usually mean "I don't know," and we try to avoid them.

Because classification in psychiatry is still at a primitive stage, there are reasonable grounds for questioning our choice of categories. In general, we lump rather than split. Hence we have two affective disorders—primary and secondary—rather than the half-dozen affective disorders cited in the official nomenclature. Schizophrenia is divided into "good prognosis" and "bad prognosis" schizophrenia rather than sliced more finely, as some prefer. Our justification for this is "the literature," meaning primarily follow-up studies.

"The follow-up is the great exposer of truth, the rock on which many fine theories are wrecked and upon which better ones can be built," wrote P. D. Scott. "It is to the psychiatrist what the post-mortem is to the physician." Not all such studies are perfect, but we feel they are better than no studies. And inevitably there are instances where our "clinical judgment" has prevailed in evaluating the merit of individual studies. No text in psychiatry could be written today without a certain amount of this, but we have tried to limit personal opinion to a minimum. Many if not most assertions have a citation, and the reader can check the references to form his own judgment.

When the term "disease" is used, this is what is meant: a disease is a cluster of symptoms and/or signs with a more or less predictable course. Symptoms are what patients tell you; signs are what you see. The cluster may be associated with physical abnormality or may not. The essential point is that it results in consultation with a physician who specializes in recognizing, preventing, and, sometimes, curing diseases.

It is hard for many people to think of psychiatric problems as diseases. For one thing, psychiatric problems usually consist of symptoms—complaints about thoughts and feelings—or behavior disturbing to others. Rarely are there signs—a fever, a rash. Almost never are there laboratory tests to confirm the diagnosis. What people say changes from time to time, as does behavior. It is usually harder to agree about symptoms than about signs. But whatever the psychiatric problems are, they have this in common with "real" diseases—they result in consultation with a physician and are associated with pain, suffering, disability, and death.

Whether homosexuality, for example, is a disease like measles is not the issue. Homosexuals see psychiatrists, occasionally for homosexuality. Homosexuality can be defined precisely and has a "natural history." It is included as a diagnostic category because it leads to psychiatric consultation, meets the criteria for a useful category, and—as long as this persists—is a subject physicians should know something about.

Another objection to the disease or medical "model" arises from a misconception about disease. Disease often is equated with physical abnormality. In fact, a disease is a category used by physicians, as "apples" is a category used by grocers. It is a useful category if precise and if the encompassed phenomena are stable over time. Diseases are conventions and may not "fit" anything in nature at all. Through the centuries, diseases have come and gone, some more useful than others, and there is no guarantee that our present "diseases"—medical or psychiatric—will represent the same clusters of symptoms and signs a hundred years from now that they do today. On the contrary, as more is learned, more useful clusters surely will emerge.

There are few explanations in this book. This is because for most psychiatric conditions there *are* no explanations. "Etiology unknown" is the hallmark of psychiatry as well as its bane. Historically, once etiology is known, a disease stops being "psychiatric." Vitamins were discovered, whereupon vitamin-deficiency psychiatric disorders no longer were treated by psychiatrists. The spirochete was found, then penicillin, and neurosyphilis, once a major psychiatric disorder, became one more infection treated by nonpsychiatrists.

Little, however, is really known about most medical illnesses.

Even infectious diseases remain puzzles in that some infected individuals have symptoms and others do not.

People continue to speculate about etiology, of course, and this is good if it produees testable hypotheses, and bad if speculation is mistaken for truth. In this book, speculation largely is avoided, since it is available so plentifully elsewhere.

A final word about this approach to psychiatry. It is sometimes called "organic." This is misleading. A better term, perhaps, is agnostic. Without evidence, we do not believe pills are better than words. Without evidence, we do not believe chemistry is more important than upbringing. Without evidence, we withhold judgment.

More arguments for this point of view can be found in Appendix A. But advocacy is not the purpose of the book. Rather, we hope it will be useful in applying current knowledge to those vexatious problems—crudely defined and poorly understood—that come within the jurisdiction of psychiatry.

St. Louis
December 1973

D.W.G.

Contents

Psychiatric Diagnosis

1. Affective Disorders

Definition

. . . There is a pitch of unhappiness so great that the goods of nature may be entirely forgotten, and all sentiment of their existence vanish from the mental field. For this extremity of pessimism to be reached, something more is needed than observation of life and reflection upon death. The individual must in his own person become the prey of pathological melancholy. . . . Such sensitiveness and susceptibility to mental pain is a rare occurrence where the nervous constitution is entirely normal; one seldom finds it in a healthy subject even where he is the victim of the most atrocious cruelties of outward fortune . . . it is positive and active anguish, a sort of psychical neuralgia wholly unknown to healthy life.

WILLIAM JAMES (27)

Depression and euphoria are not the only symptoms of affective disorders. Associated with low moods are such symptoms as insomnia, anorexia, suicidal thoughts, and feelings of worthlessness or of being a burden to others; with euphoria, such symptoms as hyperactivity and flight of ideas appear. The extent of depression or euphoria is often inappropriate to the patient's life situation, a fact sometimes as obvious to the patient as to his relatives and friends.

Primary affective disorder occurs in individuals who have had no previous psychiatric disorder or else only episodes of depression or mania. Secondary affective disorder occurs in patients with a preexisting psychiatric illness other than depression or mania. Affective disorder is defined as bipolar when mania occurs, whether depressions occur or not. Unipolar affective disorder involves depressions alone (25, 48, 71).

Historical Background

Descriptions of affective disorder began with Hippocrates. The term melancholia is usually attributed to him, as is the notion that it results from the influence of black bile and phlegm on the brain, "darkening the spirit and making it melancholy . . ." (35).

About five hundred years later, early in the second century A.D., Aretaeus of Cappadocia recognized and recorded an association between melancholia and mania: "Those affected with melancholia are not everyone of them affected according to one particular form; they are either suspicious of poisoning or flee to the desert from misanthropy, or turn superstitious, or contract a hatred of life. If at any time a relaxation takes place, in most cases hilarity supervenes . . . the patients are dull or stern, dejected or unreasonably torpid, without any manifest cause . . . they also become peevish, dispirited, sleepless, and start up from a disturbed sleep. Unreasonable fear also seizes them, if the disease tends to increase . . . they complain of life, and desire to die" (31). Aretaeus observed that affective disorder was often episodic but also occurred in a chronic, unremitting form. Like Hippocrates, he attributed the cause to a humoral imbalance: "If it [black bile] be determined upwards to the stomach and diaphragm, it forms melancholy, for it produces flatulence and eructations of the fetid and fishy nature, and it sends rumbling wind downwards and disturbs the understanding" (35).

The 19th-century French physician Falret described an episodic variety of depression with remissions and attacks of increasing duration, an illness occurring more frequently among women than men, sometimes associated with precipitating events, sometimes alternating with mania (la folie circulaire). Falret and his contemporary Baillarger (who also described recurring attacks of mania and melancholia) probably influenced Kraepelin's later concept of manic depressive psychosis.

In 1896, Kraepelin made his major contribution to psychiatry by separating the functional psychoses into two groups, dementia praecox and manic depressive psychosis. Dementia praecox was chronic and unremitting with a generally bad prognosis. Manic depressive psychosis, on the other hand, did not usually end in chronic invalidism. After publishing the sixth edition of his textbook in 1896, Kraepelin continued to define the limits of dementia praecox narrowly, but expanded those of manic depressive psychosis to include almost all abnormalities of mood. Patients with chronic depressions were included as well as those with episodic illness, manics as well as depressives (34, 65).

Kraepelin had insisted that manic depressive psychosis was generally independent of social and psychological forces, that the cause of the illness was "innate." Freud and the psychoanalysts assumed the opposite. Freud in *Mourning and Melancholia*, published in 1917, outlined his theories of the psychodynamic genesis of depression (20). He hypothesized that depression had in common with the process of mourning a response to the loss of a "love-object," that is, the loss of something greatly valued. Grief, a healthy response, differed from melancholia in that the latter involved *intense* expression of ambivalent, hostile feelings, formerly associated with the object. Upon loss of the loved person or thing, these unresolved, negative feelings were directed inward, resulting in despair, a sense of worthlessness, thoughts of self-harm, and other depressive symptoms.

Since the second decade of the 20th century there has been considerable controversy over the distinction between "endogenous" depression and "reactive" depression. This controversy had its origin partially in the differing viewpoints of the Kraepelinians and Freudians toward mental phenomena in general. Kraepelin and his followers searched for the limits of pathological behavior by describing the symptoms of syndromes in keeping with the traditions of 19th-century German medicine. Freud and his pupils searched for mental mechanisms which might be most obvious in pathological states but were not limited to those states. Such differences in attitude were augmented by the fact that Kraepelinian psychiatrists dealt chiefly with severely ill, hospitalized patients while Freudian psychiatrists tended to treat mildly ill, nonhospitalized patients. The differences have never been fully resolved. There has been classification after classification of the affective disorders, most frequently in terms of dichotomies: endogenous opposed to reactive, psychotic opposed to neurotic, agitated opposed to retarded.

A large part of the 20th-century literature on affective disorders assumes tacitly that two basic forms of depression do exist. The terms reactive and neurotic have often been equated, as have endogenous and psychotic. It has been assumed that depressions of the former type are milder, that they are more often a direct result of precipitating events or unique individual responses to social and psychological stress, and, more recently, that they are less responsive to somatic therapy. However, controversy persists about the validity of this distinction. An alternative which avoids inference about cause is the classification of affective disorders as *primary* or *secondary* (see Definition).

Reactive and endogenous depressions may be classified as either primary or secondary affective disorders. Patients with mild or severe depressions, with or without "psychotic" symptoms such as hallucinations or delusions, with many episodes or with few, and regardless of age of onset, may be diagnosed as having either primary or secondary affective disorder.

Reports have been published in the last decade indicating that primary affective disorder should be divided into bipolar and unipolar forms (10, 23, 42, 65). (One's initial impression of the terms bipolar and unipolar is that bipolar patients have had both mania and depression while unipolar patients have had either one or the other alone. "Bipolar" actually refers to patients with mania, whether or not they have also had depressions. "Unipolar" refers to patients who have had depression alone.) Patients with bipolar illness have a somewhat earlier age of onset than unipolar patients. Their histories are characterized by more frequent and shorter episodes, even when depression is considered alone. There is a greater prevalence of affective disorder among relatives of bipolar patients than among relatives of unipolar patients.

Many of the questions about affective disorders which have plagued investigators are still unresolved. At present there is no way to evaluate the importance of precipitating events in either bipolar or unipolar illness. There have been preliminary efforts to divide unipolar primary affective disorder into early onset and late onset forms (65), but as yet no generally accepted subclassification of unipolar illness exists. An abiding problem is the old question of how to separate the experience of bereavement from that of depression.

Epidemiology

Estimates of the prevalence of primary affective disorder depend on the sample or population studied and on the definition of the illness. There have been studies of large groups of patients selected from isolated areas: Iceland (26), and the Danish islands of Bornholm (19) and Samso (55). According to these studies, at least 5 percent of men and 9 percent of women can expect to have primary affective disorder at some time during their lives. A higher estimate has been made for an American urban community: a lifetime expectancy rate for definite major depressions, with sexes combined, of 18 percent (63). This suggests that affective disorders could be the most common psychiatric conditions.

These figures are high by comparison with other estimates, but the latter have varied so widely that it is difficult to know whose data are most reliable (55). Many clinicians believe that the prevalence of affective disorders in the general population has been underestimated. Many private psychiatric hospitals report that primary affective disorder is the problem for which patients are most frequently admitted. The same is true of many psychiatric clinics.

A recent study suggests that, whatever the chief diagnosis, depression is a common reason for psychiatric consultation. Among patients with anxiety neurosis in one study, for example, half presented with a secondary depression (70). Secondary depression is also frequently the reason for psychiatric consultation among alcoholics, hysterics, and other patients who come to a psychiatric clinic (25, 68, 69).

Primary affective disorder is more common in women than men (66).

Studies of hospitalized patients early in the 20th century indicated that 30 to 50 percent of patients with manic depressive psychosis had either mania or a history of previous mania. The fact that bipolar illness is so disruptive, however, increases the likelihood of hospitalization. Experience with both inpatients and outpatients suggests that approximately one in ten affectively disordered patients is bipolar, but even this may be an overestimate of the prevalence of bipolar illness.

It is not clear whether primary affective disorder is distributed evenly throughout the population or is clustered within higher socioeconomic groups. A link between bipolar affective disorder and above average occupational or educational achievement has been suggested (72). Some studies raise the possibility that primary affective disorder especially affects socially striving individuals who feel great need for social success and approval (7, 16, 21, 26).

Clinical Picture

Plutarch described a melancholic man as follows: "He looks on himself as a man whom the gods hate and pursue with their anger. A far worse lot is before him; he dares not employ any means of averting or remedying the evil, least he be found fighting against the gods. The physician, the consoling friend, are driven away. 'Leave me,' says the wretched man, 'me, the impious, the accursed, hated of the gods, to suffer my punishment.' He sits out of doors, wrapped in sackcloth or in filthy rags. Ever and anon he rolls himself, naked, in the dirt confessing about this and that sin. He has eaten or drunk something wrong. He has gone some way or other which the Divine Being did not approve of. The festivals in honor of the gods give no pleasure to him but fill him rather with fear . . ." (6).

The symptoms of primary and secondary affective disorder are the same except for those of pre-existing illness in the latter group (71).

The chief complaints of patients with primary affective disorder are usually psychological: feelings of worthlessness, despair, or ideas of self-harm. But it is also common for depressed patients to complain chiefly of pains, tachycardia, breathing difficulty, gastrointestinal dysfunction, headache, or other somatic disturbances (11).

The dysphoric mood experienced by patients with depressive illness is usually characterized as sadness or despondency, but some patients describe themselves as feeling hopeless, irritable, fearful, worried, or simply discouraged. Occasionally a patient will present with what seems to be primary affective disorder, though he reports minimal feelings of dysphoria. Such patients may complain of insomnia and anorexia. They may even cry profusely while telling the examining physician that they do not feel sad. These patients are unusual, but not unknown to psychiatrists.

Other characteristic symptoms of depression are anorexia with weight loss; insomnia; early morning awakening; loss of energy, described as general tiredness or fatigability; agitation, or its opposite, psychomotor retardation; loss of interest in usual activities, including loss of interest in sex; feelings of self-reproach or guilt which may be delusional in intensity; inability to focus one's thoughts, often with a simultaneous awareness of slowed thinking; and, recurrent thoughts of death or suicide. The range of symptoms which can occur with either primary or secondary affective disorder is illustrated in Table 1.

It is common for patients with primary affective disorder to say that "something is wrong with my mind." Patients will often tell their physician that they fear they are losing their mind or have a sense of emotions out of control. It is also common for depressed patients to have a low expectancy of recovery. Such a pessimistic outlook should serve as a warning that the patient may be de-

Table 1. Comparative prevalences of depressive symptoms in primary and secondary affective disorders

Symptoms from the current episode of illness	*Primary* (N = 54) %	*Secondary* (N = 18) %
1. Patient has felt sad	93	95
2. Cried a lot	50	61
3. Future gloomy	61	67
4. Mood worse in morning	33	28
5. Mood worse in evening	13	17
6. Feelings of self-reproach	59	56
7. Feeling illness brought on self, or is punishment	33	22
8. Feelings of persecution	7	0
9. Feelings of worthlessness	74	78
10. Feelings of hopelessness	61	67
11. Feelings of social incapacity	78	61
12. Feelings of guilt, non-delusional	24	33
13. Delusions of guilt	4	0
14. Loss of interests	89	83
15. Increased morbid interests	19	28
16. Slowed thinking	69	56
17. Poor concentration	93	95
18. Indecision	59	50
19. Suicidal ideas	41	56
20. Suicidal attempts	11	22
21. Apprehensiveness	30	28
22. Foreboding	26	17
23. Concern with body and/or fear of cancer	22	44
24. Irritability	67	83
25. Restlessness	59	56
26. Pacing and/or hand-wringing	46	28
27. Muscular tension	61	61
28. Slowed down physically	48	28
29. Tired all the time	57	83
30. Tired on arising, better later	31	44
31. Initial insomnia	59	67
32. Middle insomnia	46	83
33. Terminal insomnia	61	61
34. Anorexia	87	100
35. Weight loss of 3 or more pounds	78	78
36. Weight gain of 5 or more pounds	7	6
37. Impotence (males only)	23	50
38. Diminished sexual interest and/or activity	50	56
39. Constipation	28	17

Table 1.—*Continued*

Symptoms from the current episode of illness	*Primary* (N = 54) %	*Secondary* (N = 18) %
40. Anxiety attacks	15	11
41. Somatic symptoms nausea or vomiting, abdominal pain, diarrhea, headache, eye complaints, palpitations, smothering, anxiety attacks.	74	72
42. Depersonalization and/or derealization	4	6
43. Feeling that this illness represents a definite change—not old self at all	72	28†

† Significant at P > 0.005
From Woodruff *et al.* (71)

pressed. Medically ill patients seldom give up all hope of improvement, even if seriously ill.

In some depressed patients agitation is so overwhelming that other symptoms go almost unnoticed. These patients are brought to physicians when they are found by relatives or friends pacing, wringing their hands, bemoaning their fate, clinging to anyone who will listen. They ask for reassurance, they beg for help, yet nothing satisfies them.

In other patients retardation is prominent. Marked slowing of both thought and motor behavior occurs. Tasks that once took minutes may require hours. These patients may be so slowed that it is painful to listen to their conversation. Psychomotor retardation can be so severe that a patient becomes mute or even stuporous.

Paranoid symptoms can occur among patients with primary affective disorder. They are usually exaggerated ideas of reference associated with notions of worthlessness. Characteristic delusions of patients with depression are those of a hypochondriacal or nihilistic type. Some severely ill depressives seem to feel they are so guilty and evil that they have become the focus of universal abhorrence, or even that the world is disintegrating because of their terrible inadequacies and failures.

Depressed patients may or may not mention events which they consider important in producing their illness. When a precipitating event is described, it is sometimes surprisingly trivial, difficult for the examining physician to take seriously. Furthermore, critical evaluation of the chronology of a depressed patient's symptoms may reveal that some symptoms actually began before the so-called precipitating event (11). This suggests that some patients who begin to feel depressed search for reasons to explain their depression, unable or unwilling to believe they could feel as they do for no apparent reason.

On the other hand, the stressful events women most frequently mention as precipitants of depression are apparently pregnancy and childbirth. In one series 37 percent of female bipolars and 17 percent of female unipolars had their first episode of depression during pregnancy or postpartum (28).

A change in drinking habits often accompanies depressive illness (11). Middle-aged patients who begin to drink heavily and do not have a previous history of alcoholism may be suffering from depression. On the other hand, some patients drink less than usual when depressed.

Price (44) has written movingly about the "existential position" of the severely depressed patient:

> Firstly, it is very unpleasant: depressive illness is probably more unpleasant than any disease except rabies. There is constant mental pain and often psychogenic physical pain too. If one tries to get such a patient to titrate other pains against the pain of his depression one tends to end up with a description that would raise eyebrows even in a medieval torture chamber. Naturally, many of these patients commit suicide. They may not hope to get to heaven but they know they are leaving hell. Secondly, the patient is isolated from family and friends, because the depression itself reduces his affection for others and he may well have ideas that he is unworthy of their love or even that his friendship may harm them. Thirdly, he is rejected by others because they cannot stand the sight of his suffering. There is a limit to sympathy. Even psychiatrists have protective mechanisms for dealing with

such cases: the consultant may refer the patient to the registrar's follow-up clinic; he may allow too brief a consultation to elicit the extent of the patient's suffering; he may, on the grounds that the depression has not responded to treatment, alter his diagnosis to one of personality disorder—comforting, because of the strange but widespread belief that patients with personality disorders do not suffer. Fourthly, and finally, the patient tends to do a great cover-up. Because of his outward depression he is socially unacceptable, and because of his inward depression he feels even more socially unacceptable than he really is. He does not, therefore, tell others how bad he feels. Most depressives, even severe ones, can cope with routine work—initiative and leadership are what they lack. Nevertheless, many of them can continue working, functioning at a fairly low level, and their deficiencies are often covered up by colleagues. Provided some minimal degree of social and vocational functioning is present, the world leaves the depressive alone and he battles on for the sake of his god or his children, or for some reason which makes his personal torment preferable to death.

The cardinal features of mania are euphoria, hyperactivity, and flight of ideas. Not all manic patients are euphoric; some are irritable instead. Flight of ideas is a rapid digression from one idea to another. One's response to a manic patient is often that of sympathetic amusement. In fact, experienced clinicians who find themselves amused by a patient immediately consider the possibility that the patient is either manic or hypomanic (mildly manic). Flight of ideas, unlike the incoherence and tangentiality of schizophrenia, is usually understandable, even though some connections between ideas may be tenuous. (Comedians often use a well-controlled flight of ideas to amuse audiences.) Attention is often called to this symptom by a push of speech, that is, speech in which a great deal is said in a short period of time. Such speech may be accompanied by rhyming, punning, and jocular associations.

Mania involves more than euphoria, hyperactivity, and flight of ideas. Symptoms characteristic of schizophrenia also occur: delusions of grandeur, hallucinations, ideas of passivity (delusions that one's mind or body is under the control of an external force), ideas of reference, and derealization or depersonalization (14).

Some patients exhibit depression and mania simultaneously. They may cry while speaking euphorically or show other unusual combinations of symptoms.

Some children have episodes of depression which resemble depression in adulthood: crying, social withdrawal, hypersensitivity, and behavioral problems (43). It is not clear whether such episodes are an early manifestation of primary affective disorder.

There are contradictory opinions in the literature concerning cultural variation of depressive illness, but at least one study indicates that depressive syndromes are similar, when the same method is used to study them, in the United States, Japan, Australia, Czechoslovakia, England, Germany, and Switzerland (73).

Natural History

The natural history of primary affective disorder is variable. The age of risk extends through life. Together with the usual episodic nature of the illness, this distinguishes primary affective disorder from most other psychiatric illnesses.

The mean age of onset of primary affective disorder is approximately forty (66). For bipolar patients, the mean age of onset is in the early thirties (66). Several studies have indicated a significant correlation between family members in age of onset (28).

Some patients experience only one episode of affective disorder without recurrence. Reporting a twenty-year follow-up study of manic depressive patients, Lundquist claimed that two-thirds of depressives and half of manics had only a single attack (36). In a small percentage of patients with primary affective disorder who consult psychiatrists, the illness is chronic (54, 66). These patients, in contrast to most affectively disordered patients, are difficult for physicians to manage. Their illness may be impervious to all forms of therapy.

Between episodes of illness, patients with primary affective disorder usually function well, though there are occasional residual symptoms.

The length of individual episodes is extremely variable, ranging from a few days to many years.

Complications

Primary affective disorder is associated with a high rate of suicide. One review of seventeen studies concerning death in primary affective disorder indicated that the lifetime risk of suicide is about 15 percent (24).

The risk of suicide is not necessarily correlated with the severity of symptoms. An increased risk of suicide is associated with age greater than forty, with being male, and with communication of suicidal intent (49). Folklore that patients who talk of suicide do not commit suicide is untrue. Suicidal communication must be interpreted in light of the diagnosis. The two disorders most frequently associated with suicide are primary affective disorder and alcoholism (49).

Disregarding suicide, patients with primary affective disorder may still have an increased mortality compared with matched members of the general population. In two studies, it was found that depressed men had an increased mortality from physical disease, especially carcinoma (9, 32).

Alcoholism may be a complication of primary affective disorder. This is particularly true when a patient begins to drink heavily in mid or late life, since alcoholism usually begins earlier. Drug abuse may also be a complication of primary affective disorder.

Poor judgment is another complication of primary affective disorder. Manic patients often show poor judgment, going on spending sprees and making impulsive, unrealistic decisions. Depressed patients also make bad decisions. Decisions to leave a job, to move to a different city, or to separate from a spouse sometimes are the result of the restless dissatisfaction associated with depression. Many clinicians advise depressed patients not to make major life decisions until they are clearly in remission.

Studies of psychiatric illness in the postpartum period indicate that bipolar women are more likely to have episodes of depression or mania during the puerperium than at other times in their lives. Having had a postpartum episode of depression, the likelihood that a woman with bipolar illness will have another episode after subsequent pregnancy is high. Female relatives of bipolar women, if they have been ill, are more likely to have had episodes of illness during the puerperium than at other times (5, 47).

There is a significant relationship between unipolar affective disorder and poor academic performance, including college drop-out (39, 64). In one study at a large university, students with a high number of affective symptoms received poorer grades than did others (64). Depressed students were likely to drop courses or leave college.

Family Studies

Primary affective disorder runs in families. Not only is there an increased prevalence of affective disorder among the relatives of index patients but the type of illness tends to run true to form. Bipolar illness is common among relatives of bipolar patients, occurring less frequently among relatives of unipolar patients (42, 66).

Table 2 describes the familial nature of affective disorders. It

Table 2. Parents of patients with affective disorder and of control patients

	Patients with affective disorder (N = 366)		*Control patients* (N = 180)	
Illness	*Mothers* (%)	*Fathers* (%)	*Mothers* (%)	*Fathers* (%)
Alcoholism	1.1	9.5	0	1.7
Neurosis	3.6	1.4	1.1	0
Schizophrenia	0	0.5	0	0
Chronic brain syndrome	0.8	0.5	0.6	0
Affective disorder	22.9	13.6	1.1	2.2

From Winokur and Pitts (67)

shows a much higher prevalence of affective disorder and alcoholism among parents of affectively ill patients than among parents of a matched control group of medical, surgical, and obstetrical patients.

Twin studies indicate a genetic factor in affective disorders (30, 66). If all twin studies are taken together, there is a concordance rate of approximately 75 percent for monozygotic twins, and 20 percent for dizygotic twins.

Earlier twin studies tended to show a higher concordance between monozygotic twins than more recent studies, as shown in a review by Bertelson *et al.* (8). The twin data also suggest that bipolar and unipolar affective illnesses may be two genetically distinct diseases, but the evidence for this is not conclusive (8).

An association between unipolar affective disorder and alcoholism has been proposed by Winokur and his coworkers (59). In a series of publications they have contrasted "pure depressive illness with "depressive spectrum disease." The latter refers to families in which there is a high prevalence of alcoholism and sociopathy among the males and a high prevalence of early onset unipolar affective disorder among the females. A study of daughters of alcoholics raised by adoptive parents compared to daughters of alcoholics raised by their own alcoholic parents revealed that the latter group did indeed have a high prevalence of depression, but that daughters raised by adoptive parents had no more depression than did controls, suggesting that the association of depression with alcoholism in family members may be strongly influenced by environmental factors (22).

Differential Diagnosis

Making the distinction between grief and primary affective disorder can be difficult. However, grief usually does not last as long as an episode of primary affective disorder (12, 13, 15). The majority of bereaved persons experience fewer symptoms than do patients with primary affective disorder. Furthermore, some symptoms common in primary affective disorder are relatively rare among persons experiencing bereavement, notably fear of losing one's mind and thoughts of self-harm (12, 13). If bereavement persists for more than one year, it is likely that the individual has had a pre-existing psychiatric disorder (P. Clayton, personal communication).

Differential diagnosis between anxiety neurosis and primary affective disorder can be difficult because anxiety symptoms occur frequently in primary affective disorder, and depressive symptoms occur frequently among anxiety neurotics. The distinction depends chiefly upon chronology. If anxiety symptoms antedate the depressive symptoms, the diagnosis is anxiety neurosis. If depressive symptoms appeared first, the diagnosis is primary affective disorder. Anxiety neurosis almost always begins relatively early in life. One should be cautious about diagnosing anxiety neurosis with secondary affective disorder when illness begins in mid or late life (70).

Patients with primary affective disorder often report somatic symptoms, and hysterics often report affective symptoms. If depressive and anxiety symptoms predominate, the diagnosis of hysteria should be made with caution, particularly if the illness did not occur until the patient was thirty or older. Though patients with primary affective disorder may report many somatic symptoms, these symptoms are seldom spread throughout the system review. Furthermore, conversion symptoms (unexplained neurological symptoms) combined with sexual and menstrual symptoms are infrequent in primary affective disorder.

Obsessions occur commonly in primary affective disorder. The distinction between obsessional illness and primary affective disorder is also made on the basis of chronology. If obsessions and compulsions antedate depressive symptoms, a diagnosis of primary affective disorder should not be made.

Distinguishing between schizophrenia and primary affective disorder is usually not a problem. Schizophrenia, a chronic illness of insidious onset, is not characterized by the remitting course found in primary affective disorder. Patients with primary affective disorder do not develop the formal thought disorder characteristically seen in schizophrenia. Occasionally the distinction between mania and schizophrenia can be difficult. Bizarre and dramatic hallucinations, delusions, and other abnormalities of mental content like those seen in schizophrenia may occur in mania. A previous history of episodic illness with remission, or the presence of euphoria, hyperactivity, or flight of ideas, indicates that the diagnosis may be mania rather than schizophrenia. The physician should also be careful in making a diagnosis of schizophrenia when a patient has a family history of affective disorder. This history by itself favors the diagnosis of primary affective disorder (58).

For many years, clinicians assumed that schizophreniform illness (schizo-affective psychosis) was more closely related to schizophrenia than to primary affective disorder. Now there is increasing evidence that its relation to primary affective disorder is stronger (15, 17). Family history studies indicate that among the relatives of schizophreniform patients there is an increased prevalence of affective disorder. After remission, patients with schizophreniform illness may become ill again in episodic fashion as do patients with primary affective disorder. Further episodes of illness may be typical of depression or mania (15).

A systematic study of 88 psychiatric inpatients who were diagnosed as having either manic disorder or schizo-affective disorder revealed no differences between the two groups with regard to the clinical picture, demographic variables, individual or family history, and treatment response (2).

Organic brain syndromes are sometimes accompanied by depressive symptoms. Among patients with chronic brain syndromes, those with cerebral arteriosclerosis may be particularly likely to have episodes of secondary affective disorder (50). Physicians should be careful about making a diagnosis of primary affective disorder in patients who are disoriented or who have grossly impaired memory.

Depressive or manic symptoms are side effects of certain drugs. Reserpine or alphamethyldopa, used in the treatment of hypertension, may produce depression. Steroids may produce schizophreniform illness. Some women respond to birth control pills with mild to moderate depressive symptoms (37).

Clinical Management

The management of depression in primary affective disorder always involves supportive psychotherapy. Many clinicians believe that insight-directed psychotherapy, involving examination of motives and deep feelings, is probably not wise because it tends to increase the patient's feelings of guilt. Some recent evidence, however, indicates that certain types of psychotherapy may be useful for mild or moderate depressions. In two studies, "moderately" depressed subjects were randomly allocated to treatment or no-treatment groups (53). The treatment consisted of "cognitive therapy" which aims at "breaking down existing negative cognitions and replacing them with more positive functionally adaptive ones," or behavior therapy whereby the patient is "trained to function effectively in interpersonal interactions so as to maximize reinforcement obtained from others." The treatment groups had significantly fewer depressive symptoms after a short follow-up period. In another study, depressed outpatients were randomly assigned to cognitive therapy or antidepressant medication (51). Cognitive therapy produced significantly greater improvement, but the sample was small and the follow-up short. Still other studies indicate that psychotherapy improves social adjustment but does not prevent relapse (33, 41, 61).

There are two major somatic approaches to the management of depressive episodes: drug treatment and electrotherapy. Both are viewed by most clinicians as the "treatments of choice" for serious depressions.

Tricyclic antidepressants, such as imipramine and amitriptyline, are the most commonly used drugs. They should be administered for at least three or four weeks before shifting to other drugs or to electrotherapy if there is no improvement. The side effects of tricyclic antidepressants are usually not serious. The most common are dry mouth, orthostatic hypotension, and tremor. These effects often diminish as the drug is continued.

The monoamine oxidase inhibitors are used less frequently than tricyclic antidepressants. There is no evidence that they are more effective, and the side effects can be more serious. Patients taking these drugs should not receive other drugs containing amphetamines or sympathomimetic substances. Foods and beverages containing tyramine (a pressor substance), particularly cheese, some wines, and beer, should be avoided because of the danger of a hypertensive crisis.

Phenothiazines are occasionally useful in the treatment of agitated patients (40).

For years it was claimed that the combination of tricyclic antidepressants with monoamine oxidase inhibitors was dangerous because of reports of circulatory collapse. At least one recent study indicates that fears of combining these drugs have been exaggerated and that the combination may be useful in treating depressed patients resistant to other forms of therapy (52).

Most psychiatrists reserve electrotherapy for patients who do not respond to tricyclic antidepressants or who are so ill that they cannot be treated outside a hospital. Electrotherapy may be the most effective form of treatment available for depression (18, 66). When first introduced into clinical practice in the early 1940's, it frequently caused vertebral and other fractures. As advances in the drug modification of electrotherapy have been made, the procedure is less frightening and less commonly associated with complications (66). Patients are anesthetized briefly with a very rapid acting barbiturate and then are given a muscle relaxant, usually succinylcholine. Electrodes are placed in the frontotemporal regions, and a small, measured amount of electricity is passed between them.

The most troublesome side effect of electrotherapy is temporary loss of recent memory, which occurs in most patients. New techniques of delivering unilateral electroconvulsive therapy to the nondominant side of the brain have minimized even this side effect (1). Electrotherapy is probably no more dangerous than treatment with drugs (29). The only absolute contraindication to this mode of therapy is increased intracranial pressure. If required, electrotherapy can be given during pregnancy or postoperatively.

Mania can be treated with phenothiazines, lithium, or electrotherapy. Of these methods, electrotherapy is probably the least effective.

Lithium carbonate may be the drug of choice in the treatment of mania (45), but chlorpromazine is perhaps most useful with very active manic patients. Some clinicians begin to treat manics with both chlorpromazine and lithium, stopping chlorpromazine after four or five days when lithium has begun to take effect. If lithium is not effective within ten days, it probably will not be effective at all. Serum levels of lithium required for effective action are in the range of 1 meq/l (46). Generally, total doses of 1200 to 2400 mg of lithium per day in divided form (300 to 600 mg per dose) are required to achieve such serum levels. Because lithium is a potentially toxic drug, its use must be monitored carefully by repeatedly checking serum levels, particularly early in treatment. Some patients experience a fine tremor of the hands at therapeutic levels of lithium (0.8 to 1.5 meq/l). At higher levels, ataxia, disorientation, somnolence, seizures, and finally circulatory collapse may occur. Long-term lithium therapy has also been associated with disturbances of thyroid and renal function, and tubular changes in the kidney have been found on autopsy. Thus, the drug should be used with caution.

The usefulness of lithium may not be limited to the treatment of acute mania. There is some evidence that the drug may reduce morbidity among bipolar patients, preventing depression as well as mania (4), and that it may also prevent depression among some unipolar patients (3, 4, 38).

References

1. Abrams, R., Fink, M., Dornbush, R. L., Feldstein, S., Volavka, J., and Roubicek, J. Unilateral and bilateral electroconvulsive therapy. Arch. J. Psychiat. 27:88-91, 1972.
2. Abrams, R. and Taylor, M. A. Mania and schizo-affective disorder, manic type: A comparison. Amer. J. Psychiat. 133:12, 1976.
3. Ananth, J. Treatment approaches to mania. Int. Pharmacopsychiat. 11: 215-231, 1976.
4. Angst, J., Weis, P., Grof, P., Baastrup, P. C., and Schou, J. Lithium prophylaxis in recurrent affective disorders. Brit. J. Psychiat. 116:604-614, 1970.
5. Baker, M., Dorzab, J., Winokur, G., and Cadoret, R. Depressive disease: the effect of the postpartum state. Biol. Psychiat. 3:357-365, 1971.
6. Beck, A. T. *Depression: Clinical Experimental, and Theoretical Aspects*. New York: Harper and Row, 1967.
7. Becker, J. Achievement related to characteristics of manic-depressives. J. Abnorm. Soc. Psychol. 60:334-339, 1960.
8. Bertelson, A., Harvald, B., and Hauge, M. A Danish twin study of manic-depressive disorders. Brit. J. Psychiat. 130:330-351, 1977.
9. Bratfos, O. and Haug, J. L. The course of manic-depressive psychosis. A follow-up investigation of 215 patients. Acta Psychiat. Scand. 44:89-112, 1968.
10. Brodie, H. K. and Leff, M. J. Bipolar depression—a comparative study of patient characteristics. Amer. J. Psychiat. 127:1086-1090, 1971.
11. Cassidy, W. L., Flanigan, M. B., Spellman, M., and Cohen, M. E. Clinical observations in manic depressive disease. A quantitative study of 100 manic depressive patients in 50 medically sick controls. J.A.M.A. 164: 1535-1546, 1953.
12. Clayton, P. J., Halikas, J. A., and Maurice, W. L. The depression of widowhood. Brit. J. Psychiat. 120:71-78, 1972.
13. Clayton, P. J., Halikas, J. A., and Maurice, W. L. The bereavement of the widowed. Dis. Nerv. Syst. 32:597-604, 1971.
14. Clayton, P. J., Pitts, F. N., and Winokur, G. Affective disorder. IV. Mania. Compr. Psychiat. 6:313-322, 1965.
15. Clayton, P. J., Rodin, L., and Winokur, G. Family history studies. III. Schizo-affective disorder, clinical and genetic factors including a one to two year follow-up. Compr. Psychiat. 9:31-49, 1968.
16. Cohen, M. B., Baker, G., Cohen, R. A., Fromm-Reichmann, F., and Weigert, E. V. An intensive study of 12 cases of manic depressive psychosis. Psychiatry 17:103-137, 1954.
17. Cohen, S. M., Allen, M. G., Pollin, W., and Hrubec, Z. Relationship of schizo-affective psychosis to manic depressive psychosis and schizophrenia. Arch. Gen. Psychiat. 26:539-546, 1972.

18. Davis, J. M. Efficacy of tranquilizing and antidepressant drugs. Arch. Gen. Psychiat. 13:552-572, 1965.
19. Fremming, K. The expectation of mental infirmity in the sample of the Danish population. In *Occasional Papers of Eugenics*, Number 7. London: Cassell, 1951.
20. Freud, S. Mourning and melancholia. In *The Complete Psychological Works of Sigmund Freud*. Vol. 14, pp. 243-258. London: Hogarth Press, 1957.
21. Gibson, R. W. The family background and early life experience of the manic depressive patient. Psychiatry 21:71-90, 1968.
22. Goodwin, D. W., Schulsinger, F., Knop, J., Mednick, S., and Guze, S. B. Psychopathology in adopted and nonadopted daughters of alcoholics. Arch. Gen. Psychiat. 34, 1977.
23. Goodwin, F. K., Murphy, D. L., Dunner, D. L., and Bunney, W. E. Lithium response in unipolar vs. bipolar depression. Amer. J. Psychiat. 129:44-47, 1972.
24. Guze, S. B. and Robins, E. Suicide and primary affective disorders. Brit. J. Psychiat. 117:437-438, 1970.
25. Guze, S. B., Woodruff, R. A., and Clayton, P. J. Secondary affective disorder: a study of 95 cases. Psychol. Med. 1:426-428, 1971.
26. Helgason, T. Epidemiology of mental disorders in Iceland. A psychiatric and demographic investigation of 5395 Icelanders. Acta Psychiat. Scand. 40, Suppl. 173, 1964.
27. James, W. *The Varieties of Religious Experience*. In Silverman, C. *The Epidemiology of Depression*. Baltimore: Johns Hopkins Press, 1968.
28. Johnson, G. F. S. and Leeman, M. M. Onset of illness in bipolar manic-depressives and their affectively ill first-degree relatives. Biol. Psychiat. 12: 733-741, 1977.
29. Kalinowsky, L. B. and Hippius, H. *Pharmacological, Convulsive and Other Somatic Treatments in Psychiatry*. New York: Grune and Stratton, 1969.
30. Kallman, F. J. Genetic principles in manic depressive psychosis. In Zubin, J. and Hoch, P. (eds.), *Depression*. Proceedings of the American Psychopathological Association. New York: Grune and Stratton, 1954.
31. Kendell, R. E. *The Classification of Depressive Illnesses*, Maudsley Monographs no. 18. London: Oxford University Press, 1968.
32. Kerr, T. A., Schapira, K., and Roth, M. The relationship between premature death and affective disorders. Brit. J. Psychiat. 115:1277-1282, 1969.
33. Klerman, G. L., Dimascio, A., Weissman, M., Prusoff, B., and Paykel, E. S. Treatment of depression by drugs and psychotherapy. Amer. J. Psychiat. 131:2, 1974.
34. Kraepelin, E. *Manic Depressive Insanity and Paranoia*. Edinburgh: E. S. Livingstone, 1921.
35. Lewis, A. Melancholia: a historical review. In *The State of Psychiatry: Essays and Addresses*. New York: Science House, 1967.

36. Lundquist, G. Prognosis and course in manic depressive psychosis. A follow-up study of 319 first admissions. Acta Psychiat. et Neurol., Suppl. 35, 1945.
37. Marcotte, D. B., Kane, F. G., Obrist, P., and Lipton, M. A. Psychophysiologic changes accompanying oral contraceptive use. Brit. J. Psychiat. 116:165-167, 1970.
38. Mendels, J., Secunda, S. K., and Dyson, W. L. The controlled study of the antidepressant effects of lithium carbonate. Arch. Gen. Psychiat. 26: 154-157, 1972.
39. Nicholi, A. M. Harvard dropouts: some psychiatric findings. Amer. J. Psychiat. 124:651-658, 1967.
40. Overall, J. E., Hollister, L. E., Johnson, M., and Pennington, V. Nosology of depression and differential response to drugs. J.A.M.A. 946-948, 1966.
41. Paykel, E. S., Dimascio, A., Haskell, D., and Prusoff, B. A. Effects of maintenance amitriptyline and psychotherapy on symptoms of depression. Psychol. Med. 5:67-77, 1975.
42. Perris, C. A study of bipolar (manic-depressive) and unipolar recurrent depressive psychoses. Acta Psychiat. Scand., Suppl. 194, 1966.
43. Poznaski, E. and Zrull, J. P. Childhood depression. Clinical characteristics of overtly depressed children. Arch. Gen. Psychiat. 23:8-15, 1970.
44. Price, J. S. Chronic depressive illness. Brit. Med. J. 1:1200-1201, 1978.
45. Prien, R. F., Caffey, E. M., and Klett, C. J. Comparison of lithium carbonate and chlorpromazine in the treatment of mania. Arch. Gen. Psychiat. 26:146-153, 1972.
46. Prien, R. T., Caffey, E. M., and Klett, C. J. Relationship between serum lithium level and clinical response in acute mania treated with lithium. Brit. J. Psychiat. 120:409-414, 1972.
47. Reich, T. and Winokur, G. Postpartum psychoses in patients with manic depressive disease. J. Nerv. Ment. Dis. 151:60-68, 1970.
48. Robins, E. and Guze, S. B. Classification of affective disorders: the primary-secondary, the endogenous-reactive, and the neurotic-psychotic concepts. In *Recent Advances in Psychobiology of the Depressive Illnesses*, Proceedings of a workshop sponsored by the NIMH, Williams, T. A., Katz, M. M., and Shield, J. A. (eds.). U.S. Government Printing Office, 1972.
49. Robins, E., Murphy, G. E., Wilkinson, R. G., Gassner, S., and Kayes, J. Some clinical considerations in the prevention of suicide based on a study of 134 successful suicides. Amer. J. Public Health 49:888-899, 1959.
50. Roth, M. Natural history of mental disorder in old age. J. Ment. Sci. 101:281-301, 1955.
51. Rush, A. J., Beck, A. T., Kovacs, M., and Hollon, S. Comparative efficacy of cognitive therapy and pharmacotherapy in the treatment of depressed outpatients. Cognitive Therapy and Research. 1:17-37, 1977.
52. Schuckit, M., Robins, E., and Feighner, J. Tricyclic anti-depressants in

monoamine oxidase inhibitors. Combination therapy in the treatment of depression. Arch. Gen. Psychiat. 46:509-514, 1971.

53. Shaw, B. F. Comparison of cognitive therapy and behavior therapy in the treatment of depression. J. Consulting and Clin. Psychology. 45:543-551, 1977.

54. Shobe, F. O. and Brione, P. Long-term prognosis in manic-depressive illness. A follow-up investigation of 111 patients. Arch. Gen. Psychiat. 24:334-337, 1971.

55. Silverman, C. *The Epidemiology of Depression.* Baltimore: Johns Hopkins Press, 1968.

56. Strömgren, E. Contributions to psychiatric epidemiology and genetics. Acta Jutlandica Medical Series 16, Vol. XL, 1968.

57. Taylor, F. G. and Marshall, W. L. Experimental analysis of a cognitive-behavioral therapy for depression. Cognitive Therapy and Research. 1:59-72, 1977.

58. Vaillant, G. E. Manic-depressive heredity and remission in schizophrenia. Brit. J. Psychiat. 109:746-749, 1963.

59. VanValkenburg, C., Lowry, M., Winokur, G., and Cadoret, R. Depression spectrum disease versus pure depressive disease. J. Nerv. Ment. Dis. 165:341-347, 1977.

60. Weissman, M. M., Klerman, G. L., Paykel, E. S., Prusoff, B., and Hanson, B. Treatment effects on the social adjustment of depressed patients. Arch. Gen. Psychiat. 30:771-778, 1974.

61. Weissman, M. M., Pottenger, M., Kleber, H., Ruben, H. L., Williams, D., and Thompson, W. D. Symptom patterns in primary and secondary depression. Arch. Gen. Psychiat. 34:854-862, 1977.

62. Weissman, M. M., Myers, J. K., and Harding, P. S. Psychiatric disorders in a U.S. urban community: 1975-76. Amer. J. Psych. 135:459-462, 1978.

63. Weissman, M. M. and Myers, J. K. Affective disorders in a U.S. urban community: the use of research diagnostic criteria in an epidemiological survey. Arch. Gen. Psychiat. (in press).

64. Whitney, W., Cadoret, R. J., and McClure, J. N. Depressive symptoms and academic performance in college students. Amer. J. Psychiat. 128:766-770, 1971.

65. Winokur, G. Types of depressive illness. Brit. J. Psychiat. 120:265-266, 1972.

66. Winokur, G., Clayton, P. J., and Reich, T. *Manic Depressive Illness.* St. Louis: C. V. Mosby, 1969.

67. Winokur, G. and Pitts, F. N. Affective disorder: VI. A family history study of prevalences, sex differences, and possible genetic factors. J. Psychiat. Res. 3:113-123, 1965.

68. Woodruff, R. A., Guze, S. B., Clayton, P. J., and Carr, D. Alcoholism and depression. Arch. Gen. Psychiat. 28:97-100, 1973.

69. Woodruff, R. A., Guze, S. B., and Clayton, P. J. Alcoholics who see a

psychiatrist compared with those who do not. Quart. J. Stud. Alcohol 34: 1162-1171, 1973.

70. Woodruff, R. A., Guze, S. B., and Clayton, P. J. Anxiety neurosis among psychiatric outpatients. Compr. Psychiat. 13:165-170, 1972.

71. Woodruff, R. A., Murphy, G. E., and Herjanic, M. The natural history of affective disorders—I. Symptoms of 72 patients at the time of index hospital admission. J. Psychiat. Res. 5:255-263, 1967.

72. Woodruff, R. A., Robins, L. N., Winokur, G., and Reich, T. Manic depressive illness and social achievement. Acta Psychiat. Scand. 47:237-249, 1971.

73. Zung, W. W. A cross-cultural survey of symptoms in depression. Amer. J. Psychiat. 126:116-121, 1969.

2. Schizophrenic Disorders

Definition

Hallucinations and delusions are considered hallmarks of mental disorder and thus are of great interest to psychiatrists. These symptoms may be seen in a wide variety of illnesses, including primary affective disorders, brain syndromes, alcoholism, drug dependence, and a group of conditions that may loosely be called the schizophrenic disorders. Many investigators believe that schizophrenic disorders comprise a number of different conditions, but efforts to divide them into valid subgroups generally have not been successful, and inconsistent usage has made nomenclature confusing. Extensive work, however, has indicated that the schizophrenic disorders may be divided into two major categories: one with a relatively poor prognosis and the other with a relatively good prognosis.

When this differentiation is attempted, the labels schizophrenia, chronic schizophrenia, process schizophrenia, nuclear schizophrenia, and nonremitting schizophrenia are used to refer to the poor prognosis cases, while schizophreniform, acute schizophrenia, reactive schizophrenia, and remitting schizophrenia are used for the good prognosis cases (54).

The schizophrenic disorders are manifested, at least intermittently, by delusions and hallucinations in a clear sensorium. Other noteworthy features are a blunted, shallow, or strikingly inappropriate affect; odd, sometimes bizarre, motor behavior (termed "catatonic"); and disordered thinking in which goal-directedness and normal associations between ideas are markedly distorted (loosening of associations and tangential thinking).

While the schizophrenic disorders are generally chronic, sometimes symptoms are episodic. Such psychotic episodes tend to develop in individuals whose previous general adjustment has been good. These patients are much more likely to show striking affective symptoms during the illness than the blunted, shallow affect of the chronic schizophrenic. They may seem perplexed and bewildered during the acute illness and may be mildly disoriented. Though recovery from the psychotic episode is usual, repeated episodes are common. Subsequent episodes may be less pronounced and may sometimes resemble affective disorders (78, 79).

Historical Background

In now classic studies, Emil Kraepelin (1856-1926), a German psychiatrist, building upon the work of his countrymen, K. L. Kahlbaum (1828-99) and E. Hecker (1843-1909) who described "catatonia" and "hebephrenia," respectively, laid the groundwork for present views of schizophrenia (40). After careful follow-up of hospitalized patients, he separated "manic depressive psychosis" from "dementia praecox." The latter term referred to the disorder now called "chronic schizophrenia." Even though Kraepelin believed dementia praecox to be a chronic disorder that frequently ended in marked deterioration of the personality, he recognized that a small number of patients recovered completely. His "narrow" view of schizophrenia has been followed by most European psychiatrists, particularly those in the Scandinavian countries and Great Britain.

A "broader" approach to schizophrenia (and the name itself) was offered by Eugen Bleuler (1857-1939), a Swiss psychiatrist, who realized that he might be dealing with a group of disorders (6). His diagnostic criteria were not based upon their ability to predict course and outcome, but upon their conforming to his hypothesis concerning the basic defect, namely, the "splitting" of psychic functions. By this he meant inconsistency, inappropriateness, and disorganization of affect, thought, and action, in the absence of obvious brain disease. Despite his less strict approach to diagnosis, and the variable course that his patients experienced,

Bleuler believed that patients with schizophrenia never recovered completely, never returned to their premorbid state (*restitutio ad integrum*). Because his "fundamental" symptoms included autism (defined by Bleuler as "divorce from reality"), blunted or inappropriate affect, ambivalence, and disturbed association of thought—all often difficult to define and specify—Bleuler's work set the stage for the very broad concepts of schizophrenia developed by psychoanalysts and adopted by many American psychiatrists.

Psychoanalytic theory views schizophrenia primarily as a manifestation of a "weak ego." Unable to cope with the problems of life, and unable to use effectively the "defenses of the ego" to handle instinctual forces and anxiety, patients "regress" to a primitive psychosexual level of functioning ("primary process") manifested by thought disorder, affective poverty, disorganization, and inability to conform to the demands of "reality" (8). In this psychoanalytic view of schizophrenia, all evidence of weak ego (including a wide range of personality handicaps and abnormalities) or of primary process (such as hallucinations, delusions, poor reality-testing, tangential thinking, and ambivalence) may be a manifestation of schizophrenia. It is not surprising, therefore, that the diagnosis is used in a wide range of clinical situations.

In the late 1930's a number of European and American investigators began again to approach the problem of the schizophrenias in terms of predicting course, response to treatment, and long-term outcome. They were influenced first by the advent of electroconvulsive therapy and later by the introduction of the phenothiazines. Langfeldt (43), Astrup (3, 4), Retterstöl (52, 53), Leonhard (44), Ey (18), Stephens (70, 71), and Vaillant (78, 79) have been leaders in these efforts.

Proper evaluation of treatment requires a knowledge of the natural history of the disorder being treated, especially the factors associated with different clinical courses and outcomes. Such factors can only be identified by follow-up studies such as those carried out by the above investigators. Thus, current clinical and research approaches to the schizophrenic disorders are based upon extensive follow-up studies, supplemented by family studies (54).

Epidemiology

Chronic schizophrenia occurs in somewhat less than 1 percent of the population, but because of its early onset, chronicity, and associated disability, it is one of the most important psychiatric illnesses. It has been estimated that between one-third and one-half of all psychiatric beds in United States hospitals are occupied by such patients. The distinction between good and poor prognosis forms of schizophrenia often is not made in epidemiologic surveys, though available evidence suggests that the good prognosis cases are more common than the poor prognosis ones (53). The combined prevalence of both good and poor prognosis disorders is probably between 1 and 2 percent.

Schizophrenic disorders are found in all cultures. A number of studies have indicated that they are more prevalent among people from lower socioeconomic backgrounds. For some investigators, this means that poverty, limited education, and associated handicaps predispose to schizophrenic illness. Recent work has shown, however, that the association between schizophrenic illness and low socioeconomic status can be explained by "downward drift," a term which refers to the effect of an illness on the patient's socioeconomic status. If a disorder interferes with education and work performance so that the individual is not able to complete advanced schooling or hold positions of responsibility, his socioeconomic status—characteristically defined by income, educational achievement, and job prestige—cannot be high.

Studies in England (24), Denmark (81), Finland (60), and the United States (13) have shown that the distribution of socioeconomic class among the fathers of schizophrenics is the same as in the general population, indicating that the lower socioeconomic status of patients with schizophrenic illness is the result of "downward drift."

Another interesting observation concerning the epidemiology of schizophrenia is the reported tendency of schizophrenics in Europe and the United States to be born during the late winter and early spring months of the year (30, 76). Though most schizophrenics are not born during these months, the data suggest that something associated with such births predisposes to schizophrenic illness. These reports do not distinguish between good prognosis and poor prognosis cases, so they leave the reader uncertain as to whether the observation is equally applicable to both forms of the disorder.

Clinical Picture

Common delusions in schizophrenia are those of persecution and control in which patients believe others are spying on them, spreading false rumors about them, planning to harm them, trying to control their thoughts or actions, or reading their minds. Patients may express the belief that they are the victims of conspiracies by communists, Catholics, neighbors, the FBI, etc. Delusions of depersonalization are also common. These may be feelings that bizarre bodily changes are taking place, sometimes as a result of the deliberate but obscure actions of others.

The most common hallucinations are auditory. They may involve solitary or multiple voices. The patient may or may not recognize the voices or talk back to them. The voices may seem to come from within the patient's body or from outside sources, such as radios or walls. The voices may criticize, ridicule, or threaten; often they urge the patient to do something he believes is wrong. Visual hallucinations are also frequent (26). They may vary from frightening vague forms to images of dead or absent relatives or scenes of violence or hell. Olfactory hallucinations, which are infrequent, usually consist of unpleasant smells arising from the patient's own body. Tactile (haptic) hallucinations, also infrequent, may consist of feelings that one's genitals are being manipulated, that there are animals inside one's body, or that there are insects crawling over one's skin.

Though the so-called "typical" flat schizophrenic affect is highly characteristic when it is severe, its diagnostic value is limited because it usually has a more subtle form that makes agreement about its presence hard to achieve. Even when clearly present, it is not easy to describe. The patient seems emotionally unresponsive, without warmth or empathy. He can talk about frightening or shocking thoughts without seeming to experience their usual emotional impact. It is often difficult to feel compassion and sympathy for the patient or to believe that he can empathize with others.

Recurrent posturing, grimacing, prolonged immobility, and "waxy flexibility" are dramatic examples of catatonic behavior. These may be independent symptoms or responses to auditory hallucinations.

The impaired goal-directedness of schizophrenic thought and speech may take various forms, all likely to occur in the same patient: blocking, in which the patient's thought and speech stop for periods of time only to begin again with an apparently different subject; tangential associations, in which connections between thoughts are difficult or impossible to follow; neologisms, in which the patient makes up new words; or "word salad," in which the patient's speech consists of words without any understandable sequence or meaning.

Following Kraepelin and Bleuler (6, 40), many psychiatrists group schizophrenics into paranoid, catatonic, hebephrenic, and simple types, depending upon whether the predominant symptoms are delusions, bizarre motor behavior, disturbances in affect and association, or social withdrawal and inadequacy. In practice, however, symptoms vary with time so that a patient may seem to fit several of the subclassifications during the course of his illness (9). Attempts to identify delusions or hallucinations characteristic of good or poor prognosis cases have not been consistently successful (26).

Patients with schizophrenic disorders may display prominent alterations of mood, usually depression but sometimes euphoria during the course of illness (50). Other affective symptoms—such as insomnia, anorexia, weight loss, alterations in interest and energy, impairment of mental concentration, guilt, and suicidal preoccupation—may also be present. Often, particularly early in the course of good prognosis cases, the patient may appear confused, perplexed, somewhat disoriented.

Natural History

As chronic schizophrenia typically begins insidiously, it is often hard to determine when the disorder started. In retrospect, the majority of patients show certain prepsychotic personality abnormalities: excessive shyness, social awkwardness, withdrawal from personal relationships, and inability to form close relationships (the so-called "schizoid personality"). These traits may be present from early adolescence; often they are of concern to the patient's family for months or years before delusions or hallucinations become manifest.

A number of studies have shown that in childhood and early adolescence, long before the diagnostic symptoms of schizophrenia are evident, schizophrenics have more academic difficulty in school and achieve lower scores on intelligence tests than do their siblings and other controls (1, 42). Instead of concluding that early academic difficulty and lowered intelligence may be early manifestations of schizophrenia, some investigators (36, 48) have argued that low IQ and schizophrenia are independently transmitted, but that a low IQ is one of the factors that increases the risk of clinical schizophrenia developing in those genetically predisposed. Other work indicates that antisocial and delinquent behavior may be an early manifestation of the illness (56), as may other personality disorders involving social withdrawal and disengagement (31, 62, 80).

Delusions, hallucinations, and strange behavior usually start in the twenties. At first, these aberrations may be brief and vague, so that the family is not certain of their significance. Gradually they become more obvious and disturbing, usually leading to psychiatric consultation.

Schizophrenia infrequently begins after forty. The illness generally has a fluctuating course. One or more psychiatric hospitalizations commonly occur. Many schizophrenics spend most of their lives in psychiatric hospitals. Even when not hospitalized, schizophrenics lead disturbed lives: they usually fail to form satisfactory personal relationships, less often marry than their contemporaries, have poor job histories, and seldom achieve positions of responsibility. They may become neighborhood eccentrics or socially isolated residents of inner cities, doing irregular unskilled work or being supported by welfare.

Two recent developments have altered the general clinical course in these patients: the introduction of antipsychotics and the shift away from prolonged hospitalization. With antipsychotics, control of hallucinations, delusions, and bizzare behavior is possible in a substantial number of cases. As a result, and because of the policy of early discharge, many patients spend far less time in psychiatric hospitals than was the case in earlier years, though rehospitalization for relatively brief periods is common.

The effectiveness of the antipsychotic agents, which seem nearly always to be associated with blocking of dopamine receptors in the brain, has led to the hypothesis that many of the clinical manifestations of schizophrenia depend on certain, as yet unidentified, dopaminergic neurons. This hypothesis has stimulated much research, but must still be regarded as speculative (10, 11, 68).

Good prognosis cases generally begin more abruptly, without a history of long-standing personality abnormalities. While poor and good prognosis cases may differ somewhat clinically, the most important difference relates to outcome (15). When patients are seen for the first time, however, it may be difficult to predict what the course and prognosis will be. Several studies have identified criteria associated with the difference in prognosis among the schizophrenic disorders. Table 1 summarizes the data from these

Table 1. Nomenclature and prognostic criteria for good and poor prognosis cases

	Good prognosis	*Poor prognosis*
Diagnostic terms	Schizophreniform illness	Schizophrenia
	Acute Schizophrenia	Process Schizophrenia
	Schizoaffective Schizophrenia	Nuclear Schizophrenia
	Reactive Schizophrenia	Chronic Schizophrenia
	Remitting Schizophrenia	Nonremitting Schizophrenia
Prognostic criteria		
Mode of Onset	Acute	Insidious
Precipitating Events	Frequently reported	Usually not reported
Prepsychotic History	Good	Poor; frequent history of "schizoid" traits (aloofness, social isolation)
Confusion	Often present	Usually absent
Affective Symptoms	Often present and prominent	Often absent or minimal; affective responses usually "blunted" or "flat"
Marital Status	Usually married	Often single, especially males
Family History of Affective Disorder	Often present	May be present but less likely
Family History of Schizophrenia	Absent or rare	Increased

studies. When most of the criteria are consistent, the studies indicate that the prognosis associated with the criteria will be accurate in the great majority of cases (75 to 80 percent).

Some patients presenting with an acute schizophrenic picture lose their psychotic features during hospitalization and begin to look like depressives (34, 46, 59). Others recover from the psychotic episode and then after a prolonged remission present with typical depression (64). These observations are of great theoretical interest. Some have interpreted them to suggest that the distinction between schizophrenic and affective disorders may be too arbitrary (64); others, emphasizing the familial prevalence of affective illness in the overlapping cases, have argued that such cases are more appropriately classified as affective disorders (77).

Complications

In no illness is it more difficult than in chronic schizophrenia to distinguish between the typical clinical picture and the complications. The definition of the disorder encompasses its natural history and, at the same time, almost specifies the complications. These include impaired education, poor work history and job achievement, celibacy, and prolonged psychiatric hospitalization. An increased risk of suicide among young patients may also be a complication.

Because schizophrenia typically begins early in life and is characterized by recurrent or persistent manifestations, the patient's schooling and education suffer. Early school difficulties have been noted above, but even among those who do well in elementary school, difficulties may arise in high school or college. Social withdrawal and loss of interest in studies may become evident. These changes, coupled with the need to leave school at the onset of more dramatic symptoms, eventually lead to dropping out of school in many cases. If the illness peaks after the completion of formal education, the same clinical features may lead to marked reduction of effectiveness at work, demotions, being fired, frequent job changes, and financial dependency.

In the past, early and prolonged hospitalization was associated with high rates of celibacy among schizophrenic patients. Schizophrenic men were particularly affected, presumably because male initiative was more important than female initiative in getting married. Thus a schizophrenic man would be less successful in courtship, while a schizophrenic woman might attract a suitor despite her illness. With the advent of modern drug treatment and the reduction in prolonged psychiatric hospitalization, marriage and childbearing rates of schizophrenics have approached those of the general population, though the sex difference persists (16, 72).

Despite the great reduction in chronic psychiatric hospitalization, no group of patients spends more time in psychiatric hospitals than schizophrenics. The majority are hospitalized for repeated, *relatively* brief periods, but a substantial minority of patients, perhaps one-quarter or one-third, spend many years in hospitals.

A common fear about deluded schizophrenic patients is that they are likely to act on their delusions and commit crimes. Available data suggest, however, that there is little or no increased risk of significant crimes committed by schizophrenics (29). They may be arrested for vagrancy, disturbing the peace, or similar misdemeanors, but only rarely are involved in felonies.

Some authors have reported an increased suicide risk among young schizophrenics. Unfortunately, they did not attempt to distinguish between poor and good prognosis cases. It may be that the increased suicide risk is largely a function of the latter state, and if so this would suggest a link between at least some cases of good prognosis illness and primary affective disorders (54).

While some patients considered to be suffering from a good prognosis illness turn out, at follow-up, to show the clinical picture and natural history associated with chronic schizophrenia, most are not subject to the typical complications of chronic schizophrenia. Instead, they are subject to complications similar to those of patients with primary affective disorders.

Family Studies

All investigators have found an increased prevalence of schizophrenia among the close relatives of schizophrenics. Most studies have indicated a prevalence of between 10 and 15 percent among first-degree relatives of index cases, compared with a general population figure of under 1 percent.

All but one of a series of twin studies (Table 2) have shown significantly higher concordance rates for schizophrenia among monozygotic twins than among dizygotic twins of the same sex

Table 2. Schizophrenia concordance rates in twins

	MZ Twins		*DZ Twins (same sex)*	
	"Strict" Schizophrenia (percent)	*Including "Borderline" Cases* (percent)	*"Strict" Schizophrenia* (percent)	*Including "Borderline" Cases* (percent)
Investigator				
Luxemberger, 1928 (Germany)	50	71	0	0
Rosanoff *et al.* 1934 (U.S.A.)	44	61	9	13
Essen-Möller, 1941 (Sweden)	14	71	8	17
Kallmann, 1946 (U.S.A.)		69		17
Slater, 1953 (U.K.)		65		14
Inouye, 1963 (Japan)		60		18
Tienari, 1963 (Finland)	6	31	5	5
Kringlen, 1966 (Norway)	28	38	6	14
Gottesman and Shields, 1966 (U.K.)	42	54	9	18
Fischer *et al.*, 1968 (Denmark)	24	48	10	19
Allen *et al.*, 1972 (U.S.A.)		27		5

Adapted from Fischer *et al.* (20) and Allen *et al.* (2)

(2, 17, 20, 28, 35, 37, 41, 45, 57, 65, 75). The prevalence of schizophrenia among the latter is similar to the prevalence among ordinary siblings of the same sex. While the actual concordance rates have varied from study to study, depending largely upon methods of ascertainment (28), the rate for monozygotic twins is generally three to six times that of dizygotic twins.

The failure to find complete concordance in monozygotic twins has naturally led to the conclusion that there must be important environmental factors in the etiology of schizophrenia. Often such environmental factors are assumed to be of a social or psychological nature. A recent report (7), however, suggests that the discordance may be related to certain "brain development deviations," to which monozygotic twins may be "specially prone." The report indicates that concordance for schizophrenia in monozygotic twins is close to 100 percent when both twins are right-handed, but falls markedly when one or both of the twins is not clearly right-handed, suggesting that the risk of schizophrenia is somehow associated with the process of brain lateralization. This finding is of considerable interest, but further work to evaluate its significance is needed.

In addition, it should be noted that as discordant monozygotic twins are followed, many pairs become concordant (5), suggesting that the age of onset may be affected by nongenetic factors in some cases.

There have been two studies of children separated early in life from schizophrenic parents and raised by unrelated adoptive parents. In one of these studies, done in the United States, schizophrenia was found in 5 of 47 children of hospitalized schizophrenic mothers and no cases were found in 50 control children (33). All 5 schizophrenic children had been hospitalized, three chronically; the other two were taking antipsychotic drugs. In the other study, made in Denmark, about 32 percent of the children of schizophrenic parents received a diagnosis in the "schizophrenia spectrum," compared to about 18 percent of controls (58); none, however, had been hospitalized for schizophrenia, and it is unclear how many would be considered schizophrenic in the "narrow" sense.

Another Danish study approached the problem of hereditary predisposition to schizophrenia in a different way. Monozygotic twin pairs in which one twin was schizophrenic while the other was not were identified. The children of these discordant twins were studied. It was found that the frequency of schizophrenia was the same in children of nonaffected discordant schizophrenic twins as in children of affected members of discordant twin pairs (19). The prevalence of schizophrenia in all these children was about 10 percent, which is similar to the general figure for children of schizophrenic parents (28, 37).

The results of all these investigations point to the likelihood of a hereditary predisposition to schizophrenia.

The distinction between good and poor prognosis cases generally has not been studied in investigations of the familial transmission of schizophrenia. Available evidence suggests, however, that the prevalence of affective disorders is increased in close relatives of good prognosis cases. One interpretation given these data is that at least some good prognosis cases are atypical forms of affective illness (54).

The recognition that schizophrenic disorders are familial, and that they probably result in part from hereditary factors, has focused attention on identifying at an early age those individuals within a vulnerable family who are at greatest risk of developing the clinical disorders. Such "high-risk" studies are under way in many countries (62, 74). One of the first modern studies to begin is being conducted in Denmark, and a recent report (62) indicates that the risk of schizophrenia during a ten-year follow-up of 10- to 20-year-old children of schizophrenic mothers is about eight times greater than in matched control children. The risks of "borderline states (including schizoid and paranoid personality disorders)," psychiatric hospitalization, and suicide are also much greater in the children of schizophrenic mothers than in controls. The reported data also suggest that certain measurements of autonomic nervous system function may help identify those high-risk children who will develop the clinical disorder.

A frequent problem in studies of the familial distribution of psychiatric disorders is the failure to examine both parents of index cases. As a result, puzzling familial associations between different disorders may be observed. For example, in the adoption studies of schizophrenia described above, antisocial personality disorders have been found to be associated with schizophrenia. This may indicate that antisocial behavior can be one of the manifestations of schizophrenia, but an equally likely explanation is the tendency of some schizophrenics to mate with individuals manifesting other psychiatric disorders, especially antisocial personality (21, 22, 23, 69).

Differential Diagnosis

The differential diagnosis between poor and good prognosis cases has already been discussed (see page 36). Most studies indicate that when patients fulfill the criteria of good prognosis illness, in over 80 percent of the cases the clinical course and long-term prognosis will be consistent with the classification. On the other hand, there is less consistency when the patient meets the poor prognosis criteria. The expected course and long-term outcome will conform to the classification in between 50 and 90 percent of the cases (54). Certain data suggest that the improved outcome in some series of poor prognosis schizophrenics may be the result of improved treatment (53). To recapitulate: one may be more confident in predicting a relatively good outcome than a relatively poor one. A major element in the differentiation between good and poor prognosis cases is "premorbid adjustment." Inconsistent findings may reflect difficulties in defining and measuring such adjustment (73, 74), and additional studies are needed in which patients are clearly separated on the basis of how long they have been sick prior to psychiatric evaluation.

A small number of patients hospitalized for depression will, at follow-up, turn out to be suffering from chronic schizophrenia (55). Reports offer no guidelines for recognizing these cases when they are first seen. Some patients who present with the symptoms of hysteria (Briquet's syndrome) will show at follow-up the full clinical picture of chronic schizophrenia (82), but this also is rare.

Obsessional neurosis, early in its course, occasionally is difficult to distinguish from schizophrenia. If the obsessions are bizarre or if the patient *clearly* does not have insight into the abnormal nature of his thoughts and impulses, it may not be possible to make a confident diagnosis. The risk of schizophrenia in patients with obsessional neurosis is small after the first year or two of illness and when the obsessions are classical (27).

A clinical picture resembling schizophrenia has been described in association with temporal lobe epilepsy (66). Patients presenting this clinical picture cannot be distinguished from typical schizophrenics, but the absence of an increased prevalence of schizophrenia in their close relatives suggests that one is dealing with a separate entity—a form of "symptomatic schizophrenia."

Since many good prognosis cases are probably manifestations of affective illness, the question of differential diagnosis is often one of diagnostic convention or style. Certain delusions (those of poverty, sinfulness, disease) are common in depressions, and others (of overconfidence and unusual powers) in mania. A diagnosis of affective disorder can be made when these psychotic features are present. Different delusions (of control, persecution, depersonalization) are more likely to lead to a diagnosis of schizophrenia.

The differential diagnosis of good prognosis illness and organic brain syndrome may also at times be a matter of convention. If disorientation and memory impairment are transient and less striking than the delusions, hallucinations, and bizarre behavior, a diagnosis of schizophrenia may be made. Patients with systemic medical illnesses affecting the brain, such as lupus erythematosus, may develop psychiatric symptoms that vary over time from those of depression to those of a brain syndrome, with a schizophrenic picture in between. Most patients with brain syndromes, however, present no problem in differential diagnosis because they experience little or nothing in the way of delusions or hallucinations; even when these symptoms are present, the persistent disorientation and memory impairment point to the correct diagnosis.

Persistent alcoholic hallucinosis is a syndrome of striking hallucinations, chiefly auditory, with a clear sensorium, that follows alcohol withdrawal. It may occur either after other withdrawal symptoms have subsided or in the absence of other manifestations of withdrawal. Alcoholic hallucinosis usually subsides within a couple of weeks. Occasionally it persists and becomes chronic, thus resembling schizophrenia. Family studies have been undertaken to determine whether there is an increased prevalence of schizophrenia in close relatives (thus suggesting that the alcoholism precipitated or was superimposed upon typical schizophrenia), or whether there is no increased prevalence (suggesting that, like epilepsy, alcoholism may produce a "symptomatic schizophrenia"). Unfortunately, the findings are contradictory, and the issue cannot yet be resolved (61, 63).

Amphetamines, when taken chronically in large quantities, can cause a schizophrenia-like illness (12). This psychotic state will almost always subside within ten days after the drug is discontinued. In rare chronic cases, the situation is similar to that seen in chronic alcoholic hallucinosis, where it is uncertain which came first—the drug abuse or the schizophrenic disorder.

Clinical Management

Antipsychotic medication, coupled with a policy of early discharge from psychiatric hospitals, made possible in part because of the antipsychotics, has become the keystone of standard treatment. Occasionally, the combination of antipsychotics and electroconvulsive treatments seems to produce better results than antipsychotics alone (67). Delusions, hallucinations, and bizarre behavior may be at least partially controlled by adequate doses of antipsychotics, though these drugs probably do not affect the personality changes associated with schizophrenia. Larger doses are usually needed during acute exacerbations, but may be reduced as the patient's symptoms abate.

The prolonged use of antipsychotics may lead to certain undesirable consequences. Even at moderate dosage levels, parasympatholytic, or atropinelike, effects and Parkinsonism are common. At higher doses, lenticular opacities (14, 25, 51) and tardive dyskinesia (38) have been described in many long-term patients. Patients receiving large doses of thioridazine may develop a condition resembling retinitis pigmentosa that causes visual impairment and blindness (30). A variety of skin rashes (83), a form of intrahepatic obstructive jaundice (which may rarely lead to chronic biliary cirrhosis) (39), and bone marrow toxicity may occur (47, 49), all probably as a result of special hypersensitivity. Despite these and other untoward reactions, the introduction of the antipsychotics represents a major advance in the treatment of schizophrenia.

The drugs do not control all schizophrenic symptoms. Patients continue to suffer from intermittent delusions and hallucinations, personality changes, and general social impairment. Many experienced clinicians believe, though, that the reduction in chronic hospitalization and the greater efforts at rehabilitation resulting from an increased optimism about more effective treatment prevent some personality deterioration.

The return of chronic schizophrenic patients to the community is not without problems. Many patients are severe burdens to their families. While they may be better following drug treatment, they are not well. They continue to experience symptoms, and their adjustment to family life is difficult and stressful. Also, most chronic schizophrenic patients are not able to support themselves financially and require family or community help.

The long-term care of chronic schizophrenics requires patience and perseverance. Many patients will omit medication if not carefully supervised; some require parenteral medication at least intermittently. Rehospitalization for brief periods may be necessary to reinstitute drug treatment or to help the family through a bad period in the course of the patient's illness. Many schizophrenic patients will respond to suggestions about their symptoms and adjustment; some are able to participate in more elaborate psychotherapeutic interviews. Nearly always, the patient's family will need support, encouragement, guidance, and understanding. Without this help, many families are unable to cope with the patient, and all treatment then becomes more difficult.

Because good prognosis cases are generally episodic, they present different therapeutic problems. As in chronic schizophrenia, antipsychotics may help. In many cases, electrotherapy produces remission. The place of lithium in the treatment of some cases, particularly those with features of mania, is still unclear; some authors favor it, others do not.

Generally, after symptoms have subsided, no further treatment is indicated unless there are complications such as alcoholism or drug abuse.

References

1. Albee, G., Lane, E., and Reuter, J. M. Childhood intelligence of future schizophrenics and neighborhood peers. J. Psychol. 58:141-144, 1964.
2. Allen, M. G., Cohen, S., and Pollin, W. Schizophrenia in veteran twins: a diagnostic review. Amer. J. Psychiat. 128:939-945, 1972.
3. Astrup, C., Fossum, A., and Holmboe, R. *Prognosis in Functional Psychoses*. Springfield, Ill.: C. C. Thomas, 1962.
4. Astrup, C. and Noreik, K. *Functional Psychoses: Diagnostic and Prognostic Models*. Springfield, Ill.: C. C. Thomas, 1966.
5. Belmaker, R., Pollin, W., Wyatt, R. J., and Cohen, S. A follow-up of monozygotic twins discordant for schizophrenia. Arch. Gen. Psychiat. 30: 219-222, 1974.
6. Bleuler, E. *Dementia Praecox or the Group of Schizophrenias*, translated by J. Zinkin. New York: International Universities Press, 1950.
7. Boklage, C. E. Schizophrenia, brain asymmetry development, and twinning: cellular relationship with etiological and possibly prognostic implications. Biol. Psychiat. 12:19-35, 1977.
8. Brenner, D. *Elementary Textbook of Psychoanalysis*. New York: International Universities Press, 1955.
9. Brill, N. and Glass, J. Hebephrenic schizophrenic reactions. Arch. Gen. Psychiat. 12:545-551, 1965.

10. Carlsson, A. Does dopamine play a role in schizophrenia? Psychol. Med. 7:583-598, 1977.
11. Carlsson, A. Antipsychotic drugs, neurotransmitters, and schizophrenia. Amer. J. Psychiat. 135:164-173, 1978.
12. Connell, P. H. *Amphetamine Psychosis*, Maudsley Monograph no. 5. London: Oxford University Press, 1958.
13. Dunham, H. W. *Community and Schizophrenia*. Detroit: Wayne State University Press, 1965.
14. Edler, K., Gottfries, C. G., Haslund, J., and Ravn, J. Eye changes in connection with neuroleptic treatment especially concerning phenothiazines and thioxanthenes. Acta Psychiat. Scand. 47:377-385, 1971.
15. Eitlinger, L., Laane, C. V., and Langfeldt, G. The prognostic value of the clinical picture and the therapeutic value of physical treatment in schizophrenia and the schizophreniform states. Acta Psychiat. et Neurol. Scand. 33:33-53, 1958.
16. Erlenmeyer-Kimling, L., Nicol, S., Rainer, J. D., and Deming, E. Changes in fertility rates of schizophrenic patients in the New York State. Amer. J. Psychiat. 125:916-927, 1969.
17. Essen-Möller, E. *Psychiatrische Untersuchungen an einer Serie von Zwillingen*. Copenhagen: Munksgaard, 1941.
18. Ey, H. Unity and diversity of schizophrenia: clinical and logical analysis of the concept of schizophrenia. Amer. J. Psychiat. 115:706-714, 1959.
19. Fischer, M. Psychoses in the offspring of schizophrenic twins and their normal co-twins. Brit. J. Psychiat. 118:43-52, 1971.
20. Fischer, M., Harvald, B., and Hauge, M. A Danish twin study of schizophrenia. Brit. J. Psychiat. 115:981-990, 1969.
21. Fowler, R. C. and Tsuang, M. T. Spouses of schizophrenics: a blind comparative study. Compr. Psychiat. 16:339-342, 1975.
22. Fowler, R. C., Tsuang, M. T., and Cadoret, R. J. Parental psychiatric illness associated with schizophrenia in the siblings of schizophrenics. Compr. Psychiat. 18:271-275, 1977.
23. Fowler, R. C., Tsuang, M. T., and Cadoret, R. J. Psychiatric illness in the offspring of schizophrenics. Compr. Psychiat. 18:127-134, 1977.
24. Goldberg, E. M. and Morrison, S. L. Schizophrenia and social class. Brit. J. Psychiat. 109:785-802, 1963.
25. Gombos, G. and Yarden, P. E. Ocular and cutaneous side-effects after prolonged chlorpromazine treatment. Amer. J. Psychiat. 123:872-874, 1967.
26. Goodwin, D. W., Alderson, P., and Rosenthal, R. Clinical significance of hallucinations in psychiatric disorders. Arch. Gen. Psychiat. 24:76-80, 1971.
27. Goodwin, D. W., Guze, S. B., and Robins, E. Follow-up studies in obsessional neurosis. Arch. Gen. Psychiat. 20:182-187, 1969.
28. Gottesman, I. I. and Shields, J. Contributions of twin studies to perspectives in schizophrenia. In *Progress in Experimental Personality Research*, B. A. Maher (ed.): Vol. 3, pp. 1-84. New York: Academic Press, 1966.

29. Guze, S. B., Goodwin, D. W., and Crane, J. B. Criminality and psychiatric disorders. Arch. Gen. Psychiat. 20:583-591, 1969.
30. Hagopian, V., Stratton, D., and Busiek, R. Five cases of pigmentary retinopathy associated with thioridazine administration. Amer. J. Psychiat. 123:97-100, 1966.
31. Hanson, D. R., Gottesman, I. I., and Heston, L. L. Some possible childhood indicators of adult schizophrenia inferred from children of schizophrenics. Brit. J. Psychiat. 129:142-154, 1976.
32. Hare, E. H. Season of birth in schizophrenia and neurosis. Amer. J. Psychiat. 132:1168-1171, 1975.
33. Heston, L. Psychiatric disorders in foster home-reared children of schizophrenic mothers. Brit. J. Psychiat. 112:819-825, 1966.
34. Hoedemaker, F. S. Psychotic episodes and postpsychotic depression in young adults. Amer. J. Psychiat. 127:606-610, 1970.
35. Inouye, E. Similarity and dissimilarity of schizophrenia in twins. Proceedings of the Third World Congress on Psychiatry, Vol. 1, pp. 524-530. Montreal: University of Toronto Press, 1963.
36. Jones, M. B. and Offord, D. R. Independent transmission of IQ and schizophrenia. Brit. J. Psychiat. 126:185-190, 1975.
37. Kallmann, F. J. The genetic theory of schizophrenia. An analysis of 691 twin index families. Amer. J. Psychiat. 103:309-322, 1946.
38. Kazamatsuri, H., Chien, C., and Cole, J. O. Therapeutic approaches to tardive dyskinesia. Arch. Gen. Psychiat. 27:491-499, 1972.
39. Kohn, N. and Myerson, R. Xanthomatous biliary cirrhosis following chlorpromazine. Amer. J. Med. 31:665-670, 1961.
40. Kraepelin, E. *Dementia Praecox and Paraphrenia*, translated by R. M. Barclay and edited by G. M. Robertson. Edinburgh: E. & S. Livingstone, 1919.
41. Kringlen, E. Schizophrenia in twins. An epidemiological-clinical study. Psychiatry 29:172-184, 1966.
42. Lane, E. and Albee, G. W. Childhood intellectual differences between schizophrenic adults and their siblings. Amer. J. Orthopsychiat. 35:747-753, 1965.
43. Langfeldt, G. The prognosis in schizophrenia. Acta Psychiat. et Neurol. Scand. Suppl. 110, 1956.
44. Leonhard, K. *Aufteilung Der Endogenen Psychosen*. Berlin: Akademie-Verlag, 1966.
45. Luxenburger, H. Vorläufiger Bericht über psychiatrischen Serieuntersuchungen an Zwillingen. Z. ges. Neurol. Psychiat. 176:297-326, 1928.
46. McGlashan, T. H. and Carpenter, W. T., Jr. Postpsychotic depression in schizophrenia. Arch. Gen. Psychiat. 33:231-239, 1976.
47. McKinney, W. and Kane, F. J., Jr. Pancytopenia due to chlorpromazine. Amer. J. Psychiat. 123:879-880, 1967.
48. Offord, D. R. School performance of adult schizophrenics, their siblings and age mates. Brit. J. Psychiat. 125:12-19, 1974.

49. Pisciotta, A. V. Agranulocytosis induced by certain phenothiazine derivatives. J.A.M.A. 208:1862-1868, 1969.
50. Planansky, K. and Johnston, R. Depressive syndrome in schizophrenia. Acta Psychiat. Scand. 57:207-218, 1978.
51. Prien, R. F., DeLong, S. L., Cole, J. O., and Levine, J. Ocular changes occurring with prolonged high dose chlorpromazine therapy. Arch. Gen. Psychiat. 23:464-468, 1970.
52. Retterstöl, N. *Paranoid and Paranoiac Psychoses*. Springfield, Ill.: C. C. Thomas, 1966.
53. Retterstöl, N. *Prognosis and Paranoid Psychoses*. Springfield, Ill.: C. C. Thomas, 1970.
54. Robins, E. and Guze, S. B. Establishment of diagnostic validity in psychiatric illness: its application to schizophrenia. Amer. J. Psychiat. 126: 983-987, 1970.
55. Robins, E. and Guze, S. B. Classification of affective disorders: the primary-secondary, the endogenous-reactive, and the neurotic-psychotic concepts. In *Recent Advances in the Psychobiology of the Depressive Illnesses,* Williams, T. A., Katz, M. M., and Shield, J. A., Jr. (eds.). Washington, D.C.: NIMH, DHEW, 1972.
56. Robins, L. *Deviant Children Grown Up*. Baltimore: Williams and Wilkins, 1966.
57. Rosanoff, A. J., Handy, I. M., Plesset, I. R., and Brush, S. The etiology of so-called schizophrenic psychoses. With special reference to their occurrence in twins. Amer. J. Psychiat. 91:247-286, 1934.
58. Rosenthal, D., Wender, P. H., Kety, S. S., Welner, J., and Schulsinger, F. The adopted-away offspring of schizophrenics. Amer. J. Psychiat. 128:307-311, 1971.
59. Roth, S. The seemingly ubiquitous depression following acute schizophrenic episodes, a neglected area of clinical discussion. Amer. J. Psychiat. 127:51-58, 1970.
60. Salokangas, R. R. K. Social class of the parents of schizophrenic patients. Proceedings of the 18th Nordic Psychiatric Congress. Acta Psychiat. Scand., Suppl. 265, 30, 1976.
61. Schuckit, M. A. and Winokur, G. Alcoholic hallucinosis and schizophrenia: a negative study. Brit. J. Psychiat. 119:549-550, 1971.
62. Schulsinger, H. A ten-year follow-up of children of schizophrenic mothers. Clinical assessment. Acta Psychiat. Scand. 53:371-386, 1976.
63. Scott, D. F. Alcoholic hallucinosis—an aetiological study. Brit. J. Addict. 62:113-125, 1967.
64. Sheldrick, C., Jablensky, A., Sartorius, N., and Shepherd, M. Schizophrenia succeeded by affective illness: catamnestic study and statistical enquiry. Psychol. Med. 7:619-624, 1977.
65. Slater, E. *Psychotic and Neurotic Illnesses in Twins*. London: Her Majesty's Stationery Office, 1953.
66. Slater, E., Beard, A., and Glithero, E. The schizophrenia-like psychoses of epilepsy. Brit. J. Psychiat. 109:95-150, 1963.

67. Smith, K. ECT-chlorpromazine and chlorpromazine compared in the treatment of schizophrenia. J. Nerv. Ment. Dis. 144:284-290, 1967.
68. Snyder, S. H. The dopamine hypothesis of schizophrenia: focus on the dopamine receptor. Amer. J. Psychiat. 133:197-202, 1976.
69. Stephens, D. A., Atkinson, M. W., Kay, D. W., Roth, M., and Garside, R. F. Psychiatric morbidity in parents and sibs of schizophrenics and non-schizophrenics. Brit. J. Psychiat. 127:97-108, 1975.
70. Stephens, J. H. Long-term course and prognosis of schizophrenia. Seminars in Psychiatry 2:464-485, 1970.
71. Stephens, J. H. and Astrup, C. Prognosis in "process" and "non-process" schizophrenia. Amer. J. Psychiat. 119:945-953, 1963.
72. Stevens, B. C. *Marriage and Fertility of Women Suffering from Schizophrenia or Affective Disorders,* Maudsley Monograph No. 19. London: Oxford University Press, 1969.
73. Strauss, J. S. and Gift, T. E. Choosing an approach for diagnosing schizophrenia. Arch. Gen. Psychiat. 34:1248-1253, 1977.
74. Strauss, J. S., Kokes, R., Klorman, R., and Sacksteder, J. Premorbid adjustment in schizophrenia: concepts, measures, and implications. Symposium in Schizophrenia Bulletin 3:182-245, 1977.
75. Tienari, P. Psychiatric illnesses in identical twins. Acta Psychiat. Scand., Suppl. 171:1-195, 1963.
76. Torrey, E. F., Torrey, B. B., and Peterson, M. R. Seasonality of schizophrenic births in the United States. Arch. Gen. Psychiat. 34:1065-1070, 1977.
77. Tsuang, M. T., Dempsey, G. M., Dvoredsky, A., and Struss, A. A family history study of schizo-affective disorder. Biol. Psychiat. 12:331-338, 1977.
78. Vaillant, G. E. Prospective prediction of schizophrenic remission. Arch. Gen. Psychiat. 11:509-518, 1964.
79. Vaillant, G. E. The prediction of recovery in schizophrenia. J. Nerv. Ment. Dis. 135:534-543, 1962.
80. Watt, N. F. Patterns of childhood development in adult schizophrenics. Arch. Gen. Psychiat. 35:160-165, 1978.
81. Wender, P. H., Rosenthal, D., Kety, S. S., Schulsinger, F., and Welner, J. Social class and psychopathology in adoptees. Arch. Gen. Psychiat. 28: 318-325, 1973.
82. Woodruff, R. A., Clayton, P. J., and Guze, S. B. Hysteria: studies of diagnosis, outcome, and prevalence. J.A.M.A. 215:425-428, 1971.
83. Zelickson, A. Skin changes and chlorpromazine. J.A.M.A. 198:341-344, 1966.

3. Anxiety Neurosis

Definition

Anxiety neurosis is a chronic illness characterized by recurrent, acute anxiety attacks having a definite onset and spontaneous termination. During attacks the patient is fearful and has symptoms associated with the autonomic nervous system: palpitations, tachycardia, rapid or shallow breathing, dizziness, and tremor. Between attacks, patients may be relatively asymptomatic though some experience fatigue, headache, and individual components of anxiety attacks in a persistent fashion. Anxiety neurosis is not synonymous with anxiousness, which is a symptom rather than a syndrome. Anxiety symptoms and attacks can be part of the course of any psychiatric illness. When they occur in the absence of other significant psychiatric symptoms, the diagnosis of anxiety neurosis is made.

Anxiety is often distinguished from ordinary fear by its lack of an appropriate stimulus to explain the emotion. To highlight the apparently unmotivated nature of anxiety, the term "free-floating" anxiety is often used.

Sometimes, however, patients do experience anxiety attacks in response to a fear-provoking situation, such as facing an angry employer or giving a public speech. In these cases the clinician must decide whether the anxiety is grossly out of proportion to the fear-provoking stimulus, as well as make a diagnosis based on the overall history.

Most anxiety neurotics report that they experience some anxiety attacks without any fear-provoking stimulus, but on other occasions they overreact to situations which would produce some degree of apprehension in individuals without the disorder.

Some clinicians separate "state anxiety" from "trait anxiety."

The former refers to anxiety at any particular moment: "I feel anxious right now." "Trait anxiety" refers to a tendency to be anxious over a long period: "I generally feel anxious." The two forms of anxiety commonly occur together, with increased life stresses raising the anxiety of an already anxiety-prone individual beyond the point of tolerance (24).

Historical Background

An American physician, Beard, described neurasthenia in 1869 (2). He presented a number of cases and discussed contemporary concepts of cause. Patients now described as anxiety neurotics would have been included among Beard's neurasthenics, but some patients with hysteria or obsessional illness might also have been included (4).

In 1871 DaCosta reported a syndrome among Civil War military personnel which he called "irritable heart." His concept was probably more restricted than Beard's, and closer to our definition of anxiety neurosis (8). DaCosta noted that for more than a century previously there had been similar reports of cases from British and German military medical sources.

The term "anxiety neurosis" was first used by Freud in 1895 to refer to patients who probably would have been called neurasthenic by other physicians at that time. Over the past century many terms (Table 1) have been applied to these patients.

In 1950 Wheeler, White, Ried, and Cohen published a twenty-year follow-up study of 173 patients with anxiety neurosis diagnosed by specific checklist criteria (36). Later Cohen *et al.* reported a family study based on a similar group of anxiety neurotics (6). These studies are the basis of the clinical concept of the disorder discussed in this chapter.

In the hundred years since Beard's paper on neurasthenia was published, there have been many theories regarding the cause of the disorder, ranging from constitutional weakness of the nervous

Table 1. Terms used to describe anxiety neurosis

Terms
Neurasthenia
Neurocirculatory asthenia
Nervous exhaustion
DaCosta's syndrome
Effort syndrome
Irritable heart
Soldier's heart
Somatization psychogenic cardiovascular reaction
Somatization psychogenic asthenic reaction
Anxiety reaction
Vasomotor neurosis
La nevrose d'angoisse
Personalities with mixed psychic and physical anomalies: constitutionally labile with tendency to functional disorders of specific organ systems.

From Cohen and White (7)

system, through social and psychological factors, to more recent biochemical hypotheses. Although the cause of anxiety neurosis remains unknown, some studies have indicated that there are physiologic differences between anxiety neurotics and normal individuals (7, 18, 19, 20). Anxiety neurotics, for instance, are more responsive to painful stimuli of various types. They also have low exercise tolerance, and high blood levels of lactic acid following exercise. The latter observation has led to a recent theory that abnormal lactate levels may be responsible for producing anxiety symptoms. It is true that infusion of sodium lactate is at present the most reliable means of producing anxiety attacks among anxiety neurotics; however, the lactate theory is not accepted by all investigators (13, 17, 29). The fact that physiologic differences between anxiety neurotics and normal individuals exist does not mean that such differences are causal. They may be secondary phenomena, the result of inactivity and apprehension associated with the syndrome, whatever its cause.

Epidemiology

Anxiety neurosis is one of the most common psychiatric syndromes. A Boston study indicated that approximately 5 percent of the adult population is affected (7). Many patients, however, experience the syndrome in a mild form and probably never seek medical care for their symptoms (38). Many others consult family practitioners or internists rather than psychiatrists. Anxiety neurotics who see psychiatrists may represent a small group with a high prevalence of secondary affective disorder (38).

Anxiety neurosis affects twice as many women as men. Anxiety neurotics do not differ from the general population in educational level or socioeconomic status (38). There is no evidence that any specific type of childhood experience such as bereavement or birth order predisposes to the disorder (7, 37).

Clinical Picture

Anxiety attacks are the hallmark of the disorder. Many clinicians are reluctant to diagnose anxiety neurosis if a history of these attacks is absent. Anxiety attacks usually begin suddenly, sometimes in a public place, sometimes at home, perhaps awakening the patient from sleep. There is a sense of foreboding, fear, and apprehension; a sense that one has suddenly become seriously ill; a feeling that one's life may be threatened by such illness. Among some patients there is a disturbing sense that one's body has changed or become distorted (depersonalization). Such a feeling of alien change may extend to the surrounding world (derealization).

Symptoms of labored breathing, smothering, palpitation, blurred vision, tremulousness, and weakness usually accompany the apprehension and foreboding. If a patient is examined during such an attack, signs of distress will be present: tachycardia, sweating, tachypnea, tremor, hyperactive deep tendon reflexes, and dilated pupils. An electrocardiogram taken during such an episode usually reveals sinus tachycardia.

Anxiety attacks vary in frequency among patients. Some experience them on a daily basis; others have them only once or twice a year. Other symptoms may occur between attacks. Table 2 lists

Table 2. Symptoms of anxiety neurosis

Symptoms	*60 Patients*	*102 Controls**
Palpitation	97%	9%
Tires easily	93%	19%
Breathlessness	90%	13%
Nervousness	88%	27%
Chest pain	85%	10%
Sighing	79%	16%
Dizziness	78%	16%
Faintness	70%	12%
Aprehensiveness	61%	3%
Headache	58%	26%
Paresthesias	58%	7%
Weakness	56%	3%
Trembling	54%	17%
Breathing unsatisfactory	53%	4%
Insomnia	53%	4%
Unhappiness	50%	2%
Shakiness	47%	16%
Fatigued all the time	45%	6%
Sweating	42%	33%
Fear of death	42%	2%
Smothering	40%	3%
Syncope	37%	11%
Nervous chill	24%	0
Urinary frequency	18%	2%
Vomiting and diarrhea	14%	0
Anorexia	12%	3%
Paralysis	0	0
Blindness	0	0

* Healthy controls consisted of 50 men and 11 women from a large industrial plant, and 41 healthy postpartum women from the Boston Lying-In Hospital. From Cohen and White (7)

these symptoms and their frequency reported in one study. Again, the symptoms can occur in practically any pattern. Sometimes patients report only chronic nervousness and fatigue between attacks without other symptoms.

Cardiorespiratory symptoms are the most frequent chief complaints that anxiety neurotics report to physicians: "I have heart spells," "I think I'll smother," or "There is no way for me to get enough air." The chief complaint is occasionally psychological, but more often it indicates that the patient considers his disorder medical, frequently with the fear that the disturbance may be very serious.

Symptoms may become associated with specific situations that the patient will try to avoid. For example, he may choose aisle seats in theaters, preferably close to exits, so that if an attack occurs, he will not be confined. Or, a patient may avoid social situations in which an attack would be both frightening and embarrassing.

Phobias are common in patients with anxiety neurosis. Some clinicians, in fact, do not distinguish between anxiety neurosis and phobic neurosis. For our purposes, anxiety neurosis is diagnosed when anxiety symptoms predominate, phobic neurosis when phobias predominate.

Natural History

The age of risk for the development of anxiety neurosis extends from the midteens through the early thirties. Like other neuroses, anxiety neurosis seldom begins after age thirty-five (36, 37, 38). The age of onset is usually in the twenties. Some patients may remember the exact time and circumstances of the first attack. In a study by Winokur and Holemon, 13 of 31 anxiety neurotics were able to describe such circumstances (37). Winokur found that four subjects remembered specifically that they had been awakened at night by their first anxiety attack. Some patients remember having their first attack at times of stress (while making a speech in class, for instance). Thus, the disorder may begin acutely with a discrete anxiety attack, but it also may begin insidiously with feelings of tenseness, nervousness, fatigue, or dizziness for years before the first anxiety attack.

The patient's initial medical contact is not always helpful. If he comes to a physician complaining of cardiorespiratory symptoms, fearful of heart disease, a physician unacquainted with the natural history of anxiety neurosis may support the patient's fears by referring him to a specialist and admonishing that exercise should be limited.

While patients commonly present with cardiorespiratory symptoms, they do not do so invariably. Some patients present with symptoms of "irritable colon" (22). In fact, among patients with irritable colon, anxiety neurosis is one of the most common psychiatric illnesses found. Such patients usually consult a gastroenterologist. Among their most common presenting symptoms are abdominal cramping, diarrhea, constipation, nausea, belching, flatus, and occasionally dysphagia. ("Irritable colon" sometimes occurs in the course of other psychiatric illnesses such as hysteria or primary affective disorder. It also occurs in the absence of psychiatric illness.)

In one long-term study of patients meeting the criteria for anxiety neurosis, gastrointestinal and musculoskeletal symptoms were as frequent as cardiovascular ones (27). For example, abdominal pain or discomfort was not far behind chest pain or discomfort and muscular aching or tension in occurrence. And during anxiety attacks, noncardiovascular symptoms, such as headache or abdominal pain, often became the primary focus of concern. A shift of symptoms over the follow-up period reflected the increasing chronicity of the illness. In this series, the more acute, dramatic, and disruptive manifestations tended to drop out over time. Anxiety attacks after five years were occurring in only half of the patients, and insomnia, nausea, vomiting, light-headedness, and fainting were greatly reduced.

Anxiety neurosis can occasionally be severe, but in the majority of cases the course is mild (36). Symptoms wax and wane in an irregular pattern which may or may not be associated with events and circumstances interpreted by the patient as stressful. Despite their symptoms, most anxiety neurotics live productively without social impairment.

Seven long-term studies of patients with anxiety neurosis conducted in Boston, Oslo, England, Zurich, and Iowa show remarkably similar findings (24). On five- to 20-year follow-up, about 50 to 60 percent of patients had recovered or were much improved. About one in five patients continued to have moderate to severe disability (Table 3).

The most recent follow-up of anxiety neurotics seen by a psychiatric consultation service revealed almost identical findings, suggesting that those relatively few patients who see a psychiatrist have a prognosis as favorable as the majority who do not (27). In this study men of age thirty or more at the time of psychiatric consultation showed the poorest outcome. As the authors note, this may reflect a tendency for men to ignore lesser degrees of stress and seek medical care only when more severely impaired.

Anxiety neurosis rarely leads to hospitalization. When psychiatric hospitalization does occur, it usually results from complications of the illness, such as secondary affective disorder.

While patients with anxiety neurosis may respond favorably to reassurance, or to other forms of symptomatic treatment, there is no evidence that any form of therapy prevents recurrence of at-

Table 3. Disability from anxiety neurosis—Twenty-year follow-up

Symptoms and Disability	*60 Patients*	*22 Men*	*38 Women*
Well	12%	13%	11%
Symptoms, no disability	35%	46%	29%
Symptoms, mild disability	38%	32%	42%
Symptoms, moderate or severe disability	15%	9%	18%

From Wheeler *et al.* (36)

tacks and, thus, no evidence that the long-term prognosis can be altered (10, 36).

Complications

The complications of anxiety neurosis are less severe than those of psychiatric disorders such as affective disorder or alcoholism, in which judgment may be impaired and suicide is a risk. Judgment is not impaired by anxiety neurosis and suicide rarely occurs.

The anxiety neurotics seen by psychiatrists are probably a select group with an illness frequently complicated by either secondary affective disorder or by alcoholism (38). Otherwise, anxiety neurotics seen by psychiatrists are similar to those seen by cardiologists (see Table 2).

Depression complicating anxiety neurosis does not differ symptomatically from unipolar primary affective disorder, and thus the question whether there may be an association between anxiety neurosis and primary affective disorder has occurred to many clinicians. In one series of patients diagnosed as anxiety neurotics, 19 percent were subsequently relabeled as depressives (27). The question also arises from the great frequency with which primarily depressed patients experience anxiety symptoms. It could be that anxiety neurosis is a variant of primary affective disorder. Age of onset, however, does not distinguish between anxiety neurosis with and without secondary affective disorder. The average age of onset is twenty for both groups, and this is more consistent with anxiety neurosis than with primary affective disorder, in which the average age of onset is about forty. In addition, anxiety neurotics with secondary affective disorder infrequently end their lives by suicide. Thus it would seem that anxiety neurosis, even when complicated by depression, should be regarded as distinct from primary affective disorder.

Drug abuse may occur as a complication of anxiety neurosis, and may perhaps be the occasional result of overzealous medication by well-meaning physicians. Dependence on barbiturates and other sedatives and tranquilizers is probably the most dangerous form of drug abuse associated with anxiety neurosis.

Certain complications are *not* associated with anxiety neurosis. So-called "psychosomatic disorders" do not occur more often among anxiety neurotics than in the general population (36). Patients with anxiety neurosis are no more likely than others to develop ulcers, asthma, hypertension, heart disease, or any other illness which has been associated, however tenuously, with stress. Anxiety neurotics do not develop schizophrenia, organic brain syndromes, or other psychiatric illnesses with unusual frequency. Thus, despite the common belief that a chronic state of anxiety is likely to bring about other illnesses, there is little evidence that this actually happens. Anxiety neurotics have a life span as long as that of normal individuals (36).

Family Studies

Anxiety neurosis runs in families. Most investigators agree that at least 15 percent of parents and siblings of patients with anxiety neurosis are similarly affected (3, 6, 25, 26, 35). In one family-history study, a prevalence of anxiety neurosis of about 5 percent among adults in the general population was reported as opposed to a prevalence of 49 percent among the grown children of anxiety neurotics (35). In another study, the following rates of anxiety neurosis among relatives of anxiety neurotics were found: fathers, 18 percent; mothers, 55 percent; brothers, 13 percent; sisters, 12 percent (6). Sixty-seven percent of index cases had a positive family history of anxiety neurosis. The authors interpreted these and other data from their report as suggesting that chronic anxiety neurosis is transmitted in a pattern which approximates that of Mendelian autosomal dominance. They were careful to note that the pattern was only an approximation.

Other investigators have found that more mothers than fathers of anxiety neurotics had a history of the illness themselves (26). At the same time, there is an increased frequency of alcoholism among fathers (6, 26). Thus, it is possible that alcoholism in the fathers of anxiety neurotics could be a variant of anxiety neurosis. Support for this notion comes from a study by Pitts and his colleagues (30) of neurotics in general. These authors reported an increased prevalence of neurosis among the mothers of neurotics and an increased prevalence of alcoholism among the fathers.

There have been several twin studies of neurotics, but most of them have involved very small samples. The most extensive twin study was made at the Maudsley Hospital, where a twin registry has been maintained for many years. Of 45 twin pairs with anxiety states, Slater and Shields found that 41 percent of the 17 pairs of monozygotic twins were concordant compared with 4 percent of the 28 pairs of dizygotic twins (32). Slater and Shields concluded that "this finding argues in favor of some degree of genetic specificity of anxiety."

Differential Diagnosis

Anxiety symptoms and anxiety attacks can be part of any psychiatric illness. Anxiety symptoms often appear in primary affective disorder, obsessional illness, phobic neurosis, hysteria, and alcoholism. Ultimately, the diagnosis is based on chronology. Anxiety neurosis is diagnosed only if there are either no other symptoms or if anxiety symptoms antedated the others.

Medical illnesses that produce symptoms resembling those of anxiety neurosis include cardiac arrhythmias (especially paroxysmal atrial tachycardia), angina pectoris, hyperthyroidism, pheochromocytoma, parathyroid disease, and mitral valve prolapse. Mitral valve prolapse appears to be fairly common, perhaps afflicting 5 percent of the population (9, 23). Abnormal EKG's are usually present, together with systolic clicks and late systolic murmurs.

The diagnosis of anxiety neurosis obviously requires exclusion of medical conditions that give rise to similar symptoms. Clinicians who are not familiar with anxiety neurosis as a specific diagnostic entity may mistakenly attribute the symptoms to a physical condition. Studies show that a "false positive" diagnosis is made in 25 percent of patients considered to have angina pectoris, some of whom almost certainly have anxiety neurosis (1). The percentage of false positives actually may be higher, because of disagreement about interpreting electrocardiograms. In one study, three cardiologists interviewed 57 patients with chest pain. If any of them diagnosed angina, there was only a 55 percent chance that his two colleagues would agree with him (31). In another study, of 110 electrocardiagrams read by at least one of four cardiologists as compatible with arteriosclerotic heart disease, two of the readers agreed in 60 percent of the cases, three out of the four agreed in 40 percent, and all four agreed in less than 20 percent (15). Nearly half of patients undergoing postmortem examinations who had received a diagnosis of angina pectoris show no coronary artery narrowing (11). False positives and false negatives are even found in double-blind evaluations of the two-step exercise EKG (21).

Clearly, it is important to exclude medical illness before diagnosing anxiety neurosis, but because of disagreement among clinicians, this may not be as simple as it seems.

In any case, there appears to be no characteristic electrocardiographic abnormality associated with anxiety neurosis. This conclusion came from a Framingham study of 203 cases of anxiety neurosis and 757 control subjects free of cardiovascular disease (16).

The mistake probably made most often in the evaluation of anxiety symptoms is that of overlooking primary affective disorder. Among other factors, a family history of affective disorder should alert one to the possibility that a patient with anxiety symptoms may have primary affective disorder. Also, anxiety which begins for the first time after the age of forty is commonly part of a depressive syndrome rather than a manifestation of anxiety neurosis.

Hysteria involves a broader range of medical complaints with frequent hospitalizations and operations. Anxiety neurotics are hospitalized and operated on no more frequently than other individuals. Furthermore, anxiety neurosis is *not* characterized by dramatic and medically unexplained complaints in nearly *every* area of the review of symptoms, as is the case in hysteria. Finally, sexual and menstrual complaints and conversion symptoms (unexplained neurological symptoms), common in hysteria, do not appear frequently among patients with anxiety neurosis.

Obsessional illness and phobic neurosis can be mistaken for anxiety neurosis. Phobic neurosis is so similar that the distinction depends on whether or not phobias dominate the clinical picture. Obsessional neurosis involves obsessive ruminations and compulsive rituals. While these may occur in mild form among patients with anxiety neurosis, they are not characteristically severe.

Anxiety neurosis also should be distinguished from the so-called "postaccident anxiety syndrome." In one series (26) patients who had experienced a life-threatening accident subsequently experienced a long period of free-floating anxiety, muscular tension, irritability, impaired concentration, repetitive nightmares reproducing the accident, and social withdrawal. These symptoms persisted for six months to three years after the accident. None of the patients had cardiorespiratory or other autonomic symptoms, the hallmark of a typical anxiety neurosis. Also, in some cases referred by courts, the possibility of monetary compensation may have been a contributing factor. Supporting this possibility are a number of studies, starting with one by Heim in 1892 of survivors of falls in the Alps (14), reporting that most individuals do not have frightening dreams or anxiety after their accidents. In any event, there is no evidence that life-threatening events precipitate anxiety neurosis as defined in this chapter.

Anxiety attacks are occasionally accompanied by hyperventilation, which produces symptoms that aggravate those of anxiety neurosis. Such symptoms are caused by lowering of pCO_2 as well as other chemical alterations, including an elevation of lactic acid. Five deep breaths produced by yawning or sighing may be enough to alter pCO_2 and produce the characteristic symptoms (5): cerebral hypoxia, a slowing of the EEG, and respiratory alkalosis, which in turn can induce tetany.

It appears that there is a group of patients who have hyperventilation syndrome (HVS) but do not meet the criteria for anxiety neurosis. In contrast to studies of anxiety neurosis, it is not known whether HVS represents a discrete syndrome or is symptomatic of other psychiatric or medical conditions. Apparently, some individuals are more susceptible than others to the effects of hyperventilation.

In one study at the Yale-New Haven Hospital, the diagnosis of HVS was made on the basis of the patient's response to overbreathing (5). Each patient suspected of having HVS was asked to overbreathe for up to 3 minutes or until he or she became dizzy. If the patient's reported symptoms were reproduced in their entirety and if no other explanation for the symptoms could be adduced from physical examination, medical history, or laboratory tests, the diagnosis of HVS was considered established. However, many patients had a history of conversion reactions, hypochondriasis, or "psychosomatic" illnesses, and most were young women. Others had organic diseases, such as adrenal insufficiency and peptic ulcer. Thus, psychiatric conditions such as Briquet's syndrome (hysteria) or medical illness actually may have been the primary disorder, with hyperventilation occurring secondarily, as it sometimes does in anxiety neurosis. In short, whether or not HVS exists as a separate syndrome is still uncertain.

How far to pursue a physical explanation for symptoms that may represent an anxiety neurosis depends upon clinical judgment, but a good deal of money is often invested in tests and consultations. In one study (27), anxiety neurotics received an average of five laboratory tests and two consultations with specialists. As the authors explained: "This is not unusual, since most patients did not consider their illness as psychiatric but saw themselves as persons suffering from undiagnosed physical conditions. This almost inevitably led to a search for an organic basis for the complaints. Sometimes the search was conducted against the physicians' better judgment in order that the patient might accept psychiatric referral. Even at that, the patients as a group were demanding and not easily satisfied. One patient's remark typified the attitude of many. 'I do not want to be told what I haven't got. I want the doctor to find something.' Another patient stated, 'I know I am nervous, I have always been nervous, but don't try to tell me that is what is wrong.'"

Clinical Management

Psychiatric referral is rarely necessary for anxiety neurosis if the patient's physician has diagnosed the disorder correctly, understands its natural history, and is willing to discuss the syndrome with the patient. Telling the patient that there is nothing wrong physically is usually not enough. Some patients resent the implication that their symptoms might be psychological. Others continue to believe that they have a serious illness. The physician should agree that something is wrong and should describe the syndrome in lay terms. Many patients are relieved by such an explanation, and thereby become receptive to further reassurance.

As noted earlier in this chapter, some patients with "irritable bowel" syndrome or musculoskeletal complaints meet the criteria for anxiety neurosis. In these cases, treatment should focus primarily on the basic disorder—the anxiety neurosis—so that the presenting gastrointestinal or musculoskeletal complaints are viewed in this context and treated as conservatively as possible.

Supportive psychotherapy is almost always indicated, yet there is no evidence that psychological management more extensive than reassurance has any better effect than reassurance alone (10, 36). Prolonged and expensive forms of psychotherapy are rarely indicated.

Physicians should be careful not to introduce anxiety neurotics to drugs which are frequently misused, such as shorter-acting barbiturates. Nevertheless, sedatives can be helpful. Phenobarbital and amobarbital have been used for years and presumably have benefited many patients. The more recently developed "minor tranquilizers" of the benzodiazepine variety such as chlordiazepoxide (Librium), diazepam (Valium), and oxazepam (Serax) may also be useful in treating anxiety symptoms. There is some evidence that the beta-adrenergic blocking agent propranolol (Inderal), a drug used for cardiac arrhythmias, may be effective in the treatment of anxiety neurosis in small doses (12, 34). Propranolol has potentially serious side effects but not usually in the low doses effective in reducing anxiety symptoms (33). The only significant ones reported have been increased wheezing in asthmatic patients. Although the efficacy of propranolol in treating anxiety neurosis has not definitely been established, there is little question that it blocks some of the physiologic symptoms. In combination with a benzodiazapene to relieve the anxiety, it may constitute the best pharmacological approach to anxiety neurosis now available. Since anxiety neurosis is a chronic disease, some clinicians feel that propranolol, if effective, should be used as a preventive measure rather than reserved for acute attacks.

When depressive symptoms are prominent, it is appropriate to administer tricyclic antidepressant agents. These drugs can be used in combination with the benzodiazepine compounds. The treatment of secondary affective disorder accompanying anxiety neurosis is similar to the treatment of primary affective disorder, depressed type.

The distinction between depression and anxiety neurosis may be useful as a guide to treatment. Electroconvulsive therapy and tricyclic drugs, in one study, were significantly more effective in depressives than in patients with anxiety neurosis (27).

On occasion, severe anxiety symptoms and phobias are associated with specific situations. For instance, anxiety neurotics may find that symptoms are more severe in a closed space such as an elevator. Desensitization techniques, derived from learning theory (desensitization, reciprocal inhibition, paradoxical intention, implosion) can be used to treat such specific symptoms. These forms of treatment will be discussed at greater length in the chapter on phobic neurosis.

References

1. Banks, T. and Shugoll, G. Confirmatory physical findings in angina pectoris. J.A.M.A. 200:107-112, 1967.
2. Beard, G. M. Neurasthenia or nervous exhaustion. Boston Med. and Surg. J. 3:217, 1869.
3. Brown, F. Heredity in psychoneuroses. Proc. Roy. Soc. Med. 35:785-790, 1942.
4. Chatel, J. C. and Peele, R. A centennial review of neurasthenia. J. Psychiat. 126:1404-1413, 1970.
5. Christensen, B. Studies on hyperventilation. II Electrocardiographic changes in normal man during voluntary hyperventilation. J. Clin. Invest. 24:880, 1946.
6. Cohen, M. E., Badal, D. W., Kilpatrick, A., Ried, E. W., and White, P. D. The high familial prevalence of neurocirculatory asthenia (anxiety neurosis, effort syndrome). Amer. J. Human Genet. 3:126, 1951.
7. Cohen, M. and White, P. Life situations, emotions, and neurocirculatory asthenia (anxiety neurosis, neurasthenia, effort syndrome). Ass. Res. Nerv. Dis. Proc. 29:832-869, 1950.
8. DaCosta, J. M. On irritable heart, a clinical form of functional cardiac disorder and its consequences. Amer. J. Med. Sci. 61:17, 1871.
9. Devereux, R. B., Perloff, J. K., Reichek, N., and Josephson, M. E. Mitral valve prolapse. Circulation 54:3, 1976.
10. Eysenck, H. J. *The Effects of Psychotherapy*. New York: International Science Press, 1966.
11. Friedberg, C. K. *et al.* The two step exercise electrocardiogram: A double blind evaluation of its use in the diagnosis of angina pectoris. Circulation 26:1254-1260, 1962.
12. Granville-Grossman, K. L. and Turner, P. The effect of propranolol on anxiety. Lancet 1:788-790, 1966.
13. Grosz, H. J. and Farmer, B. B. Pitts and McClure's lactate-anxiety study revisited. Brit. J. Psychiat. 120:415-418, 1972.
14. Heim, A. Remarks on Fatal Falls. Yearbook of the Swiss Alpine Club 27:327-337, 1892. Trans. R. Noyes and R. Kletti in Omega 3:45-52, 1972.
15. Higgins, I. T. Ischemic heart disease: The problem. Milbank Mem. Fund. Quart. 43:23-31, 1965.
16. Kannel, W. B., Dawber, T. R., and Cohen, M. E. The electrocardiogram in neurocirculatory asthenia (anxiety neurosis or neurasthenia): A study of 203 neurocirculatory asthenia patients and 757 healthy controls in the Framingham study. An. Int. Med. 49: No. 6, 1351-1360, 1958.
17. Kelly, D., Mittchell-Heggs, N., and Sherman, D. Anxiety and the ef-

fects of sodium lactate assessed clinically and physiologically. Brit. J. Psychiat. 119:129-141, 1971.

18. Kelly, D. and Walter, C. J. S. A clinical and physiological relationship between anxiety and depression. Brit. J. Psychiat. 115:401-406, 1969.
19. Levander-Lindgren, M. Studies in neurocirculatory asthenia (DaCosta's syndrome). Acta Med. Scand. 172:665-683, 1962.
20. Levander-Lindgren, M. Studies in neurocirculatory asthenia (DaCosta's syndrome). Acta Med. Scand. 173:631-637, 1963.
21. Liebow, I. M. and Oseasohn, R. Relationship between selected clinical and electrocardiographic findings and post mortem lesions associated with ischemic heart disease. J. Chronic Dis. 17:609-617, 1964.
22. Liss, J., Alpers, D., and Woodruff, R. A. The "irritable colon" syndrome and psychiatric illness. Dis. Nerv. Syst. 34:151-157, 1973.
23. Markiewicz, W., Stoner, J., London, E., Hunt, S. A., and Popp, R. L. Mitral valve prolapse in one hundred presumably healthy young females. Circulation 53:464, 1976.
24. Marks, I. and Lader, M. Anxiety states (anxiety neurosis): A review. J. Nerv. Ment. Dis. 156:3-18, 1973.
25. McInnes, R. G. Observations on heredity in neurosis. Proc. Roy. Soc. Med. 30:895-904, 1937.
26. Modlin, H. C. Postaccident anxiety syndrome: psychosocial aspects. Amer. J. Psychiat. 123:1008-1012, 1967.
27. Noyes, R. and Clancy, J. Anxiety neurosis: A 5-year follow-up. J. Nerv. Ment. Dis. 162:200-205, 1976.
28. Noyes, R. and Kletti, R. Depersonalization in the face of life-threatening danger: A description. Psychiatry 39:19-27, 1976.
29. Pitts, F. N. and McClure, J. N. Lactate metabolism in anxiety neurosis. N.E.J.M. 277:1329-1336, 1967.
30. Pitts, F. N., Meyer, J., Brooks, M., and Winokur, G. Adult psychiatric illness assessed for childhood parental loss, and psychiatric illness in family members: A study of 748 patients and 250 controls. Amer. J. Psychiat. 121:Suppl. i-x, 1965.
31. Rose, G. A. Ischemic heart disease: Chest pain questionnaire. Milbank Mem. Fund. Quart. 43:32-39, 1965.
32. Slater, B. and Shields, J. Genetical aspects anxiety. Brit. J. Psychiat. Special Publication No. 3, Studies of anxiety. Ashford, Kent: Headley Bros., 1969, pp. 62-71.
33. Tanna, V. T., Penningrowth, R. P., and Woolson, R. F. Propranolol in anxiety neurosis. Compr. Psychiat. 18:319-326, 1977.
34. Wheatley, D. Comparative effects of propranolol and chlordiazepoxide in anxiety states. Brit. J. Psychiat. 115:1411-1412, 1969.
35. Wheeler, E. O., White, P. D., Ried, E. W., and Cohen, M. E. Familial incidence of neurocirculatory asthenia (anxiety neurosis, effort syndrome). J. Clin. Invest. 27:562, 1948.
36. Wheeler, E. O., White, P. D., Ried, E. W., and Cohen, M. E. Neuro-

circulatory asthenia (anxiety neurosis, effort syndrome, neuroasthenia). J.A.M.A. 142:878-889, 1950.
37. Winokur, G. and Holemon, E. Chronic anxiety neurosis: Clinical and sexual aspects. Acta Psychiat. Scand. 39:384-412, 1963.
38. Woodruff, R. A. Jr., Guze, S. B., and Clayton, P. J. Anxiety neurosis among psychiatric outpatients. Compr. Psychiat. 13:165-170, 1972.

4. Hysteria (Briquet's Syndrome)

Definition

The terms "hysteria" and "conversion symptoms" are both frequently used and, for some, they are synonymous. It is important, however, to distinguish between them.

Hysteria is a *polysymptomatic* disorder that begins early in life (usually in the teens, rarely after the twenties), chiefly affects women, and is characterized by recurrent, multiple somatic complaints often described dramatically. Characteristic features, all unexplained by other known clinical disorders, are varied pains, anxiety symptoms, gastrointestinal disturbances, urinary symptoms, menstrual difficulties, sexual and marital maladjustment, nervousness, mood disturbances, and conversion symptoms. Repeated visits to physicians and clinics, the use of a large number of medications—often at the same time—prescribed by different physicians, and frequent hospitalizations and operations result in a florid medical history (18, 19).

Conversion symptoms are unexplained symptoms suggesting neurological disease, such as amnesia, unconsciousness, paralysis, "spells," aphonia, urinary retention, difficulty in walking, anesthesia, and blindness—the so-called "pseudo-neurological" or "grand hysterical" symptoms. "Unexplained" means only that the history, neurological examination, and diagnostic tests have failed to reveal a satisfactory explanation for the symptoms. The term "conversion symptom" has no etiologic or pathogenetic implication; it refers, in a descriptive way only, to a limited group of symptoms. In order to give the term greater specificity, unexplained pains and other unexplained medical symptoms that do not suggest neurological disease are not included in the definition. If other unexplained medical symptoms, such as headaches, backaches, and abdominal pains, were included, conversion symptom would mean *any* unexplained medical symptom, and thus lose any precision it has (18, 19).

In summary, conversion symptoms comprise a limited group of individual symptoms suggesting neurological disease. Hysteria is a polysymptomatic syndrome that typically includes conversion symptoms.

One criticism of this definition of hysteria is that everyone experiences many symptoms characteristic of the syndrome. It is true that most people have experienced headaches, fatigue, anorexia, nausea, diarrhea, vomiting, nervousness, and varied pains. But when responding to a physician, few report such symptoms. Most people interpret the physician's questions to mean significant symptoms; they report only symptoms that are recent, recurrent, or otherwise troublesome. Furthermore, the physician himself evaluates the patient's responses, ignoring symptoms that are not recent, recurrent, or disabling. He does pay attention to symptoms that led the patient to consult physicians, take medicines, or alter usual routines. In addition, there are some symptoms that will be considered significant regardless of qualifying features, such as blindness and paralysis. These criteria—ones that physicians ordinarily use to evaluate symptoms—are the same as those applied in the studies of hysteria cited here. By these criteria, very few people report enough symptoms, otherwise unexplained medically, to warrant the diagnosis of hysteria.

Historical Background

The concept of hysteria is at least 4000 years old, and it probably originated in Egypt. The name, hysteria, has been in use since the time of Hippocrates.

The original Egyptian approach to hysteria was probably the most fanciful. Believing that physical displacement of the uterus caused the varied symptoms, physicians treated the patient by trying to attract the "wandering uterus" back to its proper site. Sweet smelling substances were placed in the region of the vagina to attract the errant organ; unpleasant materials were ingested or inhaled to drive it away from the upper body (33).

While Egyptian and Greek physicians applied the diagnosis whenever they believed that unusual symptoms were caused by a displaced uterus, they did not provide diagnostic criteria. This state of affairs has persisted to the present, and although speculations about pathogenesis have changed through the centuries, few authors of any century, including our own, have provided diagnostic criteria of any kind (31).

Witchcraft, demonology, and sorcery were associated with hysteria in the middle ages (33). Mysterious symptoms, spells, and odd behavior were frequently considered manifestations of supernatural, evil influences. Hysterical patients were sometimes perceived as either the active evil spirit (witch, sorceress, or demon) or as the passive victim of such an evil being. Since the middle ages there have been speculations of many kinds about the cause of hysteria. Such speculations have included ideas about neurological weakness, neurological degeneration, the effects of various toxins, and disturbances of what Mesmer called animal magnetism.

Hysteria became Freud's central concern during the early years of psychoanalysis (3). That interest had developed while Freud was working in Paris with Charcot, who was treating hysteria with hypnosis. The psychoanalytic concept of conversion as an ego defense mechanism, referring to unconscious conversion of "psychic energy" into physical symptoms, ultimately resulted in the identification of conversion symptoms with hysteria. Many psychoanalysts consider hysteria a simulation of illness designed to work out unconscious conflicts, partially through attention-getting and "secondary gain," a term that refers to possible advantages of illness such as sympathy and support, including financial support, from relatives and friends and being excused from various duties (38).

This view leads easily to the attitude, widely held by physicians though seldom stated openly, that hysteria is a term of opprobrium to be applied whenever the patient's complaints are not explained or when his demands appear excessive. The most fully developed version of this view is the concept of the "hysterical personality." Here, the emphasis is upon immature, histrionic, manipulative, seductive, and attention-getting behavior, regardless of the presenting complaint or present illness. In the absence of specific diagnostic criteria and systematic studies, however, use of the term has been inconsistent and confusing. Many clinicians believe that conversion symptoms, hysteria, and hysterical personality are different: all three may frequently be present in the same individual (22), but any combination is possible, and patients may present any one without the other two (8, 9).

The syndromatic approach to the diagnosis of hysteria began in 1859, when the French physician, Briquet, published his monograph, *Traité clinique et thérapeutique à l'hystérie* (4). Similar descriptions of the syndrome were provided in 1909 by the English physician, Savill (29), and in 1951 by the American psychiatrists, Purtell, Robins, and Cohen (25). In the past decade, a series of studies has refined and clarified the concept of hysteria as a syndrome (16, 18, 19, 24, 36, 37), and in a systematic study of women diagnosed as "having a hysterical personality or as being hysterics," Blinder (2) confirmed the clinical description and familial characteristics described below. To minimize confusion and controversy, Briquet's syndrome has been proposed as a neutral diagnostic label for this group of patients (19). This term eliminates confusion resulting from different definitions of hysteria so that agreement about the presence or absence of the syndrome should be easier to achieve regardless of philosophical orientation or adherence to particular theories of etiology or pathogenesis. It also avoids the negative or pejorative implications associated with the word hysteria.

Epidemiology

A recent study (34) indicated the prevalence of Briquet's syndrome in an urban community to be 0.4 percent. Assuming that nearly all of the cases occurred in women, and correcting for the sex distribution of the sample, the prevalence of Briquet's syndrome in urban women is just under 1 percent, according to this report. Studies of hospitalized, postpartum women whose pregnancies and deliveries were without complication, indicate that the prevalence of hysteria is between 1 and 2 percent of the female population (37). There are no data on the population frequency of hysteria in men.

A history of conversion symptoms, on the other hand, is commonly found when systematic interviewing is done among hospitalized, normal, postpartum women (14), hospitalized medically ill women (36), and male and female psychiatric outpatients (21). Table 1 indicates that about one-quarter of such patients give a history of conversion symptoms.

All authors, except those describing military experiences, report that the great majority of patients with hysteria are women (26, 32). Nearly all men with symptoms resembling hysteria in women have had histories of associated compensation factors, such as litigation following injuries, consideration for veterans' and other pensions, disability payments, or serious legal difficulties.

There is a generally held view that hysteria and conversion symptoms are more common among less sophisticated, more "primitive" people. One group of investigators found that higher education (one or more years of college) was significantly less common in patients with conversion symptoms—with or without hysteria—than in patients without conversion symptoms. This was also true for patients with hysteria compared to other psychiatric patients as a group (21). Another group reported that "hysterical neurosis,

Table 1. Prevalence of a history of conversion symptoms

Sample	*Percent*
100 normal postpartum women (14)	27
50 medically ill women (36)	30
500 men and women psychiatry clinic patients (21)	24

conversion type" was twice as frequent in nonwhites as in whites and highest in the lowest socioeconomic classes (32).

Of much interest is the work of J. C. Carothers, a British psychiatrist whose anthropological studies led to a theory that "psychopathy and hysteria" may be manifestations of the persistence in modern society of preliterate "magical" modes of thinking. On the basis of this theory, Carothers concluded that sociopathy should predominate in men, hysteria in women (see below) (7).

While a history of conversion symptoms may be elicited from patients with any psychiatric disorder, two conditions are most often associated with such a history: hysteria and sociopathy.

In summary, a history of conversion symptoms can be found among psychiatric patients of either sex suffering from any psychiatric disorder. Such a history is most likely to be associated with hysteria in women or sociopathy in men. Hysteria is much less common than conversion symptoms; it is seen infrequently among men; and, like conversion symptoms, it is infrequently associated with higher education.

Clinical Picture

When first seen by a psychiatrist, the typical patient with hysteria is a married woman in her thirties. Her history is often delivered in a dramatic, complicated fashion. She usually presents with multiple vague complaints to her general physician, and the straightforward history of a present illness is difficult to elicit. Frequently, the physician has trouble deciding when the present illness began, or even why the patient came. Table 2 presents the most common symptoms reported by hysterics. Not only do hysterics report large numbers of these and other symptoms, but they report symptoms distributed widely throughout all or nearly all organ systems. It is this range of symptoms, in addition to their number, that defines hysteria.

The dramatic, colorful, exaggerated description of symptoms in hysteria is best conveyed by quoting patients, though it should be noted that not all patients show this trait to the same degree. The following quotations are from Purtell *et al.* (25).

Vomiting: "I vomit every ten minutes. Sometimes it lasts for two to three weeks at a time. I can't even take liquids. I even vomit water. I can't stand the smell of food."

Food intolerance: "I can't eat pastries. Always pay for it. I can't eat steak now. I throw up whole milk. I always throw up the skins of tomatoes. Pudding made with canned milk makes me sick. I have to use fresh milk."

A trance: "I passed out on the bathroom floor during my period and was still on the floor when they found me the next morning."

Weight change: "I can lose weight just walking down the street. I can hold my breath and lose weight. I was down to 65 pounds at one time."

Dysmenorrhea: "I can't work. Every month I am in bed for several days. I have had to have morphine hypos. There is a throbbing pain in the legs as if the blood doesn't circulate. Can't go to the bathroom as I faint." "It's murder! I want to die. It affects my nervous system."

Sexual indifference: "Have never been interested." "It's not a normal thing to me. Disgusting!" "My husband has never bothered me." "It's just a part of my married life. I have to do it." "I was only disappointed. Never really enjoyed it, but I had to please my husband." "I have no feelings. It's just a duty."

Dyspareunia: "Every time I had intercourse I swelled up on one side. It's sore and burns, and afterwards is very painful." "I hate it. I have a severe pain on the right side and have to go to bed for a day."

Presenting complaints: "I am sore all over. I can't explain it. I have been sick all my life. Now I am alone since my husband died, and the doctor said I must come for help. It has taken $10,000 to keep me alive. This is my 76th hospitalization." "I have been taking care of my invalid mother and I get very little rest or sleep." "My father came here for a checkup on his diabetes and insisted

Table 2. The frequency of symptoms in hysteria

Symptom	%	*Symptom*	%	*Symptom*	%
Dyspnea	72	Weight loss	28	Back pain	88
Palpitation	60	Sudden fluctuations in weight	16	Joint pain	84
Chest pain	72	Anorexia	60	Extremity pain	84
Dizziness	84	Nausea	80	Burning pains in rectum, vagina, mouth	28
Headache	80	Vomiting	32	Other bodily pain	36
Anxiety attacks	64	Abdominal pain	80	Depressed feelings	64
Fatigue	84	Abdominal bloating	68	Phobias	48
Blindness	20	Food intolerances	48	Vomiting all nine months of pregnancy	20
Paralysis	12	Diarrhea	20	Nervous	92
Anesthesia	32	Constipation	64	Had to quit working because felt bad	44
Aphonia	44	Dysuria	44	Trouble doing anything because felt bad	72
Lump in throat	28	Urinary retention	8	Cried a lot	60
Fits or convulsions	20	Dysmenorrhea (premarital only)	4	Felt life was hopeless	28
Faints	56	Dysmenorrhea (prepregnancy only)	8	Always sickly (most of life)	40
Unconsciousness	16	Dysmenorrhea (other)	48	Thought of dying	48
Amnesia	8	Menstrual irregularity	48	Wanted to die	36
Visual blurring	64	Excessive menstrual bleeding	48	Thought of suicide	28
Visual hallucination	12	Sexual indifference	44	Attempted suicide	12
Deafness	4	Frigidity (absence of orgasm)	24		
Olfactory hallucination	16	Dyspareunia	52		
Weakness	84				

From M. Perley and S. B. Guze, N.E.J.M. 266:421-426, 1962

that I come along. I had a nervous breakdown in 1943 and have never gotten around to being really well."

The gynecologist, the neurologist, and the psychiatrist are likely to see hysterics with more focused complaints: the gynecologist, because of menstrual pain, irregularity, or lapses, or because of dyspareunia; the neurologist because of headaches, "spells," or other conversion symptoms; the psychiatrist, because of suicide attempts, depression, or marital discord. But even these specialists find it difficult to obtain straightforward histories from patients with hysteria.

Among the characteristic recurrent or chronic symptoms in hysteria, pains are very prominent: headaches, chest pain, abdominal pain, back pain, joint pain. Abdominal, pelvic, and back pain, in association with menstrual or sexual difficulties, account for frequent gynecologic surgery: dilatation and curettage, uterine suspension, and salpingo-oopherectomy. Abdominal pain, back pain, dysuria, and dyspareunia account for frequent catheterization and cystoscopy. Abdominal pain, indigestion, bowel difficulties, and vomiting are associated with frequent gastrointestinal X-ray examinations and rectal and gallbladder surgery.

Repeated hospitalization and surgery are characteristic of hysteria (12). Because of the dramatic and persistent symptoms, patients are hospitalized for observation, tests, X-rays, and treatment of a wide variety of medical and surgical conditions that may be mimicked by hysteria. Figures 1 and 2 illustrate the markedly increased risk of surgery in hysteria.

Nervousness and anxiety symptoms (palpitation, dyspnea, chest pain, dizziness, fatigue, tremulousness) are frequent. When chest pain is prominent, it often leads to a diagnosis of heart disease, too often supported only by nonspecific deviations in the electrocardiogram. The same nervousness and anxiety symptoms, especially when associated with globus ("lump in throat") or weight loss, frequently lead to thyroid studies and the diagnosis of thyroid abnormalities. Before the advent of modern laboratory methods for evaluating thyroid function, thyroidectomy was performed for suspected hyperthyroidism, particularly in older patients. Moodiness,

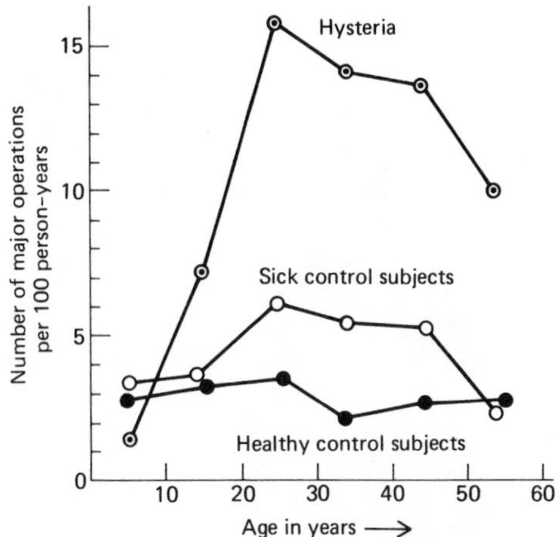

Figure 1. Comparison of incidence of major operations in hysteria patients with that in medically ill and healthy control subjects. From Cohen *et al.*, J.A.M.A. 151:977-986, 1953.

irritability, depression, suicidal ideation, and suicide attempts are common, and lead to psychiatric hospitalization. Hysteria accounts for a large portion of suicide attempts (30), but rarely leads to suicide (27).

Menstrual symptoms, sexual indifference, and frigidity are so characteristic that a diagnosis of hysteria should be made with care if the menstrual and sexual histories are normal. Marital discord, related to sexual indifference and frigidity, frequently leads to separation and divorce (16).

The question of malingering frequently arises in discussions about hysteria. While often suspected, malingering is difficult to prove. Nevertheless, malingering and factitious lesions are striking features in some cases of hysteria. Factitious fever produced by heating thermometers with matches or friction, skin lesions produced by self-injections, and "hemoptysis" and "hematuria" produced by pricking fingers and adding blood to sputum or urine may take months or years to recognize. An occasional patient will con-

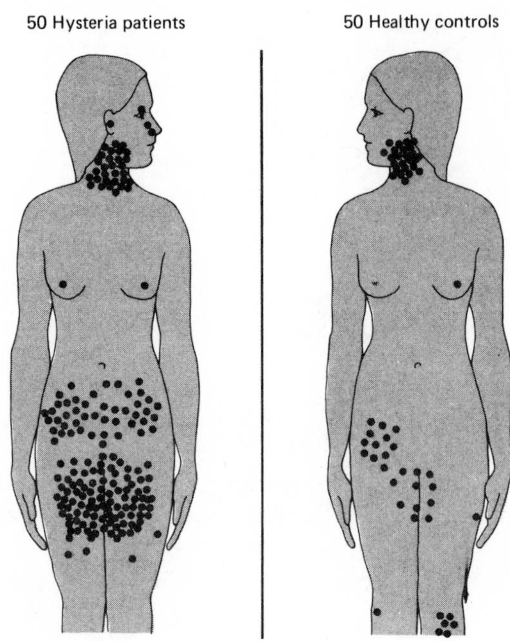

Figure 2. Comparison of number and location of major surgical procedures in 50 hysteria patients and 50 healthy control subjects. By weight, it can be calculated that the mass of organs removed in hysteria patients is more than three times that in control subjects. From Cohen *et al.*, J.A.M.A. *151*:977-986, 1953.

fide that a given symptom or sign was produced artificially in the past, but will insist that it is now real.

Another characteristic feature of hysteria is the tendency of many patients to give inconsistent histories, so that symptoms which lead to hospitalization on one occasion are denied on another. Though this inconsistency has not been studied systematically, it may be related to the patient's perception of the physician's response to her and her desire to influence his judgment about her illness.

The association between hysteria and sociopathy is of great interest. The familial aspect of this association will be discussed below (see Family Studies), but there is a clinical aspect as well. Many delinquent or antisocial adolescent girls develop hysteria as adults (28); many hysterics give a history of delinquent or antisocial behavior earlier in life (20); the medical histories of delinquent children indicate an increased prevalence of medical contacts (23); and many convicted women felons present with a mixed picture of sociopathy and hysteria (10, 11). Thus, school delinquency, repeated fighting, running away from home, a poor work record, a poor marital history, sexual promiscuity, heavy drinking, and police trouble are events found in the histories of many, though not all, hysterics. It may be pertinent that Eysenck has concluded from his studies of personality that both hysterics and psychopaths are "extroverted neurotics," a possible reason for associating the two conditions (13).

Natural History

As already noted, it is not easy to determine when the illness began. The vague and often inconsistent history makes the chronology of symptoms difficult to establish. The patient may insist that she has always been "sick," and may describe early difficulties that are hard to evaluate. Hysterics may also suffer from other illnesses, and, therefore, descriptions of childhood or adolescent disorders that allegedly were diagnosed as rheumatic fever, appendicitis, poliomyelitis, or typhoid fever can be most difficult to judge.

The symptoms fluctuate in severity, but the characteristic features persist: recurrent pains, conversion symptoms, nervousness and depression, sexual and marital discord, repeated hospitalization, and repeated surgery (16).

While systematic follow-up until death of a series of patients has not yet been reported, there is no indication that more than a minority of patients experience marked improvement or permanent remission. Twenty to thirty years of symptoms are typical, and patients who have had the illness for over forty years are not unusual.

On the other hand, the long-term course of the patient with conversion symptoms is determined by the underlying illness rather than by the nature of the symptoms themselves. Since conversion symptoms may be seen in a wide variety of medical, neurologic, and psychiatric disorders (15), patients with these symptoms have a variable prognosis and course.

Complications

The most frequent and important complications of hysteria are repeated surgical operations, drug dependence, marital separation or divorce, and suicide attempts. The first two are presumably preventable if physicians learn to recognize the disorder and manage patients properly. Knowing that hysteria is an alternate explanation for various pains and other symptoms, surgery can be withheld or postponed in cases where objective indications are equivocal or missing. Habit-forming or addicting drugs should be avoided for recurrent or persistent pain.

Whether the physician can modify marital discord through psychotherapy is uncertain, but recognizing the frequency of separation and divorce, he can certainly direct his attention to these problems. The same may be said about suicide attempts, but there the physician can approach patients with hysteria knowing that the risk of suicide is low.

Family Studies

Hysteria runs in families (1, 35). It is found in about 20 percent of first-degree (siblings, parents, children) female relatives of index cases, a tenfold increase over the prevalence in the general population of women, lending strong support to the validity of the concept of hysteria as an illness.

Family studies also indicate that a significant association exists between hysteria and sociopathy. First-degree male relatives of hysterics show an increased prevalence of sociopathy and alcoholism (1, 35). The first-degree female relatives of convicted male felons show an increased prevalence of hysteria (17). These findings, in conjunction with the observation that many female sociopaths present with, or develop, the full syndrome of hysteria (10), have suggested that at least some cases of hysteria and sociopathy share a common etiology and pathogenesis. The widely recognized observation that hysteria is predominantly a disorder of women while sociopathy is predominantly a disorder of men raises the interesting possibility that, depending upon the sex of the individual, the same etiologic and pathogenetic factors may lead to different, although sometimes overlapping, clinical pictures.

A recent study of adopted children whose biological parents showed antisocial behavior revealed greater than normal frequency in female offspring of Briquet's syndrome or other multiple unexplained somatic complaints (5, 6), thus supporting the hypothesis that hysteria and sociopathy are related disorders.

Differential Diagnosis

Three psychiatric conditions must, at times, be considered in the differential diagnosis of hysteria: anxiety neurosis, primary depression, and schizophrenia.

As already noted, the characteristic symptoms of hysteria include many that are also seen in anxiety neurosis and depression. If the patient is a young woman with menstrual and sexual difficulties who presents with a full range of anxiety or depressive symptoms, she may nearly meet the research criteria for hysteria. Age of onset, details of the symptom picture, course, and mental status will usually help clarify the diagnostic problem.

A number of patients with schizophrenia also meet the diagnostic criteria for hysteria. Also, an occasional patient with apparent hysteria, who does not show definite evidence of schizophrenia when first seen, will in time develop the typical clinical picture of schizophrenia. All the patients seen thus far with a combined hysteria-schizophrenia picture have eventually suffered from prominent and usually systematized delusions (37).

Unlike the situation in which the same patients may meet diagnostic criteria for sociopathy and hysteria, a situation in which family studies suggest that the two disorders are associated, the overlap between hysteria and schizophrenia is not accompanied by evidence of a familial association.

Clinical Management

The diagnosis of hysteria provides two advantages. For patients with the full diagnostic picture, the physician can predict, in over 90 percent of cases, that the characteristic symptoms will continue through time and that other illnesses, which in retrospect could account for the original clinical picture, will not become evident. For patients who do not present with the full diagnostic picture, especially for those who present with conversion symptoms and little else, the physician knows that in a substantial number of cases other disorders will become evident that do, in retrospect, account for the original clinical picture (24). Many, perhaps most, of the patients who resemble hysterics, but fail to meet the diagnostic criteria, will remain undiagnosed at follow-up. Enough of them, however, will turn out to have other serious medical, neurological, or psychiatric disorders to justify the kind of diagnostic open-mindedness than can lead to earlier recognition of the other illnesses.

Patients with hysteria are difficult to treat. The typical clinical picture of recurrent, multiple, vague symptoms, combined with "doctor-shopping" and frequent requests for time and attention, can frustrate and anger a physician. Few hysterics referred to a psychiatrist persist with psychiatric treatment (16). Thus, the burden of caring for these patients continues to rest with other physicians.

The physician's major goal should be to avoid the complications described earlier. Success will depend upon winning the patient's confidence without allowing the patient's symptomatic behavior to exhaust the physician's sympathy. The patient and family can be told that the patient tends to experience symptoms that suggest other disorders, but are not medically serious. On this basis the physician can approach each new complaint circumspectly and conservatively, especially with regard to elaborate or expensive diagnostic studies. As he grows familiar with the patient, the physician will become increasingly confident in his clinical judgments. Remembering that hysteria can "explain" many puzzling symptoms, the physician, always looking for objective evidence of other disorders, can avoid unnecessary hospitalization and surgery.

The physician should strive to substitute discussions of the patient's life problems, personality, and concerns for a quick-triggered response of additional tests and X-rays or yet another drug. At the same time, he must recognize the limitations resulting from the lack of knowledge concerning the causes of the disorder.

References

1. Arkonac, O. and Guze, S. B. A family study of hysteria. N.E.J.M. *268*: 239-242, 1963.
2. Blinder, M. G. The hysterical personality. Psychiatry 29:227-235, 1966.
3. Breuer, J. and Freud, S. *Studies in Hysteria,* translated by A. A. Brill. New York: Nervous and Mental Disease Monographs, 1936.
4. Briquet, P. *Traite clinique et therapeutique à l'hysterie.* Paris: J.-B. Ballière & Fils, 1859.
5. Cadoret, R. J. Psychopathology in adopted-away offspring of biologic parents with antisocial behavior. Arch. Gen. Psychiat. 35:176-184, 1978.
6. Cadoret, R. J., Cunningham, L., Loftus, R., and Edwards, J. Studies of adoptees from psychiatrically disturbed biological parents. III. Medical symptoms and illness in childhood and adolescence. Amer. J. Psychiat. 133:1316-1318, 1976.
7. Carothers, J. C. Hysteria, psychopathy and the magic word. The Mankind Quarterly 16:93-103, 1975.
8. Chodoff, P. The diagnosis of hysteria: An overview. Amer. J. Psychiat. 131:1073-1078, 1974.
9. Chodoff, P. and Lyons, H. Hysteria: the hysterical personality and hysterical conversion. Amer. J. Psychiat. 114:734-740, 1958.
10. Cloninger, C. R. and Guze, S. B. Psychiatric illness and female criminality: the role of sociopathy and hysteria in the antisocial woman. Amer. J. Psychiat. 127:303-311, 1970.

11. Cloninger, C. R. and Guze, S. B. Female criminals: their personal, familial, and social backgrounds. Arch. Gen. Psychiat. 23:554-558, 1970.
12. Cohen, M. E., Robins, E., Purtell, J. J., Altmann, M. W., and Reid, D. E. Excessive surgery in hysteria. J.A.M.A. 151:977-986, 1953.
13. Eysenck, H. *The Dynamics of Anxiety and Hysteria*. New York, Prager, 1957.
14. Farley, J., Woodruff, R. A., Jr., and Guze, S. B. The prevalence of hysteria and conversion symptoms. Brit. J. Psychiat. 114:1121-1125, 1968.
15. Gatfield, P. D. and Guze, S. B. Prognosis and differential diagnosis of conversion reactions. Dis. Nerv. Syst. 23:623-631, 1962.
16. Guze, S. B. and Perley, M. J. Observations on the natural history of hysteria. Amer. J. Psychiat. 119:960-965, 1963.
17. Guze, S. B., Wolfgram, E. D., McKinney, J. K., and Cantwell, D. P. Psychiatric illness in the families of convicted criminals: a study of 519 first-degree relatives. Dis. Nerv. Syst. 28:651-659, 1967.
18. Guze, S. B. The diagnosis of hysteria: What are we trying to do? Amer. J. Psychiat. 124:491-498, 1967.
19. Guze, S. B. The role of follow-up studies: their contribution to diagnostic classification as applied to hysteria. Seminars in Psychiatry 2:392-402, 1970.
20. Guze, S. B., Woodruff, R. A., Jr., and Clayton, P. J. Hysteria and antisocial behavior: further evidence of an association. Amer. J. Psychiat. 127: 957-960, 1971.
21. Guze, S. B., Woodruff, R. A., and Clayton, P. J. A study of conversion symptoms in psychiatric outpatients. Amer. J. Psychiat. 128:643-646, 1971.
22. Kimble, R., Williams, J. G., and Agras, S. A comparison of two methods of diagnosing hysteria. Amer. J. Psychiat. 132:1197-1199, 1975.
23. Lewis, D. O. and Shanok, S. S. Medical histories of delinquent and nondelinquent children: an epidemiologic study. Amer. J. Psychiat. 134:1020-1025, 1977.
24. Perley, M. J. and Guze, S. B. Hysteria—the stability and usefulness of clinical criteria. N.E.J.M. 266:421-426, 1962.
25. Purtell, J. J., Robins, E., and Cohen, M. E. Observations on clinical aspects of hysteria. J.A.M.A. 146:902-909, 1951.
26. Robins, E., Purtell, J. J., and Cohen, M. E. "Hysteria" in men. N.E.J.M. 246:677-685, 1952.
27. Robins, E., Murphy, G., Wilkinson, R., Gossner, S., and Kayes, J. Some clinical considerations in the prevention of suicide based on a study of 134 successful suicides. Amer. J. Pub. Hlth. 49:888-899, 1959.
28. Robins, L. *Deviant Children Grown Up*. Baltimore: Williams and Wilkins, 1966.
29. Savill, T. D. *Lectures on Hysteria and Allied Vasomotor Conditions*. London: H. J. Glaisher, 1909.
30. Schmidt, E. H., O'Neal, P., and Robins, E. Evaluation of suicide at-

tempts as guide to therapy. Clinical and follow-up study of 109 patients. J.A.M.A. 155:549-557, 1954.
31. Slater, E. Diagnosis of "hysteria." Brit. Med. J. 1:1395-1399, 1965.
32. Stefansson, J. G., Messina, J. A., and Meyerowitz, S. Hysterical neurosis, conversion type: Clinical and epidemiological considerations. Acta Psychiat. Scand. 53:119-138, 1976.
33. Vieth, I. *Hysteria. The History of a Disease*. Chicago: University of Chicago Press, 1965.
34. Weissman, M. M., Myers, J. K., and Harding, P. S. Psychiatric disorders in a U.S. urban community: 1975-76. Amer. J. Psychiat. 135:459-462, 1978.
35. Woerner, P. I. and Guze, S. B. A family and marital study of hysteria. Brit. J. Psychiat. 114:161-168, 1968.
36. Woodruff, R. A., Jr. Hysteria: an evaluation of objective diagnostic criteria by the study of women with chronic medical illnesses. Brit. J. Psychiat. 114:1115-1119, 1967.
37. Woodruff, R. A., Jr., Clayton, P. J., and Guze, S. B. Hysteria. Studies of diagnosis, outcome, and prevalence. J.A.M.A. 215:425-428, 1971.
38. Ziegler, F. J., Imboden, J. B., and Meyer, E. Contemporary conversion reactions: clinical study. Amer. J. Psychiat. 116:901-910, 1960.

5. Obsessional Neurosis

Definition

Obsessions are persistent distressing thoughts or impulses experienced as unwanted and senseless but irresistible. *Compulsions* are acts resulting from obsessions. *Obsessional neurosis* is an illness dominated by obsessions and compulsions occurring in the absence of another psychiatric disorder. Synonyms for obsessional neurosis include the following: obsessive-compulsive neurosis, obsessional state, obsessional-ruminative state, phobic-ruminative state, psychasthenia.

Historical Background

The term "obsessional neurosis" apparently originated with Karl Westphal (1833-90), a German psychiatrist who wrote about obsessional conditions and phobias. Kraepelin described obsessional neurosis (*Zwangsneurose*) in his textbooks of the early part of the 20th century, and the same term was adopted by Freud, whose classical description of the clinical picture, published in 1917, follows:

> The obsessional neurosis takes this form: the patient's mind is occupied with thoughts that do not really interest him, he feels impulses which seem alien to him, and he is impelled to perform actions which not only afford him no pleasure but from which he is powerless to desist. The thoughts (obsessions) may be meaningless in themselves or only of no interest to the patient; they are often only absolutely silly. . . (5).

Recognition of obsessional traits, however, far antedated psychiatrists' description of the syndrome. In the early 17th century Richard Flecknoe, in discussing "enigmaticall characters," described one such character as an "irresolute Person": "he hovers in his choice, like an empty Ballance with no waight of Judgement to incline him to either scale . . . everything he thinks on, is matter of deliberation . . . and he does nothing readily, but what he thinks not on . . . when he begins to deliberate, never makes an end. . . . Has some dull demon cryes, do not, do not still, when hee's on point of doing anything. . . . He plays at shall I, shall I? so long, till opportunity be past . . . and then repents at leisure" (11).

In the 17th century obsessions were often referred to as "scruples," defined by Jeremy A. Taylor (31) as "a great trouble of mind preceding from a little motive, and a great indisposition, by which the conscience though sufficiently determined by proper arguments, dares not proceed to action, or if it do, it cannot rest . . . some persons dare not eat for fear of gluttony, they fear that they shall sleep too much, and that keeps them waking, and troubles their heads more and then their scruples increase. When they are married they are afraid to do their duty, for fear it be secretly an indulgence to the flesh, and to be suspected of carnality, and yet they dare not omit it, for fear they should be unjust, and yet their fear that the very fearing it to be unclean should be a sin, and suspect that if they do not fear so it is too great a sign they adhere to "Nature more than to the Spirit. . . . *Scruple is a little stone in the foot, if you set it upon the ground it hurts you; if you hold it up you cannot go forward; it is a trouble where the trouble is over, a doubt when doubts are resolved* . . . very often it hath no reason at all for its inducement."

The content of obsessions, today as in years past, is often religious. In his monograph, *Of Religious Melancholy* (21), published in 1692, John Moore described "naughty and sometime blasphemous thoughts which start in the mind while they are exercised in the worship of God despite all their endeavors to stiffle and suppress them." In fact, he wrote, "the more they struggle with them, the more they increase." Bishop Moore had difficulty understanding this state since the sufferers were "mostly good People," whereas "bad men . . . rarely know anything of these kinds of Thoughts." Like others, he argued that this was good reason "to judge them to be Distempers of the body rather than Faults of the Mind." He was particularly concerned about the phobic avoidances that could result from such obsessions and wrote "I exhort you not to quit your Employment . . . for no business at all is as bad for you as too much: and there is always more Melancholy to be found in a Cloyster than in the Market-place."

The obsessional fear of suffering from syphilis was also well recognized as a manifestation of mental illness by clergymen and later by psychiatrists. In the past "superstition" has often been used to mean what we would consider an obsession. Samuel Johnson apparently had this in mind when he wrote that "the superstitious are often melancholic, and the melancholic almost always superstitious." As will be noted later in this chapter, obsessions are common in depressive states and vice versa.

Epidemiology

While the prevalence of obsessional neurosis in the general population is unknown, it is one of the rarest of the major treated psychiatric disorders. Less than 5 percent of psychiatric inpatients and outpatients receive the diagnosis (8). According to most studies, obsessional neurosis occurs about equally in both sexes (12, 15, 23).

When compared with all other psychiatric patients, obsessionals reportedly differ in the following ways: (a) they belong to higher social classes; (b) they make higher scores on intelligence tests; (c) they have a higher educational level (12, 18, 26). Since social class, intelligence, and educational level are interrelated, predictably if one is elevated, the others will be also. Obsessionals are often in their early or midthirties when first admitted to the hospital (4).

Clinical Picture

When obsessionals finally seek medical attention (often years after their illness began) it may be because of depression, acute anxiety, exacerbation of obsessions, or social incapacity resulting from any of these conditions (17, 23).

A life event often seems associated with the onset of symptoms: the death of a relative, a sexual conflict, overwork, or pregnancy (12, 18). Just as often, however, no precipitating factors can be identified.

A common presenting complaint is the obsessional fear of injuring oneself or another person, often a child or close relative. Fearful of losing control, the patient may develop avoidances or rituals which lead in turn to social incapacity. Perhaps he will refuse to leave the house or will avoid sharp objects or wash repeatedly.

On reflection he may identify the obsessional idea as illogical, but not always. Sometimes the ideas are not, strictly speaking, illogical (germs do produce disease), and sometimes, even when obviously absurd, the ideas are not viewed as such. What distinguishes an obsession from a delusion is not so much "insight" (recognizing the idea's absurdity) as the person's struggle against the obsessional experience itself. He strives to free himself from the obsession but cannot and feels increasingly uncomfortable until the idea temporarily "runs its course" or the obsessional act has been completed (17).

The frequency with which obsessional symptoms appear in obsessional patients has been studied systematically by three groups, and their results indicate that the illness may assume one or more of the following forms (1, 4, 30):

Obsessional ideas: thoughts which repetitively intrude into consciousness (words, phrases, rhymes), interfering with the normal train of thought and causing distress to the person. Often the thoughts are obscene, blasphemous, or nonsensical.

Obsessional images: vividly imagined scenes, often of a violent, sexual, or disgusting nature (images of a child being killed, cars colliding, excrement, parents having sexual intercourse) that repeatedly come to mind.

Obsessional convictions: notions that are often based on the magical formula of thought-equals-act ("Thinking ill of my son will cause him to die"). Unlike delusions, obsessional beliefs are characterized by ambivalence: the person believes and simultaneously does not believe. As Jaspers expressed it, there is a "constant going on between a consciousness of validity and non-validity. Both push this way and that, but neither can gain the upper hand" (14).

Obsessional rumination: prolonged, inconclusive thinking about a subject to the exclusion of other interests. The subject is often religion or metaphysics—why and wherefore questions which are as unanswerable as they are endlessly ponderable. Indecisiveness in ordinary matters is very common ("Which necktie should I wear?"). Doubt may lead to extremes in caution both irksome and irresistible ("Did I turn off the gas?" "Lock the door?" "Write the correct address"). The patient checks and rechecks, stopping only when exhausted or upon checking a predetermined "magical" number of times. Several studies suggest that obsessional doubts—*manie du doute*—may well be the most prominent feature in obsessional neurosis (1, 4).

As with other obsessions, ruminations are resisted. The person tries to turn his attention elsewhere, but cannot; often the more he tries, the more intrusive and distressing the thoughts become.

Obsessional impulses: typically relating to self-injury (leaping from a window); injury to others (smothering an infant); or embarrassing behavior (shouting obscenities in church).

Obsessional fears: often of dirt, disease, contamination; of potential weapons (razors, scissors); of being in specific situations or performing particular acts.

Obsessional rituals (compulsions): repetitive, stereotyped acts of counting, touching, arranging objects, moving in specific ways, washing, tasting, looking. Compulsions are inseparable from the obsessions from which they arise. A compulsion is an obsession expressed as action. About one-quarter of patients display no compulsions (1).

Counting rituals are especially common. The person feels compelled to count letters or words or the squares in a tile floor, or to perform arithmetical operations. Certain numbers, or their multiples, may have special significance (he "must" lay down his pencil three times or step on every fifth sidewalk crack). Other rituals concern the performance of excretory functions and such everyday acts as preparing to go to bed. Also common are rituals involving extremes of cleanliness (handwashing compulsions, relentless emptying of ashtrays) and complicated routines assuring orderliness and punctuality. Women apparently have a higher incidence of contamination phobia and of compulsive cleaning behavior than do men (4).

According to a recent study of obsessionals (30), four kinds of rituals occur most frequently: counting, checking, cleaning, and avoidance rituals. Each occurred in half of the patients. Avoidance rituals were similar to those seen in phobic neurosis (see Differential Diagnosis below). An example can be seen in a patient who avoided anything colored brown. Her inability to approach brown objects greatly limited her activities.

Other rituals which occur less often consist of "slowing," "striving for completeness," and "extreme meticulousness." With slowing, such simple tasks as buttoning a shirt or tying a shoelace might take up to 15 minutes. Striving for completeness may be seen in dressing also. Asked why he spends so much time with a single button, the patient might reply that he was trying to prove to himself that he had "buttoned the button properly."

A common form of pathological meticulousness is a concern that objects be arranged in a special way. Pencils, for example, may have to be arranged so that the points are directed away from the patient. Students may spend so much time in arranging pencils, pens, erasers, etc., that they cannot do their work.

Rituals, ridiculous as they may seem to the patient, are accompanied by a profound dread and apprehension that assure their performance, since they alone give relief. "I'll explode if I don't do it," a patient may say. Occasionally a patient believes that failure to perform a given ritual will result in harm to himself or others, but often the ritual is as inexplicable to the patient as it is to the observer.

Obsessional symptoms often are accompanied by a dysphoric mood. The patient may be irritable, tense, depressed. This may lead to an erroneous diagnosis of affective disorder, since the mood element at the time of examination may overshadow the obsessional content.

Obsessional symptoms rarely occur singly (15). As with most psychiatric illnesses, obsessional neurosis presents a cluster of symptoms which, individually, are variable and inconstant over time but as a group maintain characteristics unique to the illness. Thus a patient may now have one set of obsessional impulses, phobias, and rituals, later another set, but the symptoms remain predominantly obsessional.

Natural History

Most obsessionals develop their illness before age 25. Many obsessionals have clear-cut obsessional symptoms by age 15 and the illness may begin as early as age 6. Fewer than 15 percent of obsessionals develop their illness after age 35 (9, 12, 15).

Though the mean age of onset of symptoms is roughly 20 in both sexes, the first psychiatric contact is made on the average about seven years later. If hospitalized, most patients are in their thirties by the time they enter a hospital. Rarely are obsessionals admitted to a psychiatric hospital for the first time after age 40 (8). Since the prevalence of obsessional neurosis in the general population is unknown, it is also unknown what proportion of obsessionals are hospitalized.

The mode of onset may be acute or insidious (15). The course of obsessional neurosis may be unremitting (with or without social incapacity), episodic, or characterized by incomplete remissions which permit normal social functioning.

In one outpatient study the majority of patients had episodic courses with exacerbations usually lasting less than a year (23). Most investigators studying patients requiring hospitalization, however, have found the course to be steady, with exacerbations often attributed to fatigue or medical illness and with a tendency for the severity of the illness to wane gradually over many years (12, 18, 22).

Obsessionals with mild symptoms requiring only outpatient therapy appear to have a rather good prognosis; as many as 60 percent to 80 percent are asymptomatic or improved one to five years after diagnosis (18, 23). Hospitalized cases as a group do less well. One-third or fewer are improved symptomatically on re-examination several years after discharge; two-thirds or more, however, are functioning as well socially as before hospitalization (12, 15). Between 5 and 10 percent of clear-cut obsessionals do have a course marked by progressive social incapacity (25). Favorable prognosis is reported to be associated with three factors: (a) mild or atypical symptoms, including predominance of phobic-ruminative ideas and absence of compulsions (12, 15); (b) short duration of symptoms before treatment is begun (23); (c) good premorbid personality without childhood symptoms or abnormal personality traits (15, 16). The specific content of obsessions is not believed to have prognostic significance (Table 1).

Complications

Depression—often indistinguishable symptomatically from depression seen in primary affective disorder—is probably the most common complication of obsessional neurosis.

Failure to marry also may be a complication of obsessional neurosis, judging by two studies (12, 18) that show a higher rate of celibacy among obsessionals than in the general population.

Despite the frequency with which suicide may figure in obsessional thinking (9, 12), obsessionals rarely commit suicide. In most studies less than 1 percent of the patients committed suicide.

Obsessional patients sometimes fear they will injure someone by

Table 1. Follow-up studies of obsessional neurosis

Sample characteristics				*Length of Follow-up*	*Condition on Follow-up (%)*		
Author	*Place*	*Pt. Source**	N†	*(to nearest yr.)*	*Asymptomatic*	*Improved*	*Unimproved*
Balslev-Olesen *et al.* (2)	Denmark	I, O	52	0-8	6	58	37
Grimshaw (9)	England	O	97	1-14	40	24	35
Hastings (10)	U.S.	I	23	6-12	13	40	47
Ingram (12)	England	I	46	1-11	9	30	61
Kringlen (15)	Norway	I	85	13-20	4	45	45
Langfeldt (16)	Norway	I	27	1-11	26	41	33
Lewis (17)	England	I, O	50	>5	32	34	34
Lo (18)	Hong Kong	I, O	87	1-14	20	36	44
Luff *et al.* (19)	England	O	49	3	39	27	34
Müller (22)	Switzerland	I	57	15-35	28	50	22
Pollitt (23)	England	I, O	66	0-15	24	48	28
Rennie (24)	U.S.	I	47	20	36	38	26
Rüdin (26)	Germany	I, O	130	2-26	12	26	61

* I = inpatient; O, outpatient.

† Excluded are lobotimized cases and patients dead on follow-up. The sex ratio differs from study to study but approaches unity when all studies are combined.

Source: Goodwin *et al.* (8)

an impulsive act. They fear they will lose control and embarrass themselves in some manner. They worry about becoming addicted to drugs prescribed by their physician. These fears are generally unwarranted. There is no evidence that obsessional neurosis predisposes to homicide, criminal behavior, alcoholism, or drug addiction (12, 15).

Finally, obsessionals may fear they will "lose" their minds, become totally disabled, need chronic hospitalization. None of these events is a common complication of obsessional neurosis. If schizophrenia is clearly ruled out at the beginning, obsessionals probably become schizophrenic no more often than nonobsessionals. They infrequently become totally disabled, and they usually do not require long-term hospitalization (9, 12, 23).

Family History

Two studies comparing parents of obsessionals with parents of other psychiatric patients found the former group to be significantly more perfectionistic (18), obstinate, pedantic, and parsimonious (15). Studies without controls have yielded similar findings (2, 17). Unfortunately, such attributes as perfectionism and obstinacy are vague and resist quantification. Even in controlled studies it is unclear whether observer bias has been sufficiently eliminated to render the results meaningful.

Psychiatric illness in the families of obsessionals has been studied by several investigators. Many obsessionals have close relatives with psychiatric illness (2, 25). In one study, about 30 percent of the siblings of obsessionals had been treated for psychiatric symptoms (about one-quarter as inpatients) (17) and in another study, about 10 percent of the first degree relatives of obsessionals had received psychiatric treatment (25).

Obsessional illness probably occurs with greater frequency in the families of obsessionals than in the families of other patients (or in the general population), but so do other psychiatric illnesses, and the extent of increased familial risk is uncertain. One study comparing the families of obsessionals with those of other psychiatric and medical patients found not only a higher incidence of obsessional neurosis in the families of obsessionals (8 percent of parents, 7 percent of siblings), but also a higher incidence of other psychopathology; e.g., about 8 percent had manic-depressive disease (3).

Studies of twins with obsessional illness indicate that monozygotic twins are more concordant for obsessional illness than dizygotic twins (13). About 80 to 90 percent of monozygotic twins are concordant for obsessional illness versus a concordance rate in dizygotic twins of no more than 50 percent and probably much lower. These figures, however, derive from individual case reports and small series of cases, and should be interpreted cautiously.

Differential Diagnosis

Obsessions occur in children, in healthy adults, and in patients with a variety of psychiatric and medical illnesses.

The rituals and superstitions of children—avoidance of sidewalk cracks, insistence on a given routine, carrying of amulets and charms—may resemble the compulsive acts of obsessional neurosis, but with a difference: children usually do not complain about these acts, which seem natural to them and produce little distress.

Only a small proportion of children manifesting obsessional behavior can be classified by usual standards as having obsessional neurosis. It is not known whether children who are exceptionally ritualistic and superstitious have a greater risk of developing obsessional neurosis than their less obsessional peers.

Many adult obsessionals give a history of obsessional symptoms in childhood (12, 18, 26), but the commonness of such symptoms and the influence of retrospective distortion make such data hard to interpret. The obsessional commonly cites phobias and rituals as childhood symptoms (12, 15, 18). He rarely gives a history of stealing, truancy, or tantrums in childhood (15, 18).

"Obsessional personality" is more a description than a diagnosis. No investigator has followed a group of clearly defined obsessional personalities over time to determine their fate; hence the label has no predictive value and is not in this sense a diagnosis. The individual with an obsessional personality is punctual, orderly, scrupulous, meticulous, and dependable. He is also rigid, stubborn, pedantic, and something of a bore. He has trouble making up his mind, but once made up, is single-minded and obstinant (28).

Many individuals with obsessional neurosis have obsessional personalities antedating the illness (15, 23, 26). The proportion of obsessional personalities who develop obsessional neurosis, depression, or other psychiatric illness is not known.

Phobias are commonly associated with obsessional neurosis, and obsessionals often have anxiety symptoms. Obsessional phobias have a compulsive quality and are almost always accompanied by rituals as well as other obsessional phenomena (15). The phobias of anxiety neurosis, on the other hand, are characterized primarily by simple avoidance of the anxiety provoking object or situation.

Obsessions and depression occur together so commonly that discriminating symptom from illness may be difficult. The difficulty is compounded by the fact that obsessionals may develop a depression as florid as that seen in primary affective disorder. During the depression the obsessional symptoms may remain unchanged, worsen, or disappear. Similarly, after the depression the obsessions may be worse, better or unchanged (the last being the most common outcome) (6).

Episodes of primary depression, in a substantial number of cases, are accompanied by obsessions (6). These are usually ruminative in nature, characterized by guilt and self-deprecation, and mild by comparison with the depressed mood. In more atypical depressions, however, obsessions may dominate the picture. One-third of primary depressives have obsessional personality traits premorbidly and during remissions (17). Obsessional traits apparently precede primary depression as often as they precede obsessional neurosis (17).

Obsessional neurosis in some instances may be as cyclical as primary depression, with alternating remissions and exacerbations having no apparent relation to life events (12, 18, 23). The history may suggest affective disorder, the symptoms obsessional neurosis. Some clinicians treat patients with cyclical obsessions as if they had primary depressions, that is, with antidepressant drugs or electrotherapy. Controlled studies of the results are not available.

In distinguishing between obsessional neurosis and primary depression, the following points may be helpful: Compared with primary depressives who have obsessional symptoms, obsessionals who develop a depression do so at an earlier age, have more depressive episodes in their history, exhibit obsessional symptoms episodically during each depression, have a lower rate of attempted suicide, and lack a history of mania (6).

Family history is of diagnostic value when it includes clear-cut depressions, mania, suicide, or alcoholism, which are found more regularly in the families of primary depressives than in the families of patients with any other illness (32).

Mistaking obsessional neurosis for schizophrenia is not unusual, especially in the early stages of the illness. Error may arise from difficulty in distinguishing obsessions from delusions and from equating bizarreness or disablement with schizophrenia. Early onset and insidious development are common in both illnesses.

Schizophrenia is characterized by delusions, hallucinations, and *formal* thought disorder (form referring to the flow and connections of thought). Obsessional neurosis is primarily a disorder of thought *content*. The speech of the obsessional is understandable; his ideas are queer. The fact that he recognizes they are queer is one of the chief distinctions between obsessional neurosis and schizophrenia.

According to one study, obsessions occur in schizophrenia in about 3 percent of cases, usually early in the course and almost always in the paranoid type (29). When obsessions and schizophrenic symptoms occur together, schizophrenia is usually the most appropriate diagnosis.

Obsessions have been observed in the following organic conditions: encephalitis lethargia—especially during oculogyric crises;

early stages of arteriosclerotic dementia; posttraumatic and postencephalitic states; hearing loss with tinnitus; hypothyroidism (8).

Each of these conditions may be accompanied by the experience that one's mind is working independently, that it is not an integrated part of oneself (17), and by repetitive behavior resembling compulsions. However, the "forced thinking" and "organic orderliness" (7) occasionally observed in brain-damaged patients are said to be less well organized than those which occur in obsessional neurosis and they also lack the sense of internal compulsion that distinguishes the latter condition.

The hallmarks of organic brain disease—confusion, disorientation, memory loss—are not seen in obsessional neurosis. Their presence makes the diagnosis comparatively simple. Past history, neurological examination, blood, urine, and spinal fluid studies, plus such special techniques as EEG, brain scan, and pneumoencephalography, help establish the specific cause.

Clinical Management

The data on obsessional neurosis justify a certain measure of optimism about its natural course. Spontaneous improvement often occurs, and the patient can be informed of this. He can be reassured that his impulses to commit injury or socially embarrassing acts almost certainly will not be carried out, and that he will not—as he often fears—lose his mind. If he needs to be hospitalized, he can be assured that the hospitalization is unlikely to be a long one.

Yet, the therapist should avoid promising too much. Obsessional neurosis is a chronic illness for which there is no specific treatment. Recovery is seldom smooth, and some patients never get well. Past performance, it would appear, is the best guide to future expectations. If the patient had previous episodes from which he recovered, the prognosis is relatively good. But if the course has been steady and severely disabling, it is unreasonable to expect marked or rapid improvement.

Obsessional patients commonly attribute their symptoms to

stressful life experiences. How much credence should be accorded such interpretations? With regard to precipitating factors, follow-up studies are contradictory, as is the large anecdotal literature linking stress and obsessional illness. Some authors feel that obsessionals are unusually reactive to stress, that fatigue alone may precipitate an obsessional episode. Others believe obsessional states are rarely traceable to environmental factors. The issue of the importance of precipitants is unresolved.

At least one study indicates that behavior therapy may be useful in alleviating ritualistic behavior (20). In a two-year follow-up of 20 patients who had undergone behavior therapy for rituals, three-quarters were much improved. Although there was no control group, this improvement rate is better than one expects in untreated obsessionals. The treatment, in brief, consisted of repeatedly exposing the patients to situations about which they were obsessional or phobic so the ritualistic responses could be "extinguished" over time. About one-quarter of patients offered behavior therapy refuse it (20), probably because of apprehensiveness about confronting fear-provoking situations. Compulsive slowness presents special treatment problems but reportedly is helped by a "prompting and pacing" approach (20).

It is not known how effective antidepressant drugs are in the treatment of depression associated with obsessional neurosis. Most antidepressant drugs were introduced after the studies reviewed here were completed. One study, however, suggests that tricyclic antidepressant drugs relieve depressive symptoms in patients receiving behavior therapy for obsessional rituals (20). There was no control group and it is not clear how long improvement lasted. Chlorimipramine, a new tricyclic widely used in Europe and Latin America, reportedly has been found effective in some cases of obsessional neurosis (34). At this writing, the drug had not been released for use in the United States.

One study suggests that electroshock therapy is less effective for depression associated with obsessional neurosis than for primary depression (26). In this series, half the obsessionals receiving ECT improved and half did not.

Three follow-up studies (9, 15, 23) indicated that lobotomy produced symptomatic improvement in obsessional neurosis superior to that which occurs spontaneously. The more "typical" the obsessional illness, one investigator found, the more likely this was to be true (15). For a small minority of patients, therefore, lobotomy may warrant consideration. Before undertaking such irreversible treatment, evaluation by two or more psychiatrists is highly desirable. There is general agreement that, if used at all, lobotomy should be reserved for those severely ill obsessional patients with classical symptoms (especially rituals) who fail to respond to other treatments and are totally disabled by their illness.

References

1. Akhtar, S., Wig, N., Varma, V., Pershad, D., and Verma, S. A phenomenological analysis of symptoms in obsessive-compulsive neurosis. Brit. J. Psychiat. 127:342-348, 1975.
2. Balslev-Olesen, T. and Geert-Jorgensen, E. The prognosis of obsessive-compulsive neurosis. Acta Psychiat. Scand. 34:232-241, 1959.
3. Brown, F. W. Heredity in the psychoneuroses. Proc. Roy. Soc. Med. 35: 785-790, 1942.
4. Dowson, J. The phenomenology of severe obsessive-compulsive neurosis. Brit. J. Psychiat. 131:75-78, 1977.
5. Freud, S. Notes upon a case of obsessional neurosis. In *Standard Edition of the Complete Psychological Works of Sigmund Freud*, Vol. 10, p. 153. London: Hogarth Press, 1955.
6. Gittleson, N. L. The phenomenology of obsessions in depressive psychosis. Brit. J. Psychiat. 112:261-264, 1966.
7. Goldstein, K. *After Effects of Brain Injuries in War. Their Evaluation and Treatment*. New York: Grune and Stratton, 1942.
8. Goodwin, D. W., Guze, S. B., and Robins, E. Follow-up studies in obsessional neurosis. Arch. Gen. Psychiat. 20:182-187, 1969.
9. Grimshaw, L. The outcome of obsessional disorder: a follow-up study of 100 cases. Brit. J. Psychiat. 111:1051-1056, 1965.
10. Hastings, D. W. Follow-up results in psychiatric illness. Amer. J. Psychiat. 114:1057-1065, 1958.
11. Hunter, R. and Macalpine, I. *Three Hundred Years of Psychiatry 1535-1860*. London: Oxford University Press, 1963.

12. Ingram, I. M. Obsessional illness in mental hospital patients. J. Ment. Sci. 107:382-402, 1961.
13. Inouye, E. Similar and dissimilar manifestations of obsessive-compulsive neurosis in monozygotic twins. Amer. J. Psychiat. 121, 12:1171-1175, 1965.
14. Jaspers, K. *General Psychopathology*. Chicago: University of Chicago Press, 1963.
15. Kringlen, E. Obsessional neurotics: a long-term follow-up. Brit. J. Psychiat. 111:709-722, 1965.
16. Langfeldt, G. Studier av Tvangsfernomenenes forelomist, genese, klinik og prognose. Norsk Laegeforen 13:822-850, 1938.
17. Lewis, A. J. Problems of obsessional illness. Proc. Roy. Soc. Med. 29: 325-336, 1936.
18. Lo, W. H. A follow-up study of obsessional neurotics in Hong Kong Chinese. Brit. J. Psychiat. 113:823-832, 1967.
19. Luff, M. C. and Garrod, M. The after results of psychotherapy in 500 Adult Cases. Brit. Med. J. 11:54-59, 1935.
20. Marks, I., Hodgson, R., and Rachman, S. Treatment of chronic obsessive-compulsive neurosis by in-vivo exposure. Brit. J. Psychiat. 127:349-364, 1975.
21. Moore, J. *Of Religious Melancholy*, published by Her Majesty's special command. London, 1692.
22. Müller, C. Der Ubergang von Zwangsneurose in Schizophrenie im Lichte der Katamnese. Schweiz Arch. Neurol. Psychiat. 72:218-225, 1953.
23. Pollitt, J. Natural history of obsessional states: a Study of 150 cases. Brit. Med. J. 1:194-198, 1957.
24. Rennie, T. A. C. *Prognosis in the Psychoneurosis: Benign and Malignant Developments, Current Problems in Psychiatric Diagnosis*. New York: Grune and Stratton, pp. 66-79, 1953.
25. Rosenberg, C. M. Familial aspects of obsessional neurosis. Brit. J. Psychiat. 113:405-413, 1967.
26. Rüdin, G. Ein Beitrag zur Frage der Zwangskrankheit, insbesondere ihrer heriditaren Beziehungen. Arch. Psychiat. Nervenkr. 191:14-54, 1953.
27. Schilder, P. 'Depersonalization.' In *Introduction to Psychoanalytic Psychiatry*. Nerv. Ment. Dis. Monogr., Series 50, 1928.
28. Skoog, G. Onset of anancastic conditions. Acta Psychiat. Scand. 41, Suppl. 184, 131, 1965.
29. Stengel, E. A study of some clinical aspects of the relationship between obsessional neurosis and psychotic reaction types. J. Ment. Sci. 91:129, 1945.
30. Stern, R. and Cobb, J. Phenomenology of obsessive-compulsive neurosis. Brit. J. Psychiat. 132:233-239, 1978.
31. Taylor, J. *Ductor Dubitantium, or the Rule of Conscience*. London: Royston, 1660.
32. Winokur, G., Clayton, P. J., and Reich, T. *Manic Depressive Illness*. St. Louis: C. V. Mosby, 1969.

33. Yaryura-Tobias, J. and Neziroglu, F. The action of chlorimipramine in obsessive-compulsive neurosis: A pilot study. Current Thera. Res. 17:111-116, 1975.
34. Yaryura-Tobias, J., Neziroglu, F., and Bergman, L. Chlorimipramine, for obsessive-compulsive neurosis: An organic approach. Current Thera. Res. 20:541-548, 1976.

6. Phobic Neurosis

Definition

A phobia is an intense, recurrent, unreasonable fear. Phobic neurosis is a chronic disorder dominated by one or more phobias. The "agoraphobia syndrome" is a type of phobic neurosis characterized by multiple phobias, usually involving fear of open spaces, crowds or travel, accompanied by attacks of panic, feelings of depersonalization, and other psychiatric symptoms. A synonym for agoraphobia is "phobic-anxiety-depersonalization syndrome" (23, 32).

Historical Background

Phobos was a Greek god who frightened one's enemies. His likeness was painted on masks and shields for this purpose. Phobos, or phobia, came to mean fear or panic (23).

"Phobia" first appeared in medical terminology in Rome 2,000 years ago, when "hydrophobia" was used to describe a symptom of rabies. Though the term was not used in a psychiatric sense until the 19th century, phobic fears and behavior were described in medical literature long before that. Hippocrates described at least two phobic persons. One was "beset by terror" whenever he heard a flute, while the other could not go beside "even the shallowest ditch" and yet could walk in the ditch itself (16).

Robert Burton in his "Anatomy of Melancholy" distinguishes "morbid fears" from "normal" fears (8). Demosthenes' stage fright was normal, while Caesar's fear of sitting in the dark was morbid. Burton believed that morbid fears had little connection with will power and that psychotherapy would not help without discovery of etiology.

The term phobia appeared increasingly in descriptions of morbid fears during the 19th century, beginning with "syphiliphobia," defined in a medical dictionary published in 1848 as "a morbid dread of syphillis giving rise to fancied symptoms of the disease." Numerous theories were advanced to explain phobias, including poor upbringing (23).

In 1871 Westphal described three men who feared public places and labeled the condition agoraphobia, "agora" coming from the Greek word for place of assembly or marketplace (42). Excellent review articles on the historical development of the concept of phobia have been written by Errera (10) and Marks (23). They give Westphal credit for describing phobia in terms of a syndrome rather than an isolated symptom. Westphal even prescribed a treatment for the condition, suggesting that companionship, alcohol, or the use of a cane would be helpful.

Thereafter many clinical descriptions of phobias appeared in the literature together with attempts at classification. Among these attempts was Freud's distinction between "common" and "specific" phobias, a distinction he later denied as being important (14).

Since the late 19th century there has been a continuing controversy over the relationship of phobias to other psychiatric disorders. Janet and Kraepelin, for example, sometimes spoke of phobias and obsessions as though they were synonymous. Others, such as Henry Maudsley and Melanie Klein, considered phobias to be a manifestation of affective illness (22, 37). Clinicians agree that phobias may occur in a variety of psychiatric conditions, but there is a growing tendency to view at least particular types of phobias as the primary manifestation of a specific disorder. This trend is reflected in the inclusion of "Phobic Disorders" in the current American Psychiatric Association classification of psychiatric disorders.

Epidemiology

The prevalence of phobia in the general population was estimated at 77 in 1000 in Vermont (1). Of these disorders, 75 in 1000 were considered to be mildly disabling and 2 in 1000 severely disabling. Severe disability was defined as absence from work for an employed person, and inability to manage common household tasks for a housewife. About one-quarter of the severely disabled had received psychiatric treatment.

In psychiatric practice phobias are a main complaint in about 2 percent or 3 percent of cases in America and England (10, 38). About half of these patients, mostly women, have agoraphobia. Phobias also accompany other disorders, such as depression and obsessional neurosis. In one study, 48 percent of "neurotics," 65 percent of manic depressives, and 10 percent of schizophrenics were described as having phobias (30).

Clinical Picture

Phobias can be distinguished from "normal" fears by their intensity, duration, irrationality, and the disablement resulting from avoidance of the feared situation. As indicated by the Vermont study (1), fears sufficiently intense to be called phobias occur in only a small proportion of adults. In one study, college students felt somewhat uncomfortable when confronted with snakes, but only 20 percent reported intense fear (19).

Phobias may be isolated and specific or multiple and diffuse. In the case of isolated phobias, disablement is generally mild and other major psychiatric symptoms are not usually present. Psychiatrists rarely see patients with a chief complaint of an isolated phobia, although other physicians occasionally encounter patients who are "phobic" about injections or blood.

Animal phobias are perhaps the most common isolated phobias, or at least the most commonly studied. They occur often in childhood and are usually transient. Among adults, women are subject to animal phobias more often than men. The phobia usually involves only one kind of animal but may lead to frequent distress with mild social disablement if the animals are domestic, such as dogs or cats. In adults, these phobias may be chronic but are not associated with other psychiatric symptoms that lead to severe impairment or require psychiatric care (23).

"Social phobias" are another form of isolated phobia that generally lead to only mild forms of impairment. These include fear of eating, public speaking, urinating in the presence of others, or other behaviors that may be embarrassing but do not generally lead to avoidance of the situations. Occasionally, severe handicap may result. For example, the businessman who is phobic about airplanes may be badly inconvenienced if travel is essential to his business. Other common isolated phobias include fears of heights, thunderstorms, and darkness, none usually incapacitating.

Phobias concerning virtually any situation or object can develop, but the type of situation or object seems to be less important than whether phobias are isolated or multiple (7, 22, 33). One exception may be irrational fears of illness. Such fears are often seen in patients with affective disorders, obsessional neurosis, or anxiety neurosis. Occasionally, however, isolated phobias regarding such illnesses as cancer and heart disease may occur in the absence of other psychiatric symptoms. Little is known about the course or outcome of these monosymptomatic but sometimes disabling fears.

Multiple phobias usually involve a complex clinical picture with more ominous prognosis than that of single phobias. Patients with multiple phobias are usually agoraphobic (22). Agoraphobia sometimes is limited to fear of open places, but usually also includes fears of stores, crowds, closed spaces, travel, or of leaving the house (the "housebound housewife"). Agoraphobics almost always have other nonphobic symptoms, though phobias dominate the picture. These other symptoms include diffuse anxiety, panic attacks, feelings of depersonalization and derealization, and dizziness (32). These symptoms can make diagnosis difficult when they are intense.

Natural History

Most studies of phobias have been limited to agoraphobia. Several studies have dealt with animal phobias, but little is known about other isolated phobias.

A study of phobias at the Maudsley Hospital indicates that most animal phobias begin in early childhood before the age of eight (22). Before puberty animal phobias are found commonly in both boys and girls, but after puberty they occur predominantly in women. The phobia usually remains limited to a single type of animal species but may persist for decades. In the absence of the phobic object the patient does not experience unusual tension or anxiety. No other psychiatric features are conspicuous.

Unlike animal phobias, agoraphobia is rare in childhood, usually beginning in young adult life. The mean age of onset is about 26. Agoraphobics usually do not seek psychiatric help for some five to fifteen years after onset of the illness. Most patients are women (21).

Knowledge about phobic disorders is based mainly on studies of treated patients. Most of the studies have been retrospective and have failed to collect systematic data. An exception is Marks' follow-up of phobic patients four years after treatment (26). Regardless of the treatment received (behavioral modification vs. psychotherapy), most patients continued to have phobias and did not develop other psychiatric disorders. Other follow-up studies indicate that phobias wax and wane in severity but are rarely absent over long periods (18, 23).

A study of nonpatients (2) showed that at five-year follow-up a group of 30 phobics identified in a population survey had a course similar to that seen among treated phobics (10, 31). About half improved, a quarter were unchanged, and another quarter were worse. Isolated phobias and phobias beginning in childhood had the best prognosis. Severity of isolated phobias did not predict course or outcome.

Complications

Social, occupational, and marital disability are the main complications of phobias (33). In isolated phobias the disability tends to be mild and is limited to responses to the phobic object or situation.

Agoraphobics generally suffer greater impairment, sometimes to the point of being totally housebound.

In several series of patients, frigidity and other sexual maladjustments have been reported in association with agoraphobia. Since the frigidity often antedates the phobias, this may not represent a true "complication" of the illness. In any case, more than half of agoraphobic women have been reported to be frigid, although studies indicate that their marriages are stable (32, 40).

Follow-up studies suggest that phobics occasionally become depressed and have an affective syndrome indistinguishable from primary affective disorder except for the prior history of chronic phobias. Suicide does not appear to be a complication of phobic neurosis. One study (38) indicates that phobics are particularly susceptible to drug or alcohol dependence, but another study (36) suggests the contrary and the issue is unresolved.

Family Studies

Marks and Herst (25) found that a fifth of agoraphobics in Britain reported that they had a close relative with the same kind of phobia. Berg (5) found that school phobia occurred in the children of agoraphobic women to a greater extent than expected, but in another study Berg *et al.* (6) were unable to relate school phobia to any type of maternal psychiatric illness. Nor were Buglass *et al.* (7) able to show excessive psychiatric disturbances in the children of agoraphobic women compared to controls. Three studies indicate that phobics come from stable families in which the mothers may be overprotective (32, 38, 40).

Of five sets of monozygotic twins studied at the Maudsley Hospital in which one of each twin pair was phobic, there were no cases in which both twins were affected (23).

Differential Diagnosis

Phobias occur in psychiatric conditions other than phobic neurosis, notably obsessional neurosis and anxiety neurosis. Since all three conditions begin in early adult life and have a chronic though sometimes fluctuating course, distinguishing them may be difficult. This is particularly true of agoraphobia when multiple phobias occur together with anxiety attacks, obsessional thinking, and other nonphobic psychiatric symptoms.

Anxiety neurotics often have phobias but the most conspicuous feature of anxiety neurosis is anxiety attacks that are apparently unrelated to external situations, attacks in which the subjective experience of fear is accompanied by severe cardiorespiratory symptoms. In the case of obsessional neurosis, the condition is manifested by a panoply of obsessional symptoms, including checking and counting rituals, repetitive ideas relating to the possibility of harming oneself or others, and other recurrent thoughts viewed by the patient as bizarre but irresistible.

As with other "neurotic" patients, phobics may become depressed and may develop the full range of affective symptoms, physiological and subjective. When the phobias preceding the affective episode are isolated and nonincapacitating, it may be legitimate to view the affective disorder as "primary." With regard to agoraphobia, depressions commonly occur during the course of the illness and probably should be considered "secondary" (without giving this nosologic distinction etiological connotations). To some British authors, agoraphobia is an atypical form of affective disorder. Many of the symptoms of primary affective disorder may have phobic qualities, such as fearfulness of social situations and disease.

When phobic-like symptoms occur in schizophrenia, they are usually bizarre and unaccompanied by insight.

Clinical Management

Regardless of the theoretical orientation of the therapist, it is generally agreed that at some point the phobic patient must confront the feared situation. Freud observed that "one can hardly ever master a phobia if one waits till the patient lets the analysis influence him to give it up. One succeeds only when one can induce them through the influence of the analysis to go about alone and to struggle with their anxiety while they make the attempt" (13).

Most treatments have been designed to reduce the phobic anxiety to the extent that the patient can tolerate exposure to the phobic situation. These treatments include drugs, psychotherapy, behavior modification techniques, and (in extremely severe, chronic cases) lobotomy.

Among drugs used for phobias, tricyclic antidepressants (3, 15, 18) and MAO inhibitors (9, 41) have had advocates; controlled studies to support their use have been rare. A recent double-blind trial of phenelzine, an MAO inhibitor, did suggest that phenelzine was superior to placebo in phobic patients who completed the trial (29). This was consistent with many anecdotal reports, usually from England, indicating that MAO inhibitors are useful for phobic anxiety, particularly when there also are elements of depression. However, other studies of patients with agoraphobia and social phobias have indicated that phenelzine produces a temporary relief of symptoms in both groups, but that within a year the difference between the treated and placebo groups disappears, mainly because of spontaneous improvement in the placebo groups (28, 39). One study suggests that electrotherapy worsens phobias, again without adequate controls (4). Individual case reports indicate that some phobic patients respond favorably to psychoanalysis and other forms of psychotherapy, but no controlled studies have been made.

The most popular approach to the treatment of phobias in recent years involves techniques based on learning theory. Of these, "systematic desensitization," introduced by Wolpe, has been most widely used and extensively studied (20, 43). Nearly a score of studies, most of them controlled, suggest that systematic desensitization produces at least temporary relief of isolated phobias but is less effective in agoraphobia (23). One study indicates that desensitization may be particularly effective for flight phobia (35).

The method consists of training the patient to relax and then gradually exposing him to more and more intensive versions of the phobic stimulus. This requires that the patient imagine the feared events, starting with events that produce minimal anxiety and then progressing through a "hierarchy" to imagine events of maximal fearfulness. At this point he is expected to confront the phobic situation in reality and by relaxation be able to tolerate it. The approach is based on the concept of "reciprocal inhibition" which holds that two mutually incompatible emotions, such as fear and pleasure, cannot be simultaneously experienced. Therefore, relaxation, being "pleasurable," theoretically cancels the sensation of fear if the latter is not overwhelming.

A variation of this approach consists of "flooding" the individual with the phobic stimulus at maximal intensity without progressing through a hierarchy. The process has also been called "implosion." Although its efficacy is still a matter of debate, controlled trials indicate that flooding, like systematic desensitization, may be superior to other treatments in reducing avoidance behavior related to simple phobias (23, 24). The effectiveness of flooding apparently does not depend upon whether the phobic patient is exposed to real phobic stimuli or is asked to imagine phobic stimuli (imaginal flooding) (17).

"Paradoxical intention" was conceived by Frankl to help patients overcome their phobic fears by deliberately exaggerating them (12). This technique derived from the observation that anxiety may be increased by the endeavor to avoid anxiety. If, for example, a patient is unreasonably afraid of having a heart attack, he may be encouraged to "try as hard as possible" to have one "right on the spot" (23). This often introduces an element of humor into the situation, which may itself be helpful. It is unclear whether paradoxical intention has lasting therapeutic effect. Other techniques involve operant conditioning and hypnosis; their efficacy also remains to be demonstrated. There has been one report that phobic patients show a higher rate of improvement from hypnosis than smokers who try to quit smoking through hypnosis.

One controlled retrospective study suggests that lobotomy may produce significantly more improvement in phobias than other procedures when the patient is severely agoraphobic and has not responded to any other treatment (27). There is general agreement that lobotomy should be used as a last resort, if at all.

References

1. Agras, S., Sylvester, D., and Oliveau, D. The epidemiology of common fears and phobia. Compr. Psychiat. 10:151-156, 1969.
2. Agras, S., Chapin, H. N., and Oliveau, D. C. The natural history of phobia, course and prognosis. Arch. Gen. Psychiat. 26:315-317, 1972.
3. Ayd, F. J., Jr. Antidepressant, 1959. Psychosomatics 1:31, 1960.
4. Ayd, F. J., Jr. APA psychiatric research reports, 213, 1959.
5. Berg, I. School phobia in the children of agoraphobic women. Brit. J. Psychiat. 128:86-89, 1976.
6. Berg, I., Butler, A., and Pritchard, J. Psychiatric illness in the mothers of school phobic adolescents. Brit. J. Psychiat. 125:466-467, 1974.
7. Buglass, D., Clarke, J., Henderson, A. S., Kreitman, N., and Presley, A. S. A study of agoraphobic housewives. Psychol. Med. 7:73-86, 1977.
8. Burton, R. *The Anatomy of Melancholy* (1621), Vol. 1, 11th ed. London, 1813.
9. Dally, P. J. and Rohde, P. Comparison of antidepressant drugs in depressive illnesses. Lancet 1:18, 1961.
10. Errera, P. Some historical aspects of the concept of phobia. Psychiat. Quart. 36:325-336, 1962.
11. Frankel, F. and Orne, M. Hypnotizability and phobic behavior. Arch. Gen. Psychiat. 33:1259-1261, 1976.
12. Frankl, V. E. Paradoxical intention: a logotherapeutic technique. Amer. J. Psychother. 14:520-535, 1960.
13. Freud, S. *Collected Papers*, Vol. 2, New York: Basic Books.
14. Freud, S. Rev. neurol. 3. (Transl. in *Collected Papers*, Vol. 1, p. 128. London: International Psychoanalytic Press, 1924.)
15. Goldman, D. Clinical experience with newer antidepressant drugs and some related electroencephalographic observations. Ann. N.Y. Acad. Sci. 80:687, 1959.
16. Hippocrates on Epidemics, V, Section LXXXII.
17. Johnston, D., Lancashire, M., Mathews, A., Munby, M., Shaw, P., and Gelder, M. Imaginal flooding and exposure to real phobic situations: Changes during treatment. Brit. J. Psychiat. 129:372-377, 1976.
18. Klein, D. F. The delineation of two drug-responsive anxiety syndromes. Psychopharmacologia 5:397, 1964.
19. Lang, P. J. Fear reduction and fear behaviour. "Problems in treating a construct." In *3rd Conference on Research in Psychotherapy*, Chicago, June, 1966.
20. McConaghy, N. Results of systematic desensitization with phobias reexamined. Brit. J. Psychiat. 117:89-92, 1970.

21. Marks, I. M. Agoraphobic syndrome (phobic anxiety state). Arch. Gen. Psychiat. 23:538-553, 1970.
22. Marks, I. M. The classification of phobic disorders. Brit. J. Psychiat. 116:377-386, 1970.
23. Marks, I. M. *Fears and Phobias*. London: Academic Press, 1969.
24. Marks, I. M., Boulougouris, J., and Marset, P. Flooding versus desensitization in the treatment of phobic patients: a crossover study. Brit. J. Psychiat. 119:353-375, 1971.
25. Marks, I. M. and Herst, E. The open door: a survey of agoraphobics in Britain. Soc. Psychiat. 1:16-24, 1970.
26. Marks, I. M. Phobic disorders four years after treatment: a prospective follow-up. Brit. J. Psychiat. 118:683-688, 1971.
27. Marks, I. M., Birley, J. L. T., and Gelder, M. G. Modified leucotomy in severe agoraphobia: a controlled serial inquiry. Brit. J. Psychiat. 112:757-769, 1966.
28. Mathews, A., Johnston, D., Lancashire, M., Munby, M., Shaw, P., and Gelder, M. Imaginal flooding and exposure to real phobic situations: Treatment outcome with agoraphobic patients. Brit. J. Psychiat. 129:362-371, 1976.
29. Mountjoy, C., Roth, M., Garside, R., and Leitch, I. A clinical trial of phenelzine in anxiety depressive and phobic neuroses. Brit. J. Psychiat. 131:486-492, 1977.
30. Paskind, H. A. A study of phobias. J. Neurol. Psychopath. 12:40-46, 1931.
31. Roberts, A. H. Housebound housewives: a follow-up study of a phobic anxiety state. Brit. J. Psychiat. 110:191-197, 1964.
32. Roth, M. The phobic-anxiety-depersonalisation syndrome. Proc. Roy. Soc. Med. 52:587, 1959.
33. Shafar, S. Aspects of phobic illness—a study of 90 personal cases. Brit. J. Med. Psychol. 49:221-236, 1976.
34. Shapiro, M. B., Marks, I. M., and Fox, B. A therapeutic experiment on phobic and affective symptoms in an individual psychiatric patient. Brit. J. Soc. Clin. Psychol. 2:81-93, 1963.
35. Shaw, H. A simple and effective treatment for flight phobia. Brit. J. Psychiat. 130:229-232, 1977.
36. Sim, M. and Houghton, H. Phobic anxiety and its treatment. J. Nerv. Ment. Dis. 143:484-491, 1966.
37. Snaith, R. P. A clinical investigation of phobias. Brit. J. Psychiat. 114: 673-698, 1968.
38. Terhune, W. The phobic syndrome: a study of 86 patients with phobic reactions. Arch. Neurol. Psychiat. 62:162-172, 1949.
39. Tyrer, P. and Steinberg, D. Symptomatic treatment of agoraphobia and social phobias: A follow-up study. Brit. J. Psychiat. 127:163-168, 1975.
40. Webster, A. S. The development of phobias in married women. Psychol. Monogr. 67:367, 1953.

41. West, E. D. and Dally, P. J. Effects of iproniazid in depressive syndromes. Brit. Med. J. 1:1491, 1959.
42. Westphal, C. Die Agoraphobie: eine neuropathische Erscheinung. Arch. für Psychiatrie und Nervenkrankheiten 3:138-171, 219-221, 1871-72.
43. Wolpe, J. *Psychotherapy by Reciprocal Inhibition*. Stanford: Stanford University Press, 1958.

7. Alcoholism

Definition

Alcoholism is synonymous with problem drinking. The alcoholic is a person whose excessive use of alcohol results in serious medical, social, domestic, vocational, or legal problems. The condition is usually progressive and either chronic or characterized by frequent relapses (42).

Historical Background

The use of alcohol by man dates back at least to Paleolithic times. The evidence for this statement derives from etymology as well as studies of Stone Age cultures that survived into the 20th century.

Available to Paleolithic man, presumably, were fermented fruit juice (wine), fermented grain (beer), and fermented honey (mead). Etymological evidence suggests that mead may have been the earliest beverage of choice. The word "*mead*" derives—by way of "*mede*" (Middle English) and "*meodu*" (Anglo-Saxon)—from ancient words of Indo-European stock, such as "*methy*" (Greek) and "*madhu*" (Sanskrit). In Sanskrit and Greek, the term means both "honey" and "intoxicating drink." The association of honey, rather than grain or fruit, with intoxication may indicate its greater antiquity as a source of alcohol (74).

All but three of the numerous Stone Age cultures that survived into modern times have been familiar with alcohol. "The three exceptions," Berton Roueché writes, "are the environmentally underprivileged polar peoples, the intellectually stunted Australian aborigines, and the comparably lackluster primitives of Tierra del Fuego" (74). Early European explorers of Africa and the New World invariably discovered that alcohol was important in the local cultures. The Indians of eastern North America, for instance, were using alcohol in the form of fermented birch and sugar maple sap (74).

Alcohol was used medicinally and in religious ceremonies for thousands of years, but it also has a long history of recreational use. Noah, according to the Old Testament, "drank of the wine and was drunken." Mesopotamian civilization provided one of the earliest clinical descriptions of intoxication and one of the first hangover cures. In *A History of Medicine* (80), Sigerist translates a Mesopotamian physician's advice as follows: "If a man has taken strong wine, his head is affected and he forgets his words and his speech becomes confused, his mind wanders and his eyes have a set expression; *to cure him,* take licorice, beans, oleander . . . to be compounded with oil and wine before the approach of the goddess Gula (or sunset), and in the morning before sunrise and before anyone has kissed him, let him take it, and he will recover."

Roueché notes that "one of the few surviving relics of the Seventeenth Egyptian Dynasty, which roughly coincided with the reign of Hammurabi, is a hieroglyphic outburst of a female courtier. 'Give me eighteen bowls of wine!' she exclaims for posterity. 'Behold, I love drunkenness!' " (73). So did other Egyptians of that era. "Drunkenness was apparently not rare," Sigerist remarks, "and seems to have occurred in all layers of society from the farmers to the gods (or ruling class). Banquets frequently ended with the guests, men and women, being sick, and this did not in any way seem shocking" (80).

Not only descriptions of drunkenness fill the writings of antiquity, but also pleas for moderation. Dynastic Egypt apparently invented the first temperance tract (74). Moderation was recommended by no less an authority than Genghis Khan: "A soldier must not get drunk oftener than once a week. It would, of course, be better if he did not get drunk at all, but one should not expect the impossible." The Old Testament condemns drunkenness, but not alcohol. "Give strong drink unto him that is ready to perish," the Book of Proverbs proclaims, "and wine unto those that be of heavy hearts. Let him drink, and forget his poverty, and remember his misery no more."

The process of distillation was discovered about A.D. 800 in Arabia. ("Alcohol" comes from the arabic "*alkuhl*," meaning essence). For centuries distilled alcohol was used in medicine, but by the 17th century it had also become a drug of abuse on a large scale. By the late 17th century the annual worldwide production of distilled liquors, chiefly gin, was enormous.

The "disease concept" of alcoholism originated in the writings of Benjamin Rush and the British physician Thomas Trotter (75), and during the last half of the 19th century the notion that alcoholism was a disease became popular with physicians. In the 1830's, Dr. Samuel Woodward, the first superintendent of Worcester State Hospital, Massachusetts, and Dr. Eli Todd of Hartford, Connecticut, suggested establishing special institutions for inebriates. The first was opened in Boston in 1841. In 1904 the Medical Temperance Society changed its name to the American Medical Association for the Study of Inebriety and Narcotics. *The Journal of Inebriety*, established in 1876, was founded on the "fact that inebriety is a neurosis and psychosis." During Prohibition, however, the concept of alcoholism as a disease lost its vogue (42).

With repeal of the 18th Amendment, the "disease concept" was revived. Pioneering studies performed at the Yale School of Alcohol Studies and the writings of E. M. Jellinek were largely responsible for the popularization of this concept in the 20th century. In the mid-1960's the U.S. Government began supporting alcoholism research on a rather large scale, and by the early 1970's the federal government and most state governments were sponsoring treatment programs for alcoholics.

Epidemiology

More is known about patterns of "normal" drinking than about the prevalence of alcoholism, at least in the United States. A nationwide survey of drinking practices by Cahalan, Cissin, and Crossley (9) revealed that 68 percent of adults in America drink alcohol on occasion and that 12 percent are "heavy" drinkers. (A heavy drinker was defined as a person who drinks almost every day and becomes intoxicated several times a month.) Drinkers tend to be young, relatively prosperous, and well-educated. More live in cities and suburbs than in rural regions and small towns. To some extent religion determines whether a person is a drinker or a teetotaler: almost all urban Jews and Episcopalians drink on occasion; fewer than half of rural Baptists drink.

More men than women are "heavy" drinkers (20 percent of men versus 8 percent of women). Heavy drinkers more often come from the lower classes and are less well-educated than "normal" drinkers. The study by Cahalan and his associates indicated that drinking patterns were highly changeable. It was common for individuals to be heavy drinkers for long periods and then become moderate drinkers or teetotalers.

There have been no adequate studies of prevalence rates of alcoholism in the United States. In part, this is because of disagreement about the definition of alcoholism. Estimates of the extent of alcoholism range from five to nine million Americans. These estimates are roughly equivalent to expectancy rates obtained in studies by Luxenberger (57) in Germany, Bleuler (3) in Switzerland, Sjögren (81) in Sweden, Fremming (23) in Denmark, and Slater (82) in England. In these countries the life-long expectancy rate for alcoholism among men is about 3 to 5 percent; the rate for women ranges from 0.1 to 1 percent.

In the United States blacks in urban ghettos appear to have a particularly high rate of alcohol-related problems; whether rural blacks have comparably high rates of alcohol problems is unknown (59, 71). American Indians are also said to have high rates of alcoholism (19), but this does not apply to all tribes, and books have been written debunking the "firewater myth" (49, 58). Orientals, on the other hand, generally have low rates of alcoholism.

Alcoholism is a serious problem in France and Russia (76). Although Italy, like France, is a "vinocultural" country, where wine is a popular beverage, it is commonly asserted that Italians have a lower rate of alcoholism than the French (55). The evidence for this is scant, however. Estimates of alcoholism rates are usually based on cirrhosis rates and admissions to psychiatric hospitals for alcoholism. France has the highest cirrhosis rate in the world, but Italy also has a high rate, suggesting that alcoholism may be more common in Italy than is generally assumed. Ireland has a relatively low cirrhosis rate, despite its reputation for a high rate of alcoholism. According to de Lint and Schmidt (54), there is a positive correlation between per capita consumption of alcohol and cirrhosis rates. If cirrhosis rates are a reliable indicator of the extent of alcoholism in a particular country, then both cirrhosis and alcoholism are correlated with the total amount of alcohol consumed by the population of that country. Cirrhosis rates themselves are probably somewhat unreliable, and estimates of the prevalence of alcoholism in different countries tends to change from time to time, as new information is obtained (68).

Alcohol problems are correlated with a history of school difficulty (70). High school dropouts and individuals with a record of frequent truancy and delinquency appear to have a particularly high risk of alcoholism.

No systematic studies have explored the relationship between occupation and alcoholism, but cirrhosis data suggest that individuals in certain occupations are more vulnerable to alcoholism than those doing other types of work. Waiters, bartenders, longshoremen, musicians, authors, and reporters have relatively high cirrhosis rates; accountants, mail carriers, and carpenters have relatively low rates (54).

Age is another demographic variable correlated with alcoholism. Urban blacks begin drinking at an earlier age than whites of comparable socioeconomic status (71). Women as a rule begin heavy drinking at a later age than men (67).

Clinical Picture

Alcoholism is a behavioral disorder. The specific behavior that causes problems is the consumption of large quantities of alcohol on repeated occasions. The motivation underlying this behavior is often obscure. When asked why they drink excessively, alcoholics occasionally attribute their drinking to a particular mood, such as depression or anxiety, or to situational problems. They sometimes describe an overpowering "need" to drink, variously described as a craving or compulsion. Just as often, however, the alcoholic is unable to give a plausible explanation of his excessive drinking (56).

Like other drug dependencies, alcoholism is accompanied by a preoccupation with obtaining the drug in quantities sufficient to produce intoxication over long periods. It is especially true early in the course of alcoholism that the patient may deny this preoccupation or attempt to rationalize his need by assertions that he drinks no more than his friends. As part of this denial or rationalization, alcoholics tend to spend their time with other heavy drinkers.

Given the occurrence of denial, it would be useful to have a test for heavy drinking. Lieber and associates (53) found that heavy drinking produces a striking increase in the amino acid, alpha-amino-*n*-butyric acid. The use of this test in rehabilitation programs and industrial settings reportedly has validated its ability to indicate active alcoholism before there is social or medical disintegration (79). Further studies to replicate this work need to be done, but no one denies the importance of early diagnosis of high alcohol intake.

As alcoholism progresses and problems from drinking become more serious, the alcoholic may drink alone, sneak drinks, hide the bottle, and take other measures to conceal the seriousness of his condition. This is almost always accompanied by feelings of guilt and remorse which in turn may produce more drinking, temporarily relieving the feelings. Remorse may be particularly intense in the morning, when the patient has not had a drink for a number of hours, and this may provoke morning drinking (43).

Prolonged drinking, even if initiated to relieve guilt and anxiety, commonly produces anxiety and depression (17). The full range of symptoms associated with depression and anxiety neurosis, including terminal insomnia, low mood, irritability, and anxiety attacks with chest pain, palpitations, and dyspnea, often appears. Alcohol temporarily relieves these symptoms, resulting in a vicious cycle of drinking-depression-drinking which may ultimately result in a classical withdrawal syndrome. Often the patient makes a valiant effort to stop drinking and may succeed for a period of several days or weeks, only to "fall off the wagon" again.

Repeated experiences like this easily lead to feelings of despair and hopelessness. By the time the patient consults a physician, he has often reached "rock bottom." His situation seems hopeless and, after years of heavy drinking, his problems have become so numerous that he feels nothing can be done about them. At this point he may be ready to acknowledge his alcoholism, but feel powerless to stop drinking.

Alcohol is one of the few psychoactive drugs that produce, on occasion, classical amnesia. Nonalcoholics, when drinking, also experience this amnesia (blackouts), but much less often, as a rule, than do alcoholics (32). These episodes of amnesia are particularly distressful to the alcoholic, since he may fear that he has unknowingly harmed someone or behaved imprudently while intoxicated. Studies of blackouts (30, 83) indicate that the amnesia is anterograde. During a blackout, the person has relatively intact remote and immediate memory but experiences a specific "short-term" memory deficit in which he is unable to recall events that happened five or ten minutes before. Since his other intellectual faculties are well preserved, he can perform complicated acts and appears normal to the casual observer. Present evidence suggests that alcoholic blackouts represent impaired consolidation of new information rather that "repression" motivated by a desire to forget events that happened while drinking (30).

By the time the alcoholic consults a physician, he has often developed medical and social complications from drinking. These will be discussed under the section *Complications.*

Natural History

The natural history of alcoholism seems to be somewhat different in men and women (67). In men the onset is usually in the late teens or twenties, the course is insidious, and the alcoholic may not be fully aware of his dependency on alcohol until his thirties. The first hospitalization usually occurs in the late thirties or forties (20).

Symptoms of alcoholism rarely occur for the first time after age 45 (1). If they do occur, the physician should be alerted to the possibility of primary affective disorder or brain disease.

Alcoholism has a higher "spontaneous" remission rate than is often recognized. The incidence of first admissions to psychiatric hospitals for alcoholism drops markedly in the sixth and seventh decades as do first arrests for alcohol-related offenses. Although the mortality rate among alcoholics is perhaps two to three times that of nonalcoholics, this is probably insufficient to account for the apparent decrease in problem drinking in middle and late middle life (20).

Female alcoholics have been studied less extensively than male alcoholics, but the evidence suggests that the course of the disorder is more variable in women. The onset often occurs later and spontaneous remission apparently is less frequent (67). Female alcoholics are also more likely to have a history of primary affective disorder (77).

On the basis of questionnaire data obtained from alcoholics, Jellinek promulgated the view that manifestations of alcoholism follow a natural chronological order, with blackouts being one of the early "prodromal" symptoms of the illness (43). Later studies (32) have challenged this view, and it is now believed that problems from drinking may occur in various sequences and that blackouts have no special significance as a sign of incipient alcoholism.

Frequently, after years of heavy problem-free drinking, a person may experience a large number of problems in a brief period. Table 1 shows the mean age of onset of alcohol problems in an unselected series of male hospitalized alcoholics.

Patterns of drinking also are variable and it is a mistake to associate one particular pattern exclusively with "alcoholism." Jellinek (42) divided alcoholics into various "species" depending on their pattern of drinking. One species, the so-called gamma alcoholic, is common in America and conforms to the stereotype of the Alcoholics Anonymous alcoholic. Gamma alcoholics have problems with "control": once they begin drinking, they are unable to stop until poor health or depleted financial resources prevent them from continuing. Once the "bender" is terminated, however, the person is able to abstain from alcohol for varying lengths of time. Jellinek contrasted the gamma alcoholic with a species of alcoholic common in France. He has "control" but is "unable to abstain"; he *must* drink a given quantity of alcohol every day, although he has no compulsion to exceed this amount. He may not recognize that he has an alcohol problem until, for reasons beyond his control, he has to stop drinking, whereupon he experiences withdrawal symptoms.

Although these pure types of alcoholism do exist, many individuals who do not conform to the stereotypes still have serious drinking problems. Among American alcoholics, one drink does *not* invariably lead to a binge; a person may drink moderately for a long time before his drinking begins to interfere with his health or social functioning.

This diversity in drinking patterns explains the current emphasis on *problems* rather than a single set of symptoms, as the basis for diagnosing alcoholism.

Complications

Since alcoholism is defined by the problems it creates, symptoms and complications inevitably overlap. For present purposes, we will consider social and medical complications separately.

Alcoholics have a high rate of marital separation and divorce (91). They often have job troubles, including frequent absenteeism and job loss. They also have a high frequency of accidents—in the home, on the job, and while driving automobiles. Of the more than 55,000 highway fatalities each year in the United States, about half involve a driver who has been drinking, usually an alcoholic (78). Nearly half of convicted felons are alcoholic (31), and about half of police activities in large cities are associated with alcohol-related offenses.

Medical complications fall into three categories: (a) acute effects of heavy drinking; (b) chronic effects of heavy drinking; and (c) withdrawal effects.

Consumption of very large amounts of alcohol can lead directly to death by depressing the respiratory center in the medulla. Acute hemorrhagic pancreatitis occasionally occurs from a single heavy drinking episode.

Nearly every organ system can be affected, directly or indirectly, by chronic, heavy use of alcohol. Gastritis and diarrhea are common reversible effects. Gastric ulcer may also occur, although the evidence that alcohol directly produces ulceration is equivocal (89).

The most serious effect of alcohol on the gastrointestinal tract is liver damage. After many years of study, however, it is still not clear whether alcohol alone has a direct toxic effect on the liver. At present, it appears that cirrhosis results from the combined effect of alcohol and diet, plus other factors, possibly including heredity. Human and animal studies indicate that a single large dose of alcohol, combined with a diet rich in fat, produces a fatty liver (51, 89). Conversely, alcohol together with fasting can result in a fatty liver. The connection between fatty liver and cirrhosis, however, is unclear. The fatty changes in the liver after acute alcohol intoxication are reversible. Most patients with Laennec's cirrhosis, in Western countries, are excessive drinkers. Most severe alcoholics, however, do not develop cirrhosis (probably less than 10 percent).

Investigations of the pathogenesis of Laennec's cirrhosis until recently have been hampered by inability to produce this type of cirrhosis in animals. Recent studies show that force-feeding baboons with large amounts of alcohol over long periods results in cirrhosis (52). However, not all baboons develop cirrhosis, and these studies leave unresolved the question of the direct role of alcohol in producing cirrhosis. One complication in interpreting the finding is that large intake of alcohol also produces a malabsorption syndrome and, therefore, although the baboons had adequate diets, it is likely that important food constituents, including vitamins, were not fully absorbed during the drinking periods.

Alcoholism is associated with pathology of the nervous system, principally due to vitamin deficiencies and not to a direct toxic effect of alcohol. Peripheral neuropathy, the most common neurological complication, apparently results from multiple vitamin B deficiencies (84). It is usually reversible with adequate nutrition. Retrobulbar neuropathy may lead to amblyopia (sometimes called tobacco-alcohol amblyopia), which is also usually reversible with vitamin therapy.

Other neurological complications include anterior lobe cerebellar degenerative disease (73) and the Wernicke-Korsakoff syndrome (85). The latter results from thiamine deficiency. The acute Wernicke stage consists of ocular disturbances (nystagmus or sixth nerve palsy), ataxia, and confusion. It usually clears in a few days but may progress to a chronic brain syndrome (Korsakoff psychosis). Short-term memory loss (anterograde amnesia) is the most characteristic feature of Korsakoff's psychosis. "Confabulation" (narration of fanciful tales) may also occur. The Wernicke-Korsakoff syndrome is associated with necrotic lesions of the mammillary bodies, thalamus, and other brain stem areas. Thiamine corrects early Wernicke signs rapidly and *may* prevent development of an irreversible Korsakoff dementia.

Whether excessive use of alcohol produces cortical atrophy has been debated for many years (15). Computed tomography scans of alcoholics have been contradictory, one showing cerebral atrophy (21), one showing none (40), and one showing *reversible* atrophy (10). The extensive psychometric literature on intellectual impairment in alcoholics is also contradictory (36). Most studies performed soon after drinking bouts show intellectual deficits, but the deficits vary from study to study. The most consistent results have involved use of the categories test of the Halstead Battery, indicating that alcoholics have difficulty in "conceptual shifting." Many of the deficits found in alcoholics undergoing detoxification are reversible. No studies have reported a decline in alcoholics' IQs.

Other medical complications of alcoholism include cardiomyopathy, thrombocytopenia and anemia, and myopathy.

A possible teratogenic effect of alcohol has been suspected for centuries, but it was not until the work of Lemoine in 1968 (50) and the independent observations of Jones and Smith in 1973 (44) that a distinct, dysmorphic condition associated with maternal alcoholism during pregnancy was described in the medical literature. The abnormalities most typically associated with alcohol teratogenicity can be grouped into four categories: central nervous system dysfunction; birth deficiencies; a characteristic cluster of facial abnormalities; and variable major and minor malformations (14). Recent U.S. studies place the frequency of full expression at between one and two live births per 100,000, with frequency of partial expression at perhaps three to five live births per 100,000 (39). Animal studies have now demonstrated specific teratogenic properties of ethyl alcohol in a variety of species, many of the abnormalities being similar to those described in man (12, 69).

Despite this growing body of evidence, the so-called "fetal alcohol syndrome" remains a subject of controversy. Large-scale longitudinal studies are needed to definitely establish the teratogenicity of alcohol in humans. This is because alcoholic women are often malnourished, take other drugs, smoke heavily, and have life-styles in general that differ from those of nonalcoholic women. Most clinicians, considering present evidence, believe women should be cautioned against drinking excessively during pregnancy, and perhaps should avoid alcohol altogether, since "safe" levels of alcohol have not been ascertained.

The term "alcohol withdrawal syndrome" is preferable to "delirium tremens" (DT's). The latter refers to a specific manifestation of the syndrome. The most common withdrawal symptom is tremulousness, which usually occurs only a few hours after cessation of drinking and may even begin while the person is still drinking ("relative abstinence"). Transitory hallucinations also may occur. If so, they usually begin 12 to 24 hours after drinking stops (84). Grand mal convulsions ("rum fits") occur occasionally, sometimes as long as two or three days after drinking stops. As a rule, alcoholics experiencing convulsions do not have epilepsy; they have normal electroencephalograms when not drinking and experience convulsions only during withdrawal (60).

Delirium tremens is infrequent and when it does occur is often associated with an intervening medical illness. For a diagnosis of delirium tremens, gross memory disturbance should be present in addition to other withdrawal symptoms, such as agitation and vivid hallucinations. Classically, delirium tremens begins two or three days after drinking stops and subsides within one to five days (84). One must always suspect intercurrent medical illness when delirium occurs during withdrawal. The physician should be particularly alert to hepatic decompensation, pneumonia, subdural hematoma, pancreatis, and fractures.

So-called "chronic alcoholic hallucinosis" refers to the persistence of hallucinations, usually auditory, for long periods after other abstinence symptoms subside and after the patient has stopped heavy drinking (86). This occurs rarely and, after 75 years of debate concerning the etiology, it has not been resolved whether drinking actually produces the condition.

Suicide is an important complication of alcoholism. About one-quarter of suicides are alcoholic, predominantly men over age 35. Apparently alcoholics (unlike patients with primary affective disorder) are especially likely to commit suicide after loss of a wife, close relative, or other serious interpersonal disruption (27).

Family Studies

Every family study of alcoholism, regardless of country of origin, has shown much higher rates of alcoholism among the relatives of alcoholics than in the general population. According to a number of sudies, about 25 percent of fathers and brothers of alcoholics are themselves alcoholics (29).

Several authors have attempted to analyze their data to control for environmental factors. Dahlberg and Stenberg (16) established that in 25 percent of the alcoholics they studied at least one of the parents was also an alcoholic, and that both parents were abstainers in 12 percent of the cases. The *severity* of alcoholism in the index cases was the same whether the parents were alcoholics or abstainers. The authors interpreted this finding as indicating a hereditary influence in alcoholism, since exposure to an alcoholic parent did not appear to be a factor. Åmark (1) reported that "periodic" and "compulsive" alcoholics more frequently had alcoholic children than did relatively "mild" alcoholics. Home environments were found to be equally "good" or "bad" in both groups, again suggesting that alcoholism has a hereditary component. In a pedigree study of a single large family, Kroon (48) concluded that alcoholism was influenced by a sex-linked hereditary trait.

The possible association of alcoholism with other psychiatric illnesses, based on family data, has been studied by Brugger (7), Åmark (1), Bleuler (4), Winokur *et al.* (90), and Guze *et al.* (37), among others. There seems to be an excess of depression, criminality, sociopathy, and "abnormal personality" in the families of alcoholics. Typically, depression occurs in the female relatives, and alcoholism or sociopathy in the male relatives of alcoholics. Relatives of alcoholics apparently are no more often schizophrenic, mentally defective, manic, or epileptic than are relatives of nonalcoholics (29).

The obvious difficulty with family studies is that most individuals, including alcoholics, are raised by their progenitors; thus "nature" and "nurture" arise from the same source during early life. Several methods have been developed to circumvent this problem. Among these are twin and adoption studies.

Two twin studies of alcoholism have been conducted, one in Sweden and one in Finland. The Swedish study, using temperance board records, found that monozygotic twins were about two times more often concordant for alcoholism than were dizygotic twins of the same sex (46). The Finnish study, starting with a larger population of twins, few of whom were alcoholic, found a higher concordance rate for drinking "patterns" among monozygotic twins than among dizygotic twins, but no significant difference between monozygotic and dizygotic twins with regard to drinking "problems" (66). "Pattern" referred purely to quantity and frequency of alcohol consumption.

There have been a number of adoption studies of alcoholism. The first, by Roe and Burks (72), compared offspring of heavy drinkers with offspring of moderate drinkers, both groups having been adopted by nonrelatives. They found no adult drinking problems in either group. It was unclear, however, whether the heavy drinkers could be considered alcoholics, since none had received treatment and their heavy drinking usually occurred in the context of other antisocial behavior.

More recently a series of adoption studies of alcoholism has been conducted in Denmark. Sons of alcoholics raised by unrelated nonalcoholic adoptive parents were four times more likely to become alcoholic by an early age than were adopted-out sons of nonalcoholics. They were no more likely to have other forms of psychopathology and no more likely to be classified as "heavy drinkers." In short, transmission of alcoholism from the alcoholic parent seemed highly specific for alcoholism and did not increase the risk of another illness developing (28, 33).

Later, daughters of alcoholics were studied, both those raised by nonalcoholic adoptive parents and those raised by their own alcoholic parents (34, 35). The adopted-out daughters had a higher rate of alcoholism than exists in the general population (4 percent versus about 0.1 percent), but adopted-out controls also had a high rate of alcoholism, and the findings were equivocal. Daughters of alcoholics *raised* by their alcoholic parents more often had clinical depressions than did controls, but daughters raised by adoptive parents had rates of clinical depression no different from controls. This, of course, suggests that depression in the children of alcoholic parents may have an environmental basis.

Other studies have strengthened the original finding in this series. In the records of a cohort of adopted children followed for 25 or 30 years in Sweden, Bohman demonstrated that among the 89 males officially registered as alcoholics, 40 percent of their biological fathers were also so registered (56). This contrasted with a figure of only 13 percent of the fathers of the 723 other males in the cohort who had not been registered as alcoholics.

Cadoret and Gath reported similar findings in an adoption study conducted in Iowa (8). Among 84 adoptees, eighteen years of age and older, separated at birth from their biological parents and without further contact with them, alcoholism was found significantly more frequently in those whose relatives included an alcoholic. Adoptee alcoholism did not correlate with any other diagnosis in a biological parent.

Thus, studies conducted independently in three countries suggest that a susceptibility to alcoholism is transmitted from parent to child irrespective of whether the child is exposed to the alcoholic parent, and that this susceptibility seems specific for alcoholism and does not involve an increased susceptibility to antisocial behavior or other psychiatric disorders.

Differential Diagnosis

Chronic excessive use of alcohol produces a wide range of psychiatric symptoms which, in various combinations, can mimic other psychiatric disorders. Therefore, while a person is drinking heavily and during the withdrawal period, it is difficult to determine whether he suffers from a psychiatric condition other than alcoholism.

The diagnosis of alcoholism itself is relatively easy. However, many alcoholics also use other drugs, and it may be difficult to determine which symptoms are produced by alcohol and which by barbiturates, amphetamines, and so on. If a patient has been drinking heavily and not eating, he may become hypoglycemic (22), and this condition may produce symptoms resembling those seen in withdrawal.

The two psychiatric conditions most commonly associated with alcoholism are primary affective disorder and sociopathy. Female alcoholics apparently suffer more often from primary affective disorder than do male alcoholics (77). The diagnosis of primary affective disorder usually can be made by past history or by observing the patient during long periods of abstinence. According to one study, about one-third of patients with manic depressive illness drink more while depressed and another third drink less (11). Studies indicate that small amounts of alcohol administered to a depressed patient relieve depressive symptoms, but large amounts worsen depression (61).

Many sociopaths drink to excess, although how many would be considered "alcoholic" is uncertain. A follow-up study of convicted felons, about half of whom had alcohol problems, indicates that sociopathic drinkers have a higher "spontaneous" remission rate than do nonsociopathic alcoholics (31, 38). When sociopaths reduce their drinking, their criminal activities are correspondingly reduced.

Various personality disorders have been associated with alcoholism, particularly those in which "dependency" is a feature. The consensus at present is that alcoholism is not connected with a particular constellation of personality traits. Longitudinal studies help little in predicting what types of individuals are particularly susceptible to alcoholism (45, 62).

Clinical Management

The treatment of alcoholism and the management of alcohol withdrawal symptoms present separate problems.

In the absence of serious medical complications, the alcohol withdrawal syndrome is usually transient and self-limited; the patient recovers within several days regardless of treatment (84). Insomnia and irritability may persist for longer periods (25).

Treatment for withdrawal is symptomatic and prophylactic. Relief of agitation and tremulousness can be achieved with a variety of drugs, including barbiturates, paraldehyde, chloral hydrate, the phenothiazines, and the benzodiazepines. Currently, the benzodiazepines—chlordiazepoxide and diazepam—are widely considered the drugs of choice for withdrawal. They have little, if any, synergistic action with alcohol and, compared with barbiturates and paraldehyde, relatively little abuse potential. They can be administered parenterally to intoxicated patients without apparent risk and continued orally during the withdrawal period. There is some evidence that mortality is increased when the phenothiazines are used, reportedly from hypotension or hepatic encephalopathy.

Administration of large doses of vitamins—particularly the B vitamins—is obligatory, given the role of these vitamins in preventing peripheral neuropathy and the Wernicke-Korsakoff syndrome. The B vitamins are water-soluble and there is no apparent danger in administering them in large doses.

Unless the patient is dehydrated because of vomiting or diarrhea, there is no reason to administer fluids parenterally. Contrary to common belief, alcoholics usually are not dehydrated; actually, they may be overhydrated from consumption of large volumes of fluid (65). During the early stages of withdrawal, hyperventilation may cause respiratory alkalosis and this, together with hypomagnesemia, has been reported to produce withdrawal seizures (63). If the individual has a history of withdrawal seizures, diphenylhydantoin

(Dilantin) may be prescribed, although there is no evidence that it prevents withdrawal seizures.

If the patient develops delirium, he should be considered dangerous to himself and others, and protective measures taken. Ordinarily, tranquilizers will calm the patient sufficiently to control agitation, and restraints will not be necessary. Administration of intravenous barbiturates may be necessary for severe agitation. Most important, if delirium occurs, further exploration should be conducted to rule out serious medical illness missed in the original examination. When a patient is delirious, an attendant should always be present. It is sometimes helpful to have a friend or relative present.

The treatment of alcoholism should not begin until withdrawal symptoms subside. Treatment has two goals: (a) sobriety and (b) amelioration of psychiatric conditions associated with alcoholism. A small minority of alcoholics are eventually able to drink in moderation, but for several months after a heavy drinking bout total abstinence is desirable for two reasons. First, the physician must follow the patient, sober, for a considerable period to diagnose a coexistent psychiatric problem. Second, it is important for the patient to learn that he can cope with ordinary life problems without alcohol. Most relapses occur within six months of discharge from the hospital; they become less and less frequent after that (26).

For many patients, disulfiram (Antabuse) is helpful in maintaining abstinence. By inhibiting aldehyde dehydrogenase, the drug leads to an accumulation of acetaldehyde if alcohol is consumed. Acetaldehyde is highly toxic and produces nausea and hypotension. The latter condition in turn produces shock and may be fatal. In recent years, however, Antabuse has been prescribed in a lower dosage than was employed previously and no deaths from its use have been reported for a number of years.

Discontinuation of Antabuse after administration for several days or weeks still deters drinking for a three- to five-day period, since the drug requires that long to be excreted. Thus, it may be useful to give patients Antabuse during office visits at three- to four-day intervals early in the treatment program.

Until recent years it was recommended that patients be given Antabuse for several days and challenged with alcohol to demonstrate the unpleasant effects that follow. This procedure was not always satisfactory because some patients showed no adverse effects after considerable amounts of alcohol were consumed and other patients became very ill after drinking small amounts of alcohol. At present, the alcohol challenge test is considered optional. The principal disadvantage of Antabuse is not that patients drink while taking the drug but that they stop taking the drug after a brief period. This, again, is a good reason to give the drug on frequent office visits during the early crucial period of treatment.

In recent years, a wide variety of procedures, both psychological and somatic, have been tried in the treatment of alcoholism. None has proven definitely superior to others (5). There is no evidence that intensive psychotherapy helps most alcoholics. Nor are tranquilizers or antidepressants usually effective in maintaining abstinence or controlled drinking (18). Aversive conditioning techniques have been tried, with such agents as apomorphine and emetine to produce vomiting (88), succinylcholine to produce apnea (13), and electrical stimulation to produce pain (41). None has been shown to be effective in groups of alcoholics, although in individual cases one or more of these approaches may be helpful. Lysergic acid (LSD) has also been tried, but controlled studies (5) indicate that it is ineffective. While we do not know how many alcoholics benefit from participation in Alcoholics Anonymous, most clinicians agree that alcoholics should be encouraged to attend AA meetings on a trial basis.

In two double-blind studies, lithium carbonate was found superior to placebo in reducing drinking in depressed alcoholics (47, 64). There was a high drop-out rate in both studies and the results can only be considered preliminary. However, further investigation seems warranted.

Table 1. Onset of alcoholic manifestations among all subjects (N = 100) (ref. 32)

Manifestation	Present (*percent*)	*Mean age at onset*	*Percent of subjects reporting manifestation, by age at first occurrence**										
			<20	20-24	25-29	30-34	35-39	40-44	45-49	50-54	55-59	60-64	65-70
1. Frequent drunks	98	27	18	17	21	18	13	7	3		1	1	
2. Weekend drunks	82	28	11	18	21	32	6	8	2		1		
3. Morning drinking	84	31	2	17	15	25	17	9	11	1	1	1	
4. Benders	76	31	7	14	18	21	13	9	12	5	1		
5. Neglecting meals	86	32	2	11	14	29	15	10	10	6	1		1
6. "Shakes"	88	33	1	11	15	24	17	9	16	3	2		1
7. Job loss from drinking	69	34	3	7	19	19	26	7	9	6	3	1	
8. Separation or divorce from drinking	44	34		16	7	23	14	20	14	7			
9. Blackouts	64	35	2	6	16	28	25	8	9	3	3		
10. Joined A.A.	39	36		8	8	28	20	15	8	10	3		
11. Hospitalization for drinking	100	37	1	3	14	18	20	13	14	9	6	1	1
12. Delirium tremens	45	38		2	11	11	40	16	7	11	2		

* Figures rounded off to nearest whole number for ease of perusal. Sums may therefore not equal 100 percent.

In conclusion, it should be emphasized that relapses are characteristic of alcoholism and that physicians treating alcoholics should avoid anger or excessive pessimism when such relapses occur. Alcoholics see nonpsychiatric physicians as often as they see psychiatrists (probably more often), and there is evidence that general practitioners and internists are sometimes more helpful (24). This may be particularly true when the therapeutic approach is warm but authoritarian, with little stress on "insight" or "understanding." Since the cause of alcoholism is unknown, "understanding" in fact means acceptance of a particular theory. That may provide temporary comfort but probably rarely provides lasting benefit.

References

1. Amark, C. Study in alcoholism; clinical, social-psychiatric and genetic investigations. Acta Psych. Scand., Suppl. 70, 1951.
2. Bales, R. F. Cultural differences in rates of alcoholism. Quart. J. Stud. Alcohol 5:480, 1946.
3. Bleuler, M. Psychotische Belastung von korperlich Kranken. Z. Ges. Neurol. Psychiat. 142:780, 1932.
4. Bleuler, M. A comparative study of the constitutions of Swiss and American alcoholic patients. In *Etiology of Chronic Alcoholism*. Springfield, Ill.: C. C. Thomas, 1955.
5. Blum, E. M. and Blum, R. H. *Alcoholism*. San Francisco: Jossey-Bass, 1969.
6. Bohman, M. Some general aspects of alcoholism and criminality. Arch. Gen. Psychiat. 35:269-276, 1978.
7. Brugger, C. Familienuntersuchungen bei Alkoholdeliranten, Z. Ges. Neurol. Psychiat. 151:740, 1934.
8. Cadoret, R. J. and Gath, A. Inheritance of alcoholism in adoptees. Brit. J. Psychiat. 132:252-258, 1978.
9. Cahalan, D., Cisin, I. H., and Crossley, H. M. *American Drinking Practices: A National Survey of Behavior and Attitudes,* Monograph No. 6. New Brunswick, N.J.: Rutgers University Center of Alcohol Studies, 1969.
10. Carlen, P. L., Wortzman, G., Holgate, R. C., Wilkinson, D. A., and Rankin, J. G. Reversible cerebral atrophy in recently abstinent chronic alcoholics measured by computed tomography scans. Science. 200:1076-1078, 1978.
11. Cassidy, W. L., Flanagan, N. B., Spellman, M., and Cohen, M. E. Clinical observations in manic-depressive disease. J.A.M.A. 164:1535-1546, 1957.

12. Chernoff, G. F. The fetal alcohol syndrome in mice: an animal model. Teratology. 15:223-230, 1977.
13. Clancy, J., Vanderhoof, E., and Campbell, P. Evaluation of an aversive technique as a treatment for alcoholism. Quart. J. Stud. Alcohol 28:476-485, 1967.
14. Clarren, S. K. and Smith, D. W. The fetal alcohol syndrome. N.E.J.M. 298.No.19:1063-1067, 1978.
15. Courville, C. The effects of alcohol on the nervous system of man. Privately printed, San Lucas, Los Angeles, 1955.
16. Dahlberg, G. and Stenberg, S. Alkoholismen som Samhallsproblem. Stockholm: Oskar Eklunds, 1934.
17. Davis, D. Mood changes in alcoholic subjects with programmed and free-choice experimental drinking. In *Recent Advances in Studies of Alcoholism*. Washington, D.C.: U.S. Government Printing Office, 1971.
18. Ditman, K. S. Review and evaluation of current drug therapies in alcoholism. Int. J. Psych. 3:248-58, 1967.
19. Dozier, E. P. Problem drinking among American Indians: the role of socio-cultural deprivation. Quart. J. Stud. Alcohol 27:72-87, 1966.
20. Drew, L. R. H. Alcoholism as a self-limiting disease. Quart. J. Stud. Alcohol 29:956-967, 1968.
21. Epstein, P. S., Pisani, V. D., and Fawcett, J. A. Alcoholism and cerebral atrophy. Alcoholism: Clin., Exp., Res. 1:61-65, 1977.
22. Freinkel, N. and Arky, R. A. Effects of alcohol on carbohydrate metabolism in man. Psychosom. Med. 28:551-563, 1966.
23. Fremming, K. H. Sygdomsrisikoen for Sindslidelser og andre sjaeledige Abnormtilstande i den danske Gennemsnitsbefolkning. Copenhagen: Ejnar Munksgaard, 1947.
24. Gerard, D. L. and Saenger, G. *Out-Patient Treatment of Alcoholism*. Toronto: University of Toronto Press, 1966.
25. Gerard, D. L., Saenger, G., and Wile, R. The abstinent alcoholic. Arch. Gen. Psychiat. 6:83-95, 1962.
26. Glatt, M. M. An alcoholic unit in a metal hospital. Lancet 2:397-398, 1959.
27. Goodwin, D. W. Alcohol in suicides and homicides. Quart. J. Stud. Alcohol 34:144-156, 1973.
28. Goodwin, D. W., Schulsinger, F., Hermansen, L., Guze, S. B., and Winokur, G. Alcohol problems in adoptees raised apart from alcoholic biological parents. Arch. Gen. Psychiat. 28:238-243, 1973.
29. Goodwin, D. W. Is alcoholism hereditary? Arch. Gen. Psychiat. 25: 545-549, 1971.
30. Goodwin, D. W. Blackouts and alcohol-induced memory dysfunction. In *Recent Advances in Studies of Alcoholism*. Washington, D.C.: U.S. Department of Health, Education and Welfare, 1971.
31. Goodwin, D. W., Crane, J. B., and Guze, S. B. Felons who drink. Quart. J. Stud. Alcohol 32:136-147, 1971.
32. Goodwin, D. W., Crane, J. B., and Guze, S. B. Alcoholic "blackouts":

a review and clinical study of 100 alcoholics. Amer. J. Psychiat. 126: 191-198, 1969.

33. Goodwin, D. W., Schulsinger, F., Moller, N., Hermansen, L., Winokur, G., and Guze, S. B. Drinking problems in adopted and nonadopted sons of alcoholics. Arch. Gen. Psychiat. 31:164-169, 1974.
34. Goodwin, D. W., Schulsinger, F., Knop, J., Mednick, S., and Guze, S. B. Alcoholism and depression in adopted-out daughters of alcoholics. Arch. Gen. Psychiat. 34, 1977.
35. Goodwin, D. W., Schulsinger, F., Knop, J., Mednick, S., and Guze, S. B. Psychopathology in adopted and nonadopted daughters of alcoholics. Arch. Gen. Psychiat. 34, 1977.
36. Goodwin, D. W. and Hill, S. Y. Chronic effects of alcohol and other psychoactive drugs on intellect, learning and memory. Chronic effects of alcohol and other psychoactive drugs on cerebral function. Addict. Res. Foundation Press, Toronto, 1975.
37. Guze, S., Wolfgram, E., and McKinney, J. Psychiatric illness in the families of convicted criminals: a study of 519 first degree relatives. Dis. Nerv. Syst. 28:651-659, 1967.
38. Guze, S. B. *Criminality and Psychiatric Disorders*. New York: Oxford University Press, 1976.
39. Hanson, J. W., Streissguth, A. P., and Smith, D. W. The effects of moderate alcohol consumption during pregnancy on fetal growth and morphogenesis. J. Pediatr. 92:457-460, 1978.
40. Hill, S. Y., Reyes, R. B., Mikhael, M., and Ayre, F. A comparison of alcoholics and heroin abusers: computerized transaxial tomography and neuropsychological functioning. In *Currents in Alcoholism Sexias*, F. (ed.). In press.
41. Hsu, J. J. Electroconditioning therapy of alcoholics. Quart. J. Stud. Alcohol 26:449-459, 1965.
42. Jellinek, E. M. *The Disease Concept of Alcoholism*. New Haven: College and University Press, 1960.
43. Jellinek, E. M. Phases of alcohol addiction. Quart. J. Stud. Alcohol 13: 673-684, 1952.
44. Jones, K. L., Smith, D. W., Ulleland, C. M., *et al.* Pattern of malformation in offspring of chronic alcoholic mothers. Lancet 1:1267-1271, 1973.
45. Jones, M. C. Personality correlates and antecedents of drinking patterns in adult males. J. Consul. and Clin. Psychol. 32:2-12, 1968.
46. Kaij, L. *Studies on the Etiology and Sequels of Abuse of Alcohol*. Lund: Department of Psychiatry, University of Lund, 1960.
47. Kline, N. S., Wren, J. C., Cooper, T. B., Varga, E., and Canal, O. Evaluation of lithium therapy in chronic and periodic alcoholism. Amer. J. Med. Sci. 268:15-22, 1974.
48. Kroon, H. M. Die Erklichkeit der Trunksucht in der Familie X. Genetic 6:391, 1924.

49. Leland, Joy. *Firewater Myths*. New Brunswick, N.J.: Rutgers University Center of Alcohol Studies, 1976.
50. Lemoine, P., Harousseau, H., Borteyru, J. P., *et al.* Les enfants de parents alcooliques: anomalies observees. Quest. Med. 25:476-482, 1968.
51. Lieber, C. S. Metabolic effects produced by alcohol in the liver and other tissues. Advances Intern. Med. 14:151-199, 1968.
52. Lieber, C. S. and DeCarli, L. M. An experimental model of alcohol feeding and liver injury in the baboon. J. Med. Primatol. 3:153-163, 1974.
53. Lieber, C. S. Pathogenesis and early diagnosis of alcoholic liver injury. N.E.J.M. 298:888-893, 1978.
54. DeLint, J. and Schmidt, W. The epidemiology of alcoholism. In *Biological Basis of Alcoholism*. Toronto: Wiley-Interscience, 1971.
55. Lolli, G., Serianni, E., Golder, G. M., and Luzzatto-Fegiz, P. *Alcohol in Italian Culture,* Monogram No. 3, Yale Center of Alcohol Studies. Glencoe, Ill.: Free Press, 1958.
56. Ludwig, A. M. On and off the wagon. Quart. J. Stud. Alcohol 33:91-96, 1972.
57. Luxenberger, H. Demographische und psychiatrische Untersuchungen in der engeren biologischen Familie von Paralytikerehegatten, Z. Ges. Neurol. Psychiat. 112:331, 1928.
58. MacAndrew, C. and Edgerton, R. B. *Drunken Comportment: A Social Explanation*. Chicago: Aldine Publishing Co., 1969.
59. Maddox, G. L. and Williams, J. R. Drinking behavior of negro collegians. Quart. J. Stud. Alcohol 29:117-129, 1968.
60. Marinacci, A. A. Electroencephalography in alcoholism. In *Alcoholism*. Springfield, Ill.: C. C. Thomas, 1956, pp. 484-536.
61. Mayfield, D. G. Psychopharmacology of alcohol. I. Affective change with intoxication, drinking behavior and affective state. J. Nerv. Ment. Dis. 146:314-321, 1968.
62. McCord, W. and McCord, J. A longitudinal study of the personality of alcoholics. In *Society, Culture and Drinking Patterns*. New York: Wiley, 1962.
63. Mendelson, J. H. Biologic concomitants of alcoholism. *N.E.J.M.* 283:24-32, 1970.
64. Merry, J., Reynolds, C. M., Bailey, J., and Coppen, A. Prophylactic treatment of alcoholism by lithium carbonate. Lancet 2:481-482, 1976.
65. Ogata, M., Mendelson, J., and Mello, N. Electrolytes and osmolality in alcoholics during experimental intoxication. Psychosom. Med. 30:463-488, 1968.
66. Partanen, J., Brunn, K., and Markkanen, T. *Inheritance of Drinking Behavior*. New Brunswick, N.J.: Rutgers University Center of Alcohol Studies, 1966.
67. Pemberton, D. A. A comparison of the outcome of treatment in female and male alcoholics. Brit. J. Psychiat. 113:367-373, 1967.
68. Popham, R. E. Indirect methods of alcoholism prevalence estimation: a

critical evaluation. In *Alcohol and Alcoholism*. Toronto: University of Toronto Press, 1970.

69. Randall, C., Taylor, W., and Walker, D. Ethanol-induced malformations in mice. Alcoholism:Clin., Exp., Res. 1:219-223, 1977.
70. Robins, L. N., Bates, W. M., and O'Neil, P. Adult drinking patterns of former problem children. In *Society, Culture, and Drinking Patterns*. New York: Wiley, 1962.
71. Robins, L. N., Murphy, G. E., and Breckenridge, M. B. Drinking behavior of young negro men. Quart. J. Stud. Alcohol 29:657-684, 1968.
72. Roe, A. and Burks, B. Adult adjustment of foster children of alcoholic and psychotic parentage and the influence of the foster home. Memories of the Section on Alcohol Studies, Yale University No. 3, Quart. J. Stud. Alcohol, New Haven, 1945.
73. Romano, J., Michael, M., Jr., and Merritt, H. H. Alcoholic cerebellar degeneration. Arch. Neurol. and Psychiat. 44:1230-1236, 1940.
74. Roueché, B. *Alcohol*. New York: Grove Press, 1960.
75. Rush, B. An inquiry into the effects of ardent spirits upon the human body and mind. 6th ed. Printed for the subscribers, New York, 1811.
76. Sadoun, R., Lolli, G., and Silverman, M. *Drinking in French Culture*, Monographs of the Rutgers Center of Alcohol Studies No. 5. New Haven: College and University Press, 1965.
77. Schuckit, M., Pitts, F. N., Jr., Reich, T., King, L. J., and Winokur, G. Alcoholism. Arch. Environ. Health 18:301-306, 1969.
78. Selzer, M. L., Payne, C. E., Westervelt, F. H., and Quinn, J. Automobile accidents as an expression of psychopathology in an alcoholic population. Quart. J. Stud. Alcohol 28:505-516, 1967.
79. Shaw, S., Lue, S. L., and Lieber, C. S. Biochemical tests for the detection of alcoholism. Comparison of plasma alpha amino-n-butyric acid with other available tests. Alcoholism 2:3-7, 1978.
80. Sigerist, H. E. *On the History of Medicine*. New York: M.D. Publications, 1960.
81. Sjögren, T. Genetic-statistical and psychiatric investigations of a west Swedish population. Acta Psychiat. Neurol., Suppl. 52, 1948.
82. Slater, E. The incidence of mental disorder. Ann Eugenics 6:172, 1935.
83. Tamerin, J. S., Weiner, S., Poppen, R., Steinglass, P., and Mendelson, J. H. Alcohol and memory: amnesia and short-term memory function during experimentally induced intoxication. Amer. J. Psychiat. 127:1659 1664, 1971.
84. Victor, M. and Adams, R. D. The effect of alcohol on the nervous system. In *Proceedings of the Association for Research in Nervous and Mental Disease*. Baltimore: Williams and Wilkins, 1953.
85. Victor, M., Adams, R. D., and Collins, G. H. *The Wernicke-Korsakoff Syndrome*. Philadelphia: F. A. Davis, 1971.
86. Victor, M. and Hope, J. M. The phenomenon of auditory hallucinations in chronic alcoholism. J. Nerv. Ment. Dis. 126:451, 1958.

87. Vitols, M. M. Culture patterns of drinking in negro and white alcoholics. Dis. Nerv. Syst. 29:391-344, 1968.
88. Voegtlin, W. L. The treatment of alcoholism by estalishing a conditioned reflex. Amer. J. Med. Sci., 199:802-809, 1940.
89. Wallgren, H. and Barry, H., III. *Actions of Alcohol*. Vol. I. Amsterdam: Elsevier, 1970.
90. Winokur, G., Reich, T., Rimmer, J., and Pitts, F. N. Alcoholism: III. Diagnosis and familial psychiatric illness in 259 alcoholic probands. Arch. Gen. Psychiat. 23:104-111, 1970.
91. Woodruff, R. A., Jr., Guze, S. B., and Clayton, P. J. Divorce among psychiatric out-patients. Brit. J. Psychiat. 121:289-292, 1972.

8. Drug Dependence

Definition

Drug dependence refers to the repeated nonmedicinal use of a drug, causing harm to the user or to others. The World Health Organization recommends this term instead of "addiction" or "habituation" (13). Both these words are still widely used in the literature, however, and require definition.

Addiction is used in two senses, physical and psychological. *Physical addiction* refers to a drug-produced condition characterized by tolerance and physical dependence. *Tolerance* refers to an adaptive biological process in which "increasingly larger doses of a drug must be administered to obtain the effect observed with the original dose." *Physical dependence* refers to "the physiological state produced by the repeated administration of the drug which necessitates the continued administration of the drug to prevent the appearance of the stereotyped syndrome, the withdrawal or abstinence syndrome, characteristic for the particular drug" (17).

Psychological addiction refers to a "behavioral pattern of compulsive drug use, characterized by overwhelming involvement with the use of a drug, the securing of its supply, and a high tendency to relapse after withdrawal" (17). Physical and psychological addiction may overlap but do not necessarily occur together. For example, a person physically addicted to morphine administered for pain in a hospital may have none of the characteristics of psychological addiction. On the other hand, individuals may be psychologically addicted to drugs with little or no tolerance or physical dependence. Except for the opiates and to a lesser extent the barbiturates, no drugs produce striking degrees of both tolerance and physical dependence and therefore meet the two pharmacologic criteria for addiction.

Habituation refers to dependence on a drug for an "optimal state of well-being, ranging from a mild desire to a craving or compulsion (a compelling urge) to use the drug" (17).

More nonspecific, "drug dependence" embraces all of these definitions without exclusive adherence to any one and emphasizes *problems* from drug use rather than inferred mental states.

Historical Background

> The basic needs of the human race . . . are food, clothing, and shelter. To that fundamental trinity most modern authorities would add, as equally compelling, security and love. There are, however, many other needs whose satisfaction, though somewhat less essential, can seldom be comfortably denied. One of these, and perhaps the most insistent, is an occasional release from the intolerable clutch of reality. All men throughout recorded history have known this tyranny of memory and mind, and all have sought . . . some reliable means of briefly loosening its grip. [BERTON ROUECHÉ (35)]

Whether this fully explains the motivation behind the use of intoxicating substances, it is true they have been used by men for thousands of years in nearly every part of the world. Except in a few primitive cultures, man has discovered plants whose juices and powders, on being properly prepared and consumed, have caused desirable alterations of consciousness. In ancient times these substances were widely used in religious ceremonies (as wine is still used in the Catholic mass and peyote by the North American Church), but they also have been used for "recreational" purposes. As the sciences of medicine and chemistry progressed, the variety of drugs increased and for many years drugs have been diverted from medical use into "illicit" channels as they are today.

The analgesic drugs derived from the poppy plant were particularly susceptible to abuse, since they produced euphoria as well as analgesia. Drug "epidemics" have occurred periodically in recent centuries. The introduction of opium into England, commercially promoted as part of the Chinese opium trade, led to widespread abuse of the drug in the 19th century. With the introduction of the hypodermic needle during the American Civil War period, the use of morphine for nonmedicinal purposes became widespread, and by the turn of the century large numbers of people were apparently dependent upon the drug, taken intravenously or more often as an ingredient of patent medicines. Heroin, the diethylated form of morphine, was introduced around the turn of the century as a "heroic" solution for the opiate problem (a form of substitution therapy, as methadone is used today).

Another development of the mid-19th century was the introduction of bromides as sedatives. There was an enormous demand for these compounds and a steady increase in their use. With use came misuse, which often resulted in intoxication and psychotic reactions. The bromide problem began to abate in the 1930's as barbiturates and other sedatives became available. The first barbiturate, Veronal, was introduced in 1903 and others appeared in quick succession. The short-acting barbiturates, such as pentobarbital and amobarbital, became popular in the 1930's and 1940's, their dependence-producing qualities not having been immediately recognized (10).

During the late 19th century Westerners discovered botanicals used for mind-altering purposes elsewhere, such as cocaine and hashish (the most potent form of cannabis). Cocaine was found to be useful medically (by Freud, among others), and a number of well-known physicians and surgeons became cocaine addicts.

Ether, also discovered in the 19th century, was used recreationally, again often by medical people, as were nitrous oxide and other volatile solvents. Doctors and nurses, presumably because of their access to these drugs and their familiarity with them, were particularly prone to take them, although reliable data regarding drug abuse by physicians at any time in history, including today, are not available. Meperidine, introduced in the 1940's as a "nonaddictive" synthetic narcotic, led to a mild epidemic of abuse among physicians before its addictive potential was appreciated.

In postwar Japan, thousands of young people turned to amphetamines. Drastic measures were required to control the problem, including the establishment of special psychiatric facilities and stringent legal controls (12).

The most recent epidemic of drug abuse began in the early 1960's when "hallucinogens" became part of the American middle-class youth culture. It originated with Hofmann's discovery in 1953 that lysergic acid diethylamide (LSD) produced perceptual distortions and other aberrant mental phenomena. Again, physicians were involved in the introduction of the drug (31). It was first used on the East and West coasts experimentally because it produced symptoms resembling those seen in psychosis. It was also used therapeutically, usually by psychoanalysts who felt the drug would dissolve "repressions." Because LSD is easy to synthesize, it became widely available and has been used, at least experimentally, by several million people, the majority of them of young age and from the middle or upper-middle class (12).

As mind-altering drugs became widely publicized in the 1960's, more and more young people experimented with them. In the early adolescent group, glue-sniffing and inhalation of other volatile solvents was apparently widely practiced, while persons in late adolescence and then early twenties, particularly on college campuses, experimented with LSD and other synthetic hallucinogens, such as dimethyltryptamine (DMT) and other derivatives of the indole and catecholamines that produced "psychedelic" effects. Meanwhile, increase in the use of amphetamines produced a generation of "speed freaks" who injected methamphetamine intravenously. "Downers" such as barbiturates and other sedative-hypnotics also became popular among young people in the late 1960's. Cocaine became available in suburbia and on college campuses, although, as in the case of other "street" drugs, often the "cocaine" that people thought they were obtaining was either adulterated or completely absent. This was also the case with mescaline, the active principle of peyote (29).

Apparently because marihuana also "enhances" sensory processes (38) and also is abundantly available, it became the most widely used illicit "LSD-like" drug in America during the 1960's and

1970's. Marihuana, the "tobacco" of the hemp plant, has grown wild in America since colonial times or before, but until the past decade was used recreationally only by small minorities, such as jazz musicians in the 1930's and Mexican immigrant workers (4). Widely condemned in the 1930's as a dangerous drug, marihuana has been increasingly accepted in Western countries as a benign if not completely innocuous substance, and there has been increasing pressure to "decriminalize"" if not actually make legal the availability of the drug (12). Marihuana and its potent relative, hashish, are still, however, illegal in most countries, many of which are signitories of a United Nations treaty prohibiting its sale.

While marihuana and the hallucinogens were being widely used in middle- and upper-middle-class America in the 1960's, heroin, the fast-acting, potent form of morphine, became a serious medical and legal problem, involving mainly lower-class black urban men (12). In the late 1970's it was estimated that New York City alone had more than 100,000 opiate addicts. Because of the expense of heroin, its use led to widespread criminal activities, including corruption of police authorities. Deaths resulted from overdosage, "allergic" responses, or medical complications following unsterile intravenous injection.

The heroin "epidemic" was limited somewhat by the high price of the drug and its relative unavailability in noncoastal cities. However, during the later stages of the American involvement in the Vietnam war, pure grades of opium became widely available to American servicemen in Vietnam. One study suggests that nearly half of the American soldiers in Vietnam during 1971 experimented with opium or its derivatives and that 20 percent were frequent users (15).

Epidemiology

Epidemiological surveys of drug use not only involve the usual unreliability expected in prevalence studies but also problems peculiar to drug studies, especially the rapidly changing patterns of use. It is

Table 1. Reported experience with drug use by American youth and adults[1] (in percent)

	Youth (N = 880)	*Adults* (N = 2411)
Alcoholic beverages[2]	24	53
Tobacco, cigarettes[2]	17	38
Proprietary sedatives, tranquilizers, stimulants[3]	6	7
Ethical sedatives[3]	3	4
Ethical tranquilizers[3]	3	6
Ethical stimulants[3]	4	5
Marihuana	14	16
LSD, other hallucinogens	4.8	4.6
Glue, other inhalants	6.4	2.1
Cocaine	1.5	3.2
Heroin	.6	1.3

1. Figures are not additive, thus they do not total to 100 percent.
2. Within past 7 days.
3. Nonmedical use only.

From *Drug Use in America: Problem in Perspective* (12).

generally agreed, for example, that use of marihuana and hallucinogens has increased vastly since 1960, but data from earlier periods are lacking for comparative purposes.

As indicated in Table 1, alcohol and tobacco are still the most widely used drugs in the United States. Table 1 reflects the drug situation in recent years (12).

Drug Categories

The Opiates

Morphine is typical of this group. Other opiates include heroin, dilaudid, codeine, and paregoric. Meperidine (Demerol) is a synthetic analgesic structurally dissimilar to morphine but pharmacologically similar. Heroin is the only one of these substances not available for medical use in the United States.

In usual therapeutic doses, morphine produces analgesia, drowsiness, and a change in mood often described as a sense of well-being.

Morphine is also a respiratory depressant (often the cause of death in cases of overdose); it produces constriction of the pupils, constipation, and occasionally nausea and vomiting.

Most heroin or morphine addicts take opiates intravenously, which produces flushing and a sensation in the lower abdomen described as similar to orgasm, known as a "rush." Initial increased activity is followed by a period of drowsiness and inactivity which is called "being on the nod." During this time opium dreams occur.

Tolerance develops to most of morphine's effects, including euphoria. Libido declines; menstruation may cease. Some addicts who are able to obtain an adequate supply of opiates dress properly, maintain nutrition, and discharge social and occupational obligations without gross impairment. Other addicts become socially disabled, often because the expense of drugs may lead to theft, forgery, prostitution, and the sale of drugs to other users (12).

The first symptoms of opiate withdrawal usually appear eight to twelve hours after the last dose (Table 2). These include lacrimation, rhinorrhea, sweating, and yawning. Thereafter, the addict may fall into a fitful sleep known as "the yen" from which he awakens after several hours, restless and miserable. Additional signs and symptoms appear, reaching a peak between 48 and 72 hours after drug discontinuation. These include dilated pupils, anorexia, restlessness, insomnia, irritability, gooseflesh, nausea, vomiting, diarrhea, chills, and abdominal cramps. These manifestations subside gradually. After seven to ten days, most signs of abstinence have disappeared, although the patient may continue to experience insomnia, weakness, and nervousness.

To ameliorate withdrawal symptoms, oral methadone can be substituted for any opiate. Methadone can be discontinued gradually over a period of one or two weeks.

The course of opiate addiction varies depending on the population studied. In Vaillant's twelve-year follow-up of opiate addicts originally treated at the federal addiction treatment center at Lexington, 98 percent had returned to the use of opiates within twelve months after release (45). On the other hand, a study of Vietnam

Table 2. Abstinence signs* in sequential appearance after last dose of opiate in patients with well-established parenteral habits

Grades of abstinence	*Signs* (*observed in cool room, patient uncovered or under only a sheet*)	*Hours After Last Dose* *Morphine*	*Heroin*	*Meperidine*	*Dihydro-Morphinone*	*Codeine*
Grade 0	Craving for drug Anxiety	6	4	2-3	2-3	8
Grade 1	Yawning Perspiration Lacrimation Rhinorrhea "Yen" sleep	14	8	4-6	4-5	24
Grade 2	Increase in above signs plus: Mydriasis Gooseflesh (piloerection) Tremors (muscle twitches) Hot and cold flashes Aching bones and muscles Anorexia	16	12	8-12	7	48
	Increased intensity of above plus: Insomnia Increased blood pressure					

Grade 3	Increased temperature (1-2) Increased respiratory rate and depth Increased pulse rate Restlessness Nausea	24-36	18-24	16	12	—
Grade 4	Increased intensity of above plus: Febrile facies Position—curled up on hard surface Vomiting Diarrhea Weight loss (5 lb. daily) Spontaneous ejaculation or orgasm Hemoconcentration leukocytosis, eosinopenia, increased blood sugar	36-48	24-36	—	16	—

Note: Racemorphan (Dromoran) and levorphanol (Levodromoran), although 3 times and 6 times as strong as morphine sulfate, show same time curve as morphine sulfate. Similarly do paregoric, laudanum, and hydrochlorides of opium alkaloids (Pantopon), depending on their relative content of morphine.

* Not all signs are necessary to diagnose any particular grade.

From Amer. J. Psych., Jan., 1966 (ref. 3).

veterans who used opium and its products extensively during their tour in Vietnam revealed that less than 2 percent continued using the drug in the year after their return to the United States (15). This suggests that circumstances of exposure and availability are important factors in maintaining use.

In America, most heroin addicts are men and, at least in "inner cities" on the two coasts, a majority are nonwhite (12). There is some evidence that heroin users from this population who do not die as a result of drugs or criminal activities may "spontaneously" stop using the drug after their mid-thirties. School problems, such as delinquency and truancy, frequently antedate heroin use (6).

Except perhaps for sociopathy, there is little evidence that opiate users have other diagnosable psychiatric illnesses, although many of them take other drugs, such as alcohol and barbiturates. Multiple drug use, based on observation in methadone clinics (see below), is considered a bad prognostic sign in heroin addicts.

The mortality from opiate withdrawal is negligible despite the unpleasantness of the withdrawal syndrome. Deaths occurring among addicts are mainly due to infection, overdose, and apparent hypersensitivity reactions, possibly from diluents such as quinine. Unsterile injections may produce septicemia, hepatitis, subacute bacterial endocarditis, and tetanus.

In studies in metropolitan Chicago, Hughes and his colleagues have found that heroin addiction occurs in epidemics, that heroin use spreads from peer to peer, and that newly involved cases are more "contagious" than chronic cases. Microepidemics—5 to 15 new cases over a five-year period—are seen in some locales, and macroepidemics—more than 50 new cases over a five-year period—in others. Hughes and his associates believe macroepidemics are most likely to occur in areas of high unemployment and crime, deterioration in housing, poor or absent neighborhood leadership, a large recent influx of poor people, and the many other expressions of urban blight (19). Their observations parallel those of Leighton *et al.* (26), who found a positive correlation between social disorganization and opiate use.

Hughes has provided some evidence that an "outreach" effort by community action groups can be used to abort an epidemic of heroin addiction. However, this was accomplished in a predominantly white neighborhood and was limited to "microepidemics" (20).

The superiority of one treatment over another with regard to treating opiate addiction has not been established. Some years ago, methadone maintenance was introduced as a long-term treatment for narcotic users. Methadone is given in gradually increasing doses over a period of weeks until a high degree of cross-tolerance to all opiates is established. The euphoric effects of intravenous narcotics are blocked. Some previous drug users have become stabilized as productive citizens with this treatment. Apparently methadone alone is not enough for this outcome in many addicts; a complete program of rehabilitation is necessary.

The original methadone program of Dole and Nyswander (11) was considered impressively successful but has been criticized in that multiple drug users and other presumed poor prognosis cases were not accepted in the program. The approach also has been challenged in that it involves substituting one addiction for another, and has led to wide dissemination of methadone through illicit channels. The consensus at present is that high doses of methadone are usually required for the program to be effective.

Self-help groups made up of former addicts have stimulated enthusiastic responses from some participants, but their efficacy in general remains unknown.

Hypnotics and Sedatives

Barbiturates are the prototype, but many newer synthetic hypnotics and minor tranquilizers produce similar dependence and withdrawal symptoms. Drugs for which this is documented are glutethimide (Doriden), methyprylon (Noludar), ethchlorvynol (Placidyl), ethinamate (Valmid), and meprobamate (Miltown, Equanil). Chlordiazepoxide (Librium) and diazepam (Valium) infrequently produce serious withdrawal symptoms.

In contrast to opiates, barbiturates are usually taken orally. The short- and intermediate-acting barbiturates are most frequently used for nonmedical purposes. With both acute and chronic intoxications as well as the withdrawal syndrome, the clinical picture resembles that produced by alcohol. An intoxicated patient may show lethargy, difficulty in thinking, poor memory, irritability, and self-neglect. Nystagmus, ataxia, and a positive Romberg sign are often present (10).

Withdrawal symptoms may occur when patients take over 400 mg of barbiturates per day (16). The patient becomes anxious, restless, and weak during the first 12 to 16 hours after withdrawal. Tremors of the hands are prominent; deep tendon reflexes are hyperactive. During the second or third day, grand mal seizures may occur, sometimes followed by delirium. Deaths have been reported. The syndrome clears in about a week (10). Long-acting barbiturates such as phenobarbital rarely if ever produce major withdrawal symptoms.

Withdrawal manifestations may be prevented or treated with large doses of a short-acting barbiturate such as secobarbital (800-1000 mg per 24 hours in divided doses) with gradual reduction of the dose over a period of seven to ten days (16). If a patient shows evidence of intoxication with the first or second dose (of 200 mg each), the diagnosis of barbiturate abuse should be questioned in view of the absence of tolerance. Because of cross-tolerance between barbiturates and other sedatives and hypnotics, withdrawal from these drugs may also be accomplished with a short-acting barbiturate.

The prevalence of barbiturate abuse is unknown. A survey by the Food and Drug Administration indicated that about one million pounds of barbituric acid derivatives were available in the United States per year (10). This inventory is enough to supply about 24 100-mg doses to every man, woman, and child in the country. About half of these drugs were of the short- and intermediate-acting variety.

With regard to individuals particularly vulnerable to barbiturate abuse, there is little agreement about a so-called "addictive personality" other than the application of ambiguous and poorly defined terms such as "passive-dependent personality." It is often said that drug dependence reflects an "underlying" mental disorder, but the nature of the disorder is usually not specified. As with alcoholism, barbiturate dependence leads to physical and social complications that may involve loss of health, family, and job; accidents; and traffic offenses. Also, there is evidence that barbiturates compete with alcohol in their propensity to promote crimes of violence (42).

Little is known about the natural history of barbiturate dependence but clinical experience indicates that, in common with alcoholism, the course is characterized by relapse and chronicity. There is no specific treatment, and it is not known whether individual or group psychotherapy or drug "substitution" (e.g., prescribing tranquilizers) is helpful. Where barbiturates are used to counteract the effects of stimulant drugs, such as amphetamines, it is imperative that the multiple drug abuse pattern be attacked. Particularly in young people today, multiple drug abuse seems to have a mutually reciprocating, cyclical pattern of stimulation-sedation (12). Some individuals in this group try to achieve both effects simultaneously. Barbiturates and other sedatives also are frequently used with alcohol and opiates. These compounds have a synergistic effect with alcohol, and "accidental" suicides have been attributed to their combined use.

It may be unwise to prescribe barbiturates to depressed patients unless dosage is carefully controlled. Patients often accumulate large amounts of drugs by hoarding. Unintentional deaths may result from slow absorption rates, since large quantities of barbiturates in the stomach diminish gastric and intestinal function (10). The user, not getting the desired effect in what seems a long time, continues to take tablet after tablet until he is unconscious. In the process, he may ingest a lethal dose.

Like alcoholics, sedative-dependent individuals often deny the extent of their drug problem. When use of the drug is denied or minimized, it may be difficult to distinguish the condition from depression, organic brain syndrome, or other psychiatric or neurological disorders. When a patient has a grand mal seizure, it should alert the physician to possible sedative dependence. Seizures are most likely to occur one or two days after withdrawal, although in the case of certain newer synthetic hypnotics, such as glutethimide (Doriden), seizures may occur after a longer period of time. Occasional deaths have been reported during withdrawal, but it is often unclear whether the patient had an intercurrent medical condition at the time of death. Ordinarily, the withdrawal syndrome is self-limited.

Two recent members of the minor tranquilizer and sedative group appear to have a particularly high potential for abuse. One is meprobamate, the first minor tranquilizer to become available, and the other is an even more recent sedative, methaqualone. Both have a risk potential roughly equivalent to that of the short-acting barbiturates. Methaqualone abuse is common among adolescents (21).

In part, abuse of barbiturates and other sedative-hypnotics is iatrogenic. Unlike most of the other drugs discussed in this chapter, these compounds are primarily available by prescription (10). In prescribing such drugs there is a particular responsibility to administer the minimum necessary to control the patient's symptoms. Generally, prescriptions should be nonrefillable.

Sympathomimetic Drugs

This group of stimulants includes D-amphetamine (Dexadrine), D-l-amphetamine (Benzadrine), and methamphetamine (Desoxyn, Methedrine). Cocaine is also included because it has amphetamine-like effects while differing from amphetamine structurally.

Amphetamine effects include elevated mood, increased energy and alertness, decreased appetite, and slight improvement in task performance. Amphetamines may be taken orally or injected intravenously (12).

Drug-induced psychosis is common among individuals taking large doses of amphetamines (over 50 mg per day). Such psychosis may resemble paranoid schizophrenia with persecutory delusions occurring despite a clear sensorium. Hallucinations are common. Usually the psychosis subsides one or two weeks after drug use stops. When an apparent amphetamine psychosis persists, a hidden source of drugs or the diagnosis of schizophrenia should be considered.

No specific amphetamine withdrawal syndrome has been described; however, users complain of fatigue and depression after discontinuing the drug. Tolerane may be striking. "Speed freaks" sometimes take as much as one or two grams per day (the usual therapeutic dose is 5-15 mg per day).

As with alcohol and barbiturates, studies indicate a relationship between amphetamine use and crime. Most research indicates that amphetamine users are disproportionately involved in crimes of violence, such as assaults and robbery (12). The former may be related to the paranoid state produced by the drug. A correlation has been reported between amphetamine use and violent crime in Japan during the "epidemic" of amphetamine use in that country in the post-World War II period. Since violent behavior is relatively rare among the Japanese, its correlation with amphetamines has added significance (12).

Since their introduction in the early 1930's amphetamines have been prescribed by doctors for a variety of conditions, including depression, overweight, and narcolepsy. In recent years, increasingly more of the substance has found its way into illegal distribution channels and has been available for purchase on the street. By the early 1970's one-fifth of senior high school students had used amphetamines at least once and there was a trend toward increasing use among younger adolescents (12).

Phenothiazines may be used to treat the symptoms of amphetamine psychosis. Antidepressants may be used to treat associated depressive symptoms. Abrupt withdrawal of amphetamines is possible; the dose need not be tapered off.

Cocaine differs from amphetamine in that it is of botanical origin, deriving from shrubs grown in the Andes. Its effects last for a shorter period than do those of amphetamines, and little tolerance occurs. Like amphetamines, however, cocaine is a powerful stimulant of the nervous system, increasing alertness and suppressing fatigue and boredom. After regular, heavy use of the drug, a mild withdrawal syndrome may occur, in which formication (sensation of bugs crawling under the skin) is frequent, together with depression and lassitude.

Hallucinogens

Perceptual distortions are the primary effect of "hallucinogenic" drugs, which include LSD, mescaline, psilocybin, and a family of compounds resembling either LSD or the amphetamines chemically (e.g., DMT and STP). Except for mescaline and psilocybin, most hallucinogens are synthetic. Since LSD has been the most widely used and studied hallucinogen, our discussion will focus on it.

Together with perceptual distortions, including illusions and hallucinations, LSD "trips" produce altered time sense, disturbed judgment, and sometimes confusion and disorientation (9). Some LSD trips are unpleasant. LSD users may be brought to emergency rooms for "bad trips" characterized by panic and sometimes persecutory delusions. There are reports of prolonged or "flashback" effects (a resurgence of the drug effect days, weeks, or months subsequent to the end of a "trip") in the literature. Although "flashbacks" have not been studied systematically, they are reported so commonly that some authorities believe certain individuals do experience them. A number of deaths have been attributed to LSD, primarily from suicide or homicide, although the causal connection remains unclear (25, 40).

Repeated use of LSD results in marked tolerance. No withdrawal syndrome has been reported. The drug usually produces euphoria, but dysphoria may occur. No deaths have been reported from LSD overdosage. Evidence that LSD produces chromosomal damage is equivocal (43).

Despite the national concern about LSD and other hallucinogens, apparently only a small percentage of people have used them. According to the National Commission on Marihuana and Drug Abuse, less than 1 in 20 individuals had tried LSD or other hallucinogens even once (12). In the survey, respondents were asked what they would do if drugs of this type were legal. Only about 1 percent said they would probably try them. This suggests that the abuse potential of LSD and other hallucinogens may be considerably lower than that of alcohol, nicotine, barbiturates, and amphetamines (12, 31).

Treatment for acute adverse reactions to LSD consists of reassurance, and, if this fails, tranquilizers. Diazepam (Valium) appears to be as effective as phenothiazines and is somewhat safer because it is less likely to produce hypotension.

Hallucinogens have complicated the problem of diagnosing psychiatric disorders among young drug users. Prolonged psychotic episodes are probably more often attributable to schizophrenia or other psychiatric illness than to LSD toxicity. To determine whether a patient has a psychiatric illness that is not associated with drug abuse, the patient must be drug-free for a lengthy period.

Phencyclidine

Phencyclidine (PCP, "angel dust") has become an important drug of abuse in recent years (23, 39). Apparently it has caused a number of deaths (23, 34, 44). Though PCP is obtainable as a veterinary anesthetic (Sernylan), most of the illegal supply is manufactured in home laboratories. The drug is available in many forms—tablet, powder, leaf, rock crystal—and can be ingested, snorted, smoked, or injected. It is often sold under false guise as THC (tetrahydrocannabinol), LSD, or mescaline. Marihuana and other street drugs are often adulterated with PCP (33).

Moderate doses of PCP may produce bizarre behavior that is often accompanied by a blank stare. Users become confused, combative, stuporous, or comatose. Large doses can produce seizures and very large doses respiratory depression. Myoclonic jerks are common. Deaths are believed to be caused by hypertensive crises. One way to distinguish PCP intoxication from that of other street drugs, such as LSD and mescaline, is to inspect the pupils. Patients intoxicated with most hallucinogens have dilated pupils; with PCP the pupils are normal or small. Ataxia, nystagmus, muscular rigidity, and normal or small pupils in a combative or stuporous parient suggest the diagnosis of phencyclidine intoxication (8).

Phenothizines, the usual drug class of choice for agitated and uncontrollable patients, can cause severe postural hypotension and may increase muscle rigidity in patients intoxicated with phencyclidine. Intramuscular benzodiazepines may be a better choice. "Talking down" a patient intoxicated with PCP may not be as effective as with LSD and other hallucinogens, and can instead overstimulate the patient (8).

Marihuana

Cannabis sativa (hemp) contains chemicals called cannabinoids, one of which, delta-9-tetrahydrocannabinol (THC), is believed to be the main psychoactive constituent of marihuana.

The effects of THC depend on dosage and range from mild euphoria with small doses to LSD-like effects with high doses. Most marihuana grown wild in the United States contains insufficient amounts of THC to produce measurable psychological effects. Cannabis imported from Mexico, South America, and India often contains sufficient THC to produce marked euphoria, and, depending on the plant preparation used, paranoid delusions and other psychotomimetic effects. However, THC deteriorates at the rate of 5 percent per month at room temperature, and even imported cannabis eventually loses its potency (27).

There are two generally available cannabis preparations: marihuana and hashish. The former consists of a mixture of plant products (leaves, stems, etc.). The latter consists of the resin of the female plant and is more potent.

In parts of the world where concentrated cannabis preparations have been used by millions of people for hundreds of years, constant use is said to be associated with serious medical and psychiatric illnesses (7).

However, studies conducted in Jamaica, Costa Rica, and Greece—countries where cannabis has been used regularly for many years—

failed to reveal any serious pathology associated with the use of the drug (36). The subjects were lower-class laborers and no conclusions could be drawn about deleterious effects in other societies and in other classes. The studies did report a decrease in respiratory capacity and minor hematological abnormalities among users. The authors warned against extrapolating their findings to other societies. In a survey of the literature, "The Cannabis Habit," Murphy stated: "It seems probable that cannabis has a highly complex influence, dependent on personality and culture as well as the drug itself" (32). In a similar vein, Jones has pointed out that "the effects of psychoactive drugs on behavior and experience are often independent of the drugs' pharmacologic effect" (24).

Acute psychotic episodes apparently have resulted from cannabis use in this country, but they have been infrequent. Psychiatrists have also described a condition among chronic users of marihuana called the "amotivational syndrome" characterized by lassitude, apathy, and lack of ambition (30, 37). The evidence for a causal relationship with cannabis remains anecdotal.

However, recent evidence indicates that marihuana does have a certain abuse potential for some users (46). In a follow-up study of 97 regular users, 9 percent met operational criteria for abuse similar to criteria used in alcohol studies (see Appendix A). In other words, marihuana use was associated with a variety of social, psychological, and medical problems in these individuals. Of the abusers, two-thirds had had traffic violations which they attributed *solely* to marihuana intoxication; one-third had engaged in fights, again blaming marihuana. The latter finding was particularly interesting in view of the widespread observation that marihuana typically has antiaggressive effects. This indeed may be the case in most instances, but "set and setting" notoriously influence the effects of drugs, and it cannot be said any longer that marihuana has exclusively "taming" effects.

The difficulty of isolating marihuana effects is compounded by the fact that many regular users of marihuana also take other drugs. Furthermore, as previously mentioned, most marihuana available in this country contains small amounts of THC. Therefore, even though marihuana has been widely used in the United States (see Table 1), it is impossible to predict the consequences of prolonged use of high potency cannabis by large numbers of people.

Simultaneous use of alcoholic beverages and marihuana is common. Combining moderate doses of alcohol and marihuana sometimes produces nausea, vomiting, autonomic nervous system lability, and psychological distress (41). Although the syndrome is self-limiting, it could be dangerous for some individuals under certain conditions, e.g., in the presence of cardiac or central nervous system disorders. The mechanism of the interaction is not known and no treatment for the adverse reaction is available at the present time.

Another problem with isolating marihuana effects is that some marihuana is contaminated with the herbicide, Paraquat. This herbicide has been widely used in Mexico to destroy cannabis crops. Acute effects from Paraquat-contaminated marihuana include fever, hemoptysis, pain in the chest, and headache. Chronic effects include a reduction of respiratory capacity and shortness of breath over months or years. The amount of the herbicide required to produce these effects is not known, and, since marihuana smoking is associated with bronchitis, cough, and reduced lung capacity, diagnosing herbicide effects is difficult.

References

1. *Adverse Reactions to Hallucinogenic Drugs,* prepared by R. E. Meyer. National Institute of Mental Health. Washington: Superintendent of Documents, U.S. Government Printing Office, p. 111, 1967.
2. Bakker, C. B. The clinical picture in hallucinogen intoxication. Hospital Medicine, pp. 102-114, 1969.
3. Blachly, P. H. Management of the opiate abstinence syndrome. Amer. J. Psychiat. 122:742-744, 1966.
4. Bloomquist, E. R. *Marijuana.* Toronto, Canada: Glencoe Press, 1968.
5. Blum, R. H. *et al. The Utopiates: The Use and Users of LSD-25.* New York: Atherton Press, p. 304, 1964.
6. Bucky, S. F. The relationship between background and extent of heroin use. Amer. J. Psychiat. 130:707-708, 1973.

7. Chopra, G. S. Man and marijuana. Int. J. Addict. 4:215, 1969.
8. Cohen, S. Angel dust. J.A.M.A. 238:515-516, 1977.
9. Cohen, S. and Edwards, A. E. LSD and organic brain impairment. Drug Dependence, pp. 1-4, 1968.
10. Dependence on barbiturates and other sedative drugs. J.A.M.A. 193:107-111, 1965.
11. Dole, V. Research on methadone maintenance treatment. Proceedings of the Second National Conference on Methadone Maintenance, pp. 359-370, 1969.
12. *Drug Use in America: Problem in Perspective*. Second Report of the National Commission on Marihuana and Drug Abuse, 1973.
13. Eddy, N. B., Halback, H., Isbell, H., and Seevers, M. H. Drug dependence: its significance and characteristics. Bulletin of the World Health Organization 32:721-33, 1965.
14. Efron, V. and Keller, M. *Selected Statistics on Consumption of Alcohol* (1850-1968) *and on Alcoholism* (1930-1968). New Brunswick, N.J.: Rutgers University Center of Alcohol Studies, 1970.
15. *Follow-up of Vietnam Drug Users* (Lee N. Robins, Principal Investigator) Special Action Office Monograph, Series A, No. 1, 1973.
16. Fraser, H. F., Wikler, A., Essig, C. F., and Isbell, H. Degree of physical dependence induced by secobarbital or pentobarbital. J.A.M.A. 166:126-129, 1958.
17. Goodman, L. S. and Gilman, A. *The Pharmacological Basis of Therapeutics*. New York: Macmillan, 1965.
18. *Health Consequences of Smoking*. U.S. Department of Health, Education, and Welfare. Washington, D.C.: U.S. Government Printing Office, 1968.
19. Hughes, P. H. *et al.* The social structure of a heroin coping community. Amer. J. Psychiat. 128:551-558, 1971.
20. Hughes, P. H., Senay, E. C., and Parker, R. The medical management of a heroin epidemic. Arch. Gen. Psychiat. 27:585-593, 1972.
21. Inaba, D. S., Gay, G. R., Newmeyer, J. A., and Whitehead, C. Methaqualone abuse "luding out." J.A.M.A. 224:1505-1514, 1973.
22. Jaffe, J. H. Drug addiction and drug abuse. In *The Pharmacological Basis of Therapeutics*, Goodman, L. S. and Gilman, A. (eds.). New York: Macmillan, 1965.
23. Jain, N. C., Budd, R. D., and Budd, B. S. Growing abuse of phencyclidine: California "angel dust." N.E.J.M. 297:673, 1977.
24. Jones, R. T. Tetrahydrocannabinol and the marijuana-induced social "high," or the effects of the mind on marijuana. Annals of the Amer. Acad. of Sci. 191:155-165, 1971.
25. Klepfisz, A. and Racy, J. Homicide and LSD. J.A.M.A. 223:429-430, 1973.
26. Leighton, D. C. *et al. The Character of Danger: Psychiatric Systems in Selected Communities*. New York: Basic Books, 3:322-353, 1963.

27. Lerner, P. The precise determination of tetrahydrocannabinol in marihuana and hashish. Bull. Narc. 21:39-42, 1969.
28. Liden, C. B., Lovejoy, F. H., and Costello, C. E. Phencyclidine: nine cases of poisoning. J.A.M.A. 234:513-516, 1975.
29. Many "street" drugs are phony. American Druggist, pp. 35-44, 1971.
30. *Marihuana and Health.* Second Annual Report to Congress from the Secretary of Health, Education, and Welfare, 1972.
31. McGlothlin, W. H. and Arnold, D. O. LSD revisited–a 10 year follow-up of medical LSD use. Arch. Gen. Psychiat. 24:35, 1971.
32. Murphy, H. B. M. The cannabis habit: A review of recent psychiatric literature. United Nations Bulletin on Narcotics. 15:15-23, 1963.
33. Rainey, J. M., Jr. and Crowder, M. K. Prevalence of phencyclidine in street drug preparations. N.E.J.M. 290:466-467, 1974.
34. Reed, D., Cravey, R. H., and Sedgwick, P. R. A fatal case involving phencyclidine. International Assn. of Forensic Toxicologists Bulletin. 7, 7, 1972.
35. Roueché, B. *Alcohol.* New York: Grove Press, 1962.
36. Rubin, V. and Comitas, L. *Ganja in Jamaica.* The Hague, Paris: Mouton & Co., Publishers, 1975.
37. Scher, J. The marihuana habit. J.A.M.A. 214:1120, 1970.
38. Sharma, T. D. Clinical observations of patients who used tetrahydrocannabinol (THC) intravenously. Behavioral Neuropsychiatry 4, 1972.
39. Showalter, C. V. and Thornton, W. E. The increasing abuse of phencyclidine. Ill. Med. J. 151:387-389, 1977.
40. Smart, R. G. and Bateman, K. Unfavorable reactions to LSD: a review and analysis of available case reports. Canad. Med. Assoc. J. 97:1214-21, 1967.
41. Sulkowski, A. and Vachon, L. Side effects of simultaneous alcohol and marijuana use. Amer. J. Psychiat. 134:6, 691-692, 1977.
42. Tinklenberg, J. R. and Woodrow, K. M. Drug use among youthful assaultive and sexual offenders. In *Human Aggression*, Frazier, S. H. (ed.). Baltimore: Williams & Wilkins, 1974.
43. Tjio, J., Pahnke, W. N., and Kurland, A. A. LSD and chromosomes. J.A.M.A. 210:849-856, 1969.
44. Tong, T. G., Benowitz, N. L., Becker, C. E., *et al.* Phencyclidine poisoning. J.A.M.A. 234:512-513, 1975.
45. Vaillant, G. E. A 12-year follow-up of New York narcotic addicts. Arch. Gen. Psychiat. 15:599, 1966.
46. Weller, R. A. and Halikas, J. A. Objective criteria for the diagnosis of marihuana abuse. Arch. Gen. Psychiat. In press.
47. Wikler, A. Diagnosis and treatment of drug dependence of the barbiturate type. Amer. J. Psychiat. 125:6, 1968.

9. Sociopathy (Antisocial Personality)

Definition

Sociopathy (sociopathic personality or antisocial personality) is a pattern of recurrent antisocial, delinquent, and criminal behavior that begins in childhood or early adolescence and is manifested by disturbances in many areas of life: family relations, schooling, work, military service, and marriage.

Historical Background

Prichard's monograph of 1835, *A Treatise on Insanity and Other Disorders Affecting the Mind,* is often cited as furnishing the first description of what is now called sociopathic personality (41). Under the label "moral insanity" he defined the disorder in this way: "The intellectual faculties appear to have sustained little or no injury, while the disorder is manifested principally or alone in the state of the feelings, temper, or habits. In cases of this description the moral and active principles of the mind are strongly perverted and depraved, the power of self government is lost or impaired and the individual is found to be incapable . . . of conducting himself with decency and propriety, having 'undergone a morbid change.'" As Craft makes clear (12), Prichard included under this rubric many examples of "temporary mental illness," and most of his cases were probably patients with affective disorder. Craft quotes Clouston (10): "Prichard quoted many such cases and vividly described the disease, but I should place most of his cases in my category of simple mania."

Clouston referred also to children "so constituted that they cannot be educated in morality on account of an innate brain deficiency . . . incapable of knowing . . . right and wrong. . . . Such moral idiots I, like others, have met with frequently . . . and persons with this want of development we may label under moral insanity. . . ."

Craft points out that Prichard used "moral" in three ways: first, in referring to "moral" treatment, meaning psychological treatment; second, in referring to emotional or affective responses in contrast to intellectual ones; and third, in an ethical sense of right or wrong. Most of the time, Prichard used the term in the first two ways and only incidentally in the last way.

As Craft also notes, Benjamin Rush, in 1812, described "derangement of the moral faculties" as follows (44): "The moral faculty, conscience, and sense of deity are sometimes totally deranged. The Duke of Sully has given us a striking instance of this universal moral derangement in the character of a young man who belonged to his suite, of the name of Servin, who, after a life uncommonly distinguished by every possible vice, died, cursing and denying his God. Mr. Haslam has described two cases of it in the Bethlem Hospital, one of whom, a boy of 13 years of age, was perfectly sensible of his depravity, and often asked 'why God had not made him like other men.' . . . In the course of my life, I have been consulted in three cases of the total perversion of the moral faculties. One of them was in a young man, the second in a young woman, both of Virginia, and the third was in the daughter of a citizen of Philadelphia. The last was addicted to every kind of mischief. Her mischief and wickedness had no intervals while she was awake, except when she was kept busy in some steady and difficult employment. In all of these cases of innate, preternatural moral depravity, there is probably an original defective organization in those parts of the body which are occupied by the moral faculties of the mind."

It is Craft's conclusion that "Rush appears to give the first description of those with sound reason and good intellect who have an innate or lifelong irresponsibility without shame, being unchanged in affect, or by the consequences or by regard for others."

Thus Craft challenges the appropriateness of crediting Prichard with the first description.

Controversy over the concept of "moral insanity" developed partly in regard to the question whether the "morally insane" should be committed to mental hospitals or considered mentally ill in a court of law. The terms were gradually dropped as interest in the whole range of personality disorders grew.

In 1889, Koch (30) introduced the term "psychopathic inferiority" to imply a constitutional predisposition for many deviations of personality, including at least some that are now classified as neuroses. Kraepelin (32), Kahn (29), and Schneider (46) proposed various classifications of personality disorders. Schneider's definition of psychopathic personalities as "all those abnormal personalities who suffer from their abnormalities or cause society to suffer" clearly included much more than "moral imbecility."

The term psychopathic personality was used inconsistently, sometimes to refer to the whole spectrum of deviant personalities and sometimes to a subgroup of antisocial or aggressive "psychopaths." Finally, to reduce confusion, the term "Sociopathic Personality Disturbance" was introduced for the latter group and was adopted by the American Psychiatric Association in its 1952 edition of the Diagnostic and Statistical Manual (DSM-1). Nevertheless, many went on using the terms "psychopathy" and "sociopathy" interchangeably, while others continued to regard sociopathy as only one form of psychopathy. In a further attempt to reduce confusion, "Antisocial Personality" was adopted, in the later revisions of the American Psychiatric Association's Diagnostic and Statistical Manual and the International Classification of Disease, as the official diagnosis for the aggressive or antisocial psychopath or sociopath. Sir Aubrey Lewis recently summarized the history of the concept (34).

Epidemiology

Satisfactory data on the prevalence of antisocial personality are lacking. This is partly the result of the failure to reach a general agreement about a definition. It also stems from the difficulty of adequate ascertainment; we do not know what proportion of sociopaths comes to the attention of physicians. Nevertheless, sociopathy is seen frequently in psychiatric facilities, usually because of associated alcoholism and depression or because psychiatric care is made a condition of parole. In one series, 15 percent of male and 3 percent of female psychiatric outpatients were sociopaths (50).

Indirect estimates of population frequency, based upon figures for juvenile delinquency and police trouble of all kinds, suggest that sociopathy is common, probably increasingly so, much more frequent in males than females, and in urban than rural environments, and most common in low socioeconomic groups (35).

Sociopaths usually come from grossly disturbed families. Parental separation or divorce, early death, desertion, alcoholism, and criminality are characteristic. Only a small minority of sociopaths, in fact, come from families that are not characterized by one or more of these phenomena (11, 23, 28, 31).

Clinical Picture

Sociopathy begins in childhood or early adolescence. The first manifestations may be those of the hyperactive child syndrome (39, 45). Restlessness, a short attention span, and unresponsiveness to discipline are common. Frequent fighting, often leading to conflicts with adults, and a history of being a general neighborhood nuisance are also common (7, 42).

A disturbed school history is characteristic of early sociopathy. In fact, a history of satisfactory school adjustment through high school is so unusual among sociopaths that either the diagnosis or the history should be questioned if it is present. Disruption of classes by talking out of turn, failure to pay attention to the teacher, fighting with classmates, arguing with the teacher, and even fighting with the teacher occur. Academic failures, truancy, and suspension often lead to school dropout or permanent expulsion (7, 24, 42).

Running away from home is also common, though it may be limited to a few one-night episodes. Occasionally, adolescent sociopaths will disappear for weeks or months. During such absences, they may wander over the country, hitchhiking, doing odd jobs, "bumming around" (42).

The sociopath's job history is characterized by poor performance. Undependability (being late, missing work, quitting without warning), inability to accept criticism and advice, frequent job changes without advancement, and being fired are typical (7, 42). Poor job performance coupled with limited and incomplete education result in low socioeconomic status, low income, and frequent need for financial assistance from family or society.

Sociopaths begin heterosexual experiences earlier than others and are much more likely to be promiscuous and indiscriminate in their sexual behavior. Homosexuality is probably more common among sociopaths than in the general population (8). Prostitution is frequent among female sociopaths, and homosexual prostitution is common among male sociopaths.

Early marriage is typical, especially among women. Very few sociopathic women, in fact, fail to marry. Their marriages are marked by infidelity, separation, and divorce. Male sociopaths have similar marital difficulties. Sociopaths tend to marry sociopaths; this is particularly true of women (8, 21).

Judges used to handle male delinquents by suspending punishment if the delinquent enlisted in the armed services. Generally, however, sociopaths do not do well in military service. Undependable and unable to conform to military discipline, they go AWOL, have difficulty with their superiors, are subjected to courtsmartial, and receive various nonhonorable discharges. The type of discharge is usually determined by the nature of the offenses, the philosophy of the commanding officer, and general military policy at the time.

Sooner or later most sociopaths have trouble with the police. Some investigators, in fact, have required police trouble for the diagnosis of sociopathy (20). Stealing money from mother's purse or father's wallet or from a schoolmate may be an early sign of a budding criminal career. Shoplifting, peace disturbance (usually associated with drunkenness and fighting), various traffic offenses, auto theft, burglary, larceny, rape, robbery, and homicide may all occur. A sociopathic pattern of behavior is found in most convicted male felons (20, 22) and in about half of convicted female felons (8).

Many sociopaths engage in lying and the use of aliases, usually as understandable responses to social or legal difficulties, but sometimes without any obvious need to avoid punishment or retaliation. Such behavior has been called "pathological lying." Elaborate stories may be told to confuse or impress relatives. This behavior can take extreme forms, such as masquerading as a physician, military officer, or businessman. In time, relatives, friends, parole officers, and physicians learn to discount a good deal of what they are told by sociopaths.

Conversion symptoms (unexplained neurological symptoms) are common among sociopaths; in fact, sociopathy is second only to hysteria in producing such symptoms (25). Among sociopaths, conversion symptoms are characteristically associated with obvious social stresses such as police trouble. The full Briquet's syndrome (hysteria) may also be seen in association with sociopathy. Many female hysterics give a history of previous or concurrent sociopathy (8), and many young delinquent and antisocial girls become hysterics as adults (8, 36, 42).

Most studies of delinquents and sociopaths indicate that their average IQ is below normal, but only a minority of delinquents and sociopaths suffer from significant mental deficiency, with an IQ less than 70 (12, 35). These studies have not all been adequately controlled for socioeconomic status, sibship size, and other variables correlated with intelligence. Low intelligence probably is not an important factor in the etiology of sociopathy.

Some studies have attempted to assess "constitutional" factors in sociopathy (48). Nonspecifically disordered electroencephalograms have been reported more frequently among sociopaths than controls, but many, if not most, sociopaths do not have abnormal electroencephalograms (2, 18). Many studies have explored psychophysiological response patterns in sociopaths, and a theory of low autonomic and cortical arousal has been formulated to account for a persistent "stimulus hunger" or for the inability to learn socially approved behavior. The theory is thought to explain the sociopath's impulsive, excitement-seeking, and antisocial behavior (26, 38, 45). The research findings have not been entirely consistent (38), and some authors (37) have emphasized "a wider degree of variability in arousal levels and reactivity than [in] normal individuals." Reports have suggested an association between criminal behavior and chromosomal abnormalities. In particular, XYY karyotype, unusual height, and impulsive crimes have been associated, but not all studies are consistent (1, 15, 27, 40). Studies of hormone levels, including androgens and adrenal steroids, have revealed no consistent differences between sociopathic and nonsociopathic subjects (16, 33).

A charming manner, lack of guilt or remorse, absence of anxiety, and a failure to learn by experience are said to be characteristic of sociopathy. The easygoing, open, and winning style, when present, presumably accounts for the sociopath's success as a "confidence man." At best, however, the charm and appeal are superficial, and often they are entirely absent.

When seen by psychiatrists, many sociopaths report anxiety symptoms, depression, and guilt (50). These frequently occur with alcoholism. The guilt and remorse do not seem to lead to reduction of sociopathic behavior, however. This persistence of sociopathic behavior, despite repeated failure and punishment, is the basis for the statement that sociopaths "do not learn from experience."

Natural History

Sociopathy begins early in life. In some cases it may begin before the child starts attending school. Few, if any, sociopaths get through high school without recurrent difficulties. If the antisocial and delinquent pattern has not begun before age fifteen or sixteen, it is unlikely to occur.

The disorder is recurrent and varies in severity. Some sociopaths, generally milder cases, may remit during the early or mid-twenties. In other instances, sociopathic behavior persists into early middle age and then remits. Some sociopaths never improve. Attempts to explain remission have been based on hypothetical "maturing" or "burning-out."

Remission, when it occurs, usually comes only after years of sociopathic behavior, during which education and work achievement have been severely compromised. Sociopaths rarely recover sufficiently to compensate for the "lost years." Thus "remission" usually means no more than a marginal social adjustment. Among many sociopaths, even if sociopathic behavior subsides, alcoholism and drug abuse persist and influence long-term adjustment.

Complications

The complications of sociopathy explain why the disorder is legitimately a medical concern. High rates of venereal disease, out-of-wedlock pregnancies, injuries from fights and accidents, alcoholism and drug dependence, and various medical complications of these conditions mean that sociopaths often come to the attention of doctors. Furthermore, increased mortality from accidents and homicide contribute to a reduced life-expectancy, particularly in early adulthood (20, 43).

Family Studies

As noted, sociopaths generally come from families that show severe social disturbances and disruption. Much of this family pathology consists of sociopathy and alcoholism.

In a study of male felons, most of whom were sociopaths, one-fifth of the first-degree male relatives were sociopaths and one-third were alcoholics (23). In a study of female felons, half of whom were sociopaths, one-third of the male relatives were sociopaths and one-half were alcoholics (9). In a study of children seen in a child guidance clinic (42), one-third of the fathers and one-tenth of the mothers of sociopaths were either sociopathic or alcoholic.

Among the attempts to determine whether this familial pattern reflects genetic factors have been investigations of twins and adoptees.

Twin studies generally have focused on antisocial behavior, delinquency, or criminality, without distinguishing between sociopaths and others who show these behavior patterns. Nevertheless, since most criminals apparently are sociopaths (20), this approach appears justified. In twin studies, the concordance rate with regard to behavior difficulties, delinquency, and criminality have nearly always been higher for monozygotic than dizygotic twins (38, 49). However, the differences have not been as great as those seen in other psychiatric illnesses where a genetic predisposition is suspected. Furthermore, all of the series have been small, and the monozygotic-dizygotic difference in some does not reach statistical significance.

Twin studies of psychiatric illness may involve bias in ascertainment of cases, since concordant cases may come to the attention of physicians more often than discordant cases. Population twin registries have been proposed as more suitable for unbiased ascertainment. Christiansen, having access to a register of all Danish twin births, was able to obtain a presumably unselected series of criminal twins (6). He found that monozygotic twins had a significantly higher concordance rate than dizygotic twins (36 percent versus 12 percent).

Several follow-up studies of children of criminals and "psychopaths" indicate that these children, when adopted early in life by non-relatives, are more likely to reveal psychopathic and criminal behavior as adults than are adopted children whose biological parents were not criminals or psychopaths (4, 5, 13, 14, 47). Another study (3), however, failed to provide evidence in favor of a genetic predisposition to criminality. The association between sociopathy and hysteria (Briquet's syndrome) within families and in the same individual has been discussed in Chapter 4.

In summary, twin and adoptee studies at least suggest a genetic predisposition in some cases of sociopathy.

Differential Diagnosis

The differential diagnosis of sociopathy includes alcoholism, drug dependence, hysteria, schizophrenia, mania, and organic brain syndrome.

Alcoholism and drug abuse are frequent complications of sociopathy, and they aggravate antisocial and criminal patterns. In addition, however, some alcoholics and drug abusers who did not show sociopathic behavior in childhood or adolescence, before the onset of alcoholism or drug dependence, do show such behavior as a manifestation of the alcoholism or drug dependence. In these cases, the crucial diagnostic feature is the age of onset of antisocial and delinquent behavior; it is usually after age fifteen and coincident with or following the onset of the alcohol and drug abuse. When sociopathic behavior and alcohol or drug abuse all begin about the same time and before age fifteen, only follow-up may clarify the diagnosis, and often it is not possible to separate the sociopathy from the alcoholism or drug dependence.

The familial and clinical associations between sociopathy and hysteria have already been noted. Many female sociopaths and an occasional male sociopath develop the picture of hysteria (24, 36).

Moreover, there is an increased frequency of antisocial behavior and delinquency in the past histories and family histories of hysterics who are not sociopaths (24). Finally, hysteria and sociopathy cluster in the same families. All these observations suggest that the differential diagnosis between the two conditions may involve the recognition of overlapping manifestations of similar etiologic factors (19).

A small minority of male schizophrenics gives a history of sociopathic patterns in adolescence, and a small number of young sociopaths, at follow-up, turn out to be schizophrenics (42). If evidence of schizophrenia has not appeared by the early twenties, however, it is unlikely to develop.

The behavior of some early onset manics may mimic that of sociopaths, especially in women. Occasionally it will be difficult to distinguish mania from sociopathy when the latter is complicated by amphetamine or other drug abuse. Follow-up should clarify the issue. Since mania before age fifteen is rare, a history of antisocial and delinquent behavior before that age would suggest sociopathy rather than mania.

While antisocial and criminal behavior may accompany an organic brain syndrome, the latter rarely develops in childhood or early adolescence.

Clinical Management

A major problem in treating sociopathy is the patient's lack of motivation for change. Few sociopaths volunteer for treatment. They are nearly always brought to the physician's attention by pressure from schools, parents, or judges. Moreover, the commonly disturbed family situation and poor socioeconomic circumstances provide little support for any treatment program. Many therapists believe that early institutional therapy offers the only hope for success, but there is no consensus about this.

It is particularly difficult to carry out treatment if associated alcoholism or drug dependence cannot be controlled. In many cases, remission of the alcoholism or drug abuse is accompanied by a reduction in antisocial and criminal behavior (20). Since sociopathy begins early and individuals at high risk can be readily recognized (17, 42), early case finding and treatment may ultimately offer hope of prevention.

References

1. Åkesson, H. O., Forssman, H., Wahlström, J., and Wallin, L. Sex chromosome aneuploidy among men in three Swedish hospitals for the mentally retarded and maladjusted. Brit. J. Psychiat. 125:386-389, 1974.
2. Arthurs, R. and Cahoon, E. A clinical and electroencephalographic survey of psychopathic personality. Amer. J. Psychiat. 120:875-877, 1964.
3. Bohman, M. Some genetic aspects of criminality. Arch. Gen. Psychiat. 35:269-276, 1978.
4. Cadoret, R. J. Psychopathology in adopted-away offspring of biologic parents with antisocial behavior. Arch. Gen. Psychiat. 35:176-184, 1978.
5. Cadoret, R. J., Cunningham, L., Loftus, R., and Edwards, J. Studies of adoptees from psychiatrically disturbed biological parents. II. Temperament, hyperactive, antisocial and developmental variables. J. Pediatr. 87: 301-306, 1975.
6. Christiansen, K. O. Crime in a Danish twin population. Acta Genet. Med. Gemellol. 19:323-326, 1970.
7. Cleckley, H. *The Mask of Sanity*. St. Louis: C. V. Mosby, 1950.
8. Cloninger, C. R. and Guze, S. B. Psychiatric illness and female criminality: the role of sociopathy and hysteria in the antisocial woman. Amer. J. Psychiat. 127:303-311, 1970.
9. Cloninger, C. R. and Guze, S. B. Psychiatric illness in the families of female criminals: a study of 288 first-degree relatives. Brit. J. Psychiat. 122:697-703, 1973.
10. Clouston, T. S. *Clinical Lectures on Mental Diseases*. London: Churchill, 1883.
11. Cowie, J., Cowie, V., and Slater, E. *Delinquency in Girls*. London: Humanities Press, 1968.
12. Craft, M. *Ten Studies into Psychopathic Personality*. Bristol: John Wright and Sons, 1965.
13. Crowe, R. R. The adopted offspring of women criminal offenders. Arch. Gen. Psychiat. 27:600-603, 1972.
14. Crowe, R. R. An adoption study of antisocial personality. Arch. Gen. Psychiat. 31:785-791, 1974.
15. Editorial. What becomes of the XYY male? Lancet 2:1297-1298, 1974.
16. Ehrenkranz, J., Bliss, E., and Sheard, M. H. Plasma testosterone: correlation with aggressive behavior and social dominance in man. Psychosom. Med. 36:469-475, 1974.

17. Glueck, S. and Glueck, E. *Predicting Delinquency and Crime*. Cambridge, Mass.: Harvard University Press, 1959.
18. Gottlieb, J. S., Ashby, M. C., and Knott, J. R. Primary behavior disorders and psychopathic personality. Arch. Neurol. and Psychiat. 56:381-400, 1946.
19. Guze, S. B. The role of follow-up studies: their contribution to diagnostic classification as applied to hysteria. Seminars in Psychiatry 2:392-402, 1970.
20. Guze, S. B., Goodwin, D. W., and Crane, J. B. Criminality and psychiatric disorders. Arch. Gen. Psychiat. 20:583-591, 1969.
21. Guze, S. B., Goodwin, D. W., and Crane, J. B. A psychiatric study of the wives of convicted felons: an example of assortative mating. Amer. J. Psychiat. 126:1773-1776, 1970.
22. Guze, S. B., Goodwin, D. W., and Crane, J. B. Criminal recidivism and psychiatric illness. Amer. J. Psychiat. 127:832-835, 1970.
23. Guze, S. B., Wolfgram, E. D., McKinney, J. K., and Cantwell, D. P. Psychiatric illness in the families of convicted criminals. A study of 519 first-degree relatives. Dis. Nerv. Syst. 28:651-659, 1967.
24. Guze, S. B., Woodruff, R. A., and Clayton, P. J. Hysteria and antisocial behavior: further evidence of an association. Amer. J. Psychiat. 127:957-960, 1971.
25. Guze, S. B., Woodruff, R. A., and Clayton, P. J. A study of conversion symptoms in psychiatric out-patients. Amer. J. Psychiat. 128:643-646, 1971.
26. Hare, R. D. *Psychopathy: Theory and Research*. New York: Wiley, 1970.
27. Hook, E. B. Behavioral implications of the human XYY genotype. Science 179:139-150, 1973.
28. Jonsson, G. Delinquent boys, their parents and grandparents. Acta Psychiat. Scand., Suppl. 195:43, 1967.
29. Kahn, E. *Psychopathic Personalities*. New Haven: Yale University Press, 1931.
30. Koch, J. L. A. *Leitfaden der Psychiatrie*, 2nd ed., Ravensburg: Dorn, 1889.
31. Koller, K. M. and Castanos, J. N. Family background in prison groups: a comparative study of parental deprivation. Brit. J. Psychiat. 117:371-380, 1970.
32. Kraepelin, E. *Psychiatrie*. Leipzig: J. A. Banth, 1909.
33. Kreuz, L. E. and Rose, R. M. Assessment of aggressive behavior and plasma testosterone in a young criminal population. Psychosom. Med. 34:321-332, 1972.
34. Lewis, A. Psychopathic personality: a most elusive category. Psychol. Med. 4:133-140, 1974.
35. Lunden, W. A. *Statistics on Delinquents and Delinquency*. Springfield, Ill.: C. C. Thomas, 1964.

36. Maddocks, P. D. A five-year follow-up of untreated psychopaths. Brit. J. Psychiat. 116:511-515, 1970.
37. Mawson, A. R. and Mawson, C. D. Psychopathy and arousal: a new interpretation of the psychophysiological literature. Biol. Psychiat. 12: 49-74, 1977.
38. Mednick, S. and Christiansen, K. O., *eds. Biosocial Bases of Criminal Behavior*. New York: Gardner Press, 1977.
39. Mendelson, W., Johnson, N., and Stewart, M. A. Hyperactive children as teenagers: a follow-up study. J. Nerv. Ment. Dis. 153:273-279, 1971.
40. Nielsen, J. and Henriksen, F. Incidence of chromosome aberrations among males in a Danish youth prison. Acta Psychiat. Scand. 48:87-102, 1972.
41. Prichard, J. C. *A Treatise on Insanity and Other Disorders Affecting the Mind*. London: Sherwood, Gilbert, and Piper, 1835.
42. Robins, L. N. *Deviant Children Grown Up*. Baltimore: Williams & Wilkins, 1966.
43. Robins, L. and O'Neal, P. Mortality, mobility, and crime: problem children thirty years later. Amer. Sociol. Rev. 23:162-171, 1958.
44. Rush, B. *Medical Inquiries and Observations Upon the Diseases of the Mind*. New York: Hafner, 1962.
45. Satterfield, J. H. The hyperactive child syndrome: a precursor of adult psychopathy. Proceedings of the NATO Advanced Study Institute on Psychopathic Behavior, Les Arcs, France, September 1975. In *Psychopathic Behavior*, R. D. Hare and D. Schalling (eds.). New York: Wiley, 1978.
46. Schneider, K. *Psychopathic Personalities*. London: Cassell, 1958.
47. Schulsinger, F. Psychopathy, heredity, and environment. Int. J. Ment. Health 1:190-206, 1972.
48. Shah, S. A. and Roth, L. H. Biological and psychophysiological factors in criminality. In *Handbook of Criminology*, D. Glaser (ed.). Chicago: Rand McNally, 1974.
49. Slater, E. and Cowie, V. *The Genetics of Mental Disorders*. London: Oxford University Press, 1971.
50. Woodruff, R. A., Jr., Guze, S. B., and Clayton, P. J. The medical and psychiatric implications of antisocial personality (sociopathy). Dis. Nerv. Syst. 32:712-714, 1971.

10. Brain Syndrome

Definition

Organic brain syndrome, or simply brain syndrome, is a clinical diagnosis based primarily on the mental status examination and usually applied to patients with recognizable medical and neurological disorders affecting brain structure and function. The diagnosis depends on finding impairment of orientation, memory, and other intellectual functions. Additional psychiatric symptoms may occur, including hallucinations, delusions, depression, obsessions, and personality change. Judgment is impaired. Patients may or may not be aware of the disorder.

Brain syndromes may be divided into acute and chronic forms. An acute brain syndrome is brief and presumably reversible. *Delirium* is an acute brain syndrome associated with excitement and agitation, and often with hallucinations and delusions as well. A chronic brain syndrome, or *dementia*, is often progressive and chances of recovery are limited.

Historical Background

It is not known with any certainty when the clinical picture of brain syndrome was first recognized as distinct from other psychiatric disorders. On this subject, much interesting material is presented in a recent annotated anthology of selected medical texts (23).

One of the earliest descriptions in English was provided in 1615 by a clergyman, Thomas Adams, in his treatise *Mystical Bedlam* (1). He referred to "some *mad*, that can rightly judge of the things they see, as touching *imagination and phantasie*: but for *cogitation* and *reason*, they swarve from naturale judgement. . . ."

In 1694 William Salmon (36) described in detail a case of dementia and noted that the patient was "not mad, or distracted like a man in Bedlam . . . (but) decayed in his Intellectuals."

In 1761, Giovanni Battista Morgagni, the great Italian pioneer in morphologic pathology, who first systematically correlated clinical features and course with postmortem findings, described certain areas of "hardness" in the brains of former mental patients (30). He emphasized, however, that the correlation between clinical picture and anatomical findings was not consistent.

Morgagni's work set the stage for Antoine Laurant Jessé Bayle who, in 1822, published the first systematic clinicopathologic study of paresis. In this study the clinical symptoms, including progressive dementia, were correlated with changes in brain parenchyma and meninges (5). Bayle's findings were confirmed in 1826 by Louis Florentin Calmeil (9).

Another milestone in the understanding of brain syndrome was Korsakoff's investigation of the disorder that bears his name (41). His observations, reported between 1887 and 1891, correlated a particular form of dementia manifested by extreme amnesia with lesions of the brainstem.

Over the years the accumulation of case reports and clinical experience indicated that disorientation and memory impairment were the hallmarks of a clinical syndrome seen frequently in the presence of demonstrable brain damage, systemic infections, or intoxications. But systematic investigations were infrequent. Two modern studies based upon autopsy results indicate that brain syndromes are associated with brain pathology in the majority of cases (10, 18).

Epidemiology

There have been few epidemiologic studies of the acute brain syndrome. It occurs commonly in the presence of pneumonia, systemic infections, congestive heart failure, high fever, fluid and electrolyte imbalance, stroke, the postoperative state, and intoxication with alcohol or other drugs, but the exact frequency is unknown. Reports have dealt with cases referred for psychiatric consultation because of disturbed behavior, rather than with the frequency of the syndrome as determined by systematic study.

Since vascular disease of the brain and senile dementia are two of the most common causes of chronic brain syndromes, it is not surprising that their prevalence increases with age. But epidemiologic studies of chronic brain syndrome have had serious flaws. Most have been based upon hospitalization rates; different rates related to urban versus rural status, sex, race, educational achievement, and marital status have been reported. Many authors, however, emphasize the need for caution in extrapolating from hospitalization rates to true prevalence (12, 28). A review of recent field surveys indicates inconsistent findings in regard to these same social and economic factors (12), making it clear that most such correlations can only be regarded as tentative.

Clinical Picture

The acute brain syndrome is nearly always associated with medical, surgical, or neurological disorders, or with drug intoxications. This association is so consistent that an unexplained acute brain syndrome should alert the physician to the likelihood that such a disorder exists or is developing. A patient with pneumonia, for example, will sometimes present with an acute brain syndrome hours before the other clinical findings appear.

An acute brain syndrome may vary clinically, but two features are of special diagnostic importance: disorientation and impairment of recent memory. Without at least one of these, the diagnosis can only be suspected. Other common clinical features include a depressed or fearful mood, apathy, irritability, impaired judgment, suspiciousness, delusions, hallucinations, and combative, uncooperative, or frightened behavior.

The combination of disorientation, impaired memory, suspiciousness, hallucinations, and combative or frightened behavior constitutes delirium. This is the most dramatic, clinically severe form of the acute brain syndrome. It may develop rapidly without any preceding manifestations or gradually in a patient who has been quietly confused and apathetic for many hours or days. Sometimes it may complicate a chronic state of dementia.

An acute brain syndrome may fluctuate strikingly from day to day and even from hour to hour. Some patients show a diurnal pattern with the most obvious and severe manifestations at night. They may appear normal in the morning except for haziness about the night before and yet be frankly disoriented, confused, and hallucinating that night. In some cases, the patient's mental status must be checked repeatedly to elicit disorientation or recent memory difficulty.

Disorientation may relate to time, place, or person. The first is the most common, the last the least common. Minor errors by patients who have been sick or hospitalized for some time should not receive undue emphasis. But persistent inability to recall the month or year correctly, especially if the correct answers have been offered recently, recurrent failure to identify where the patient is, or repeated inability to recall recent events correctly, are diagnostic. Because the manifestations are often more definite at night, the first indication of an acute brain syndrome may be recorded in the nurse's notes. A report of the patient mistaking the nurse for someone else, such as a neighbor or relative, or experiencing hallucinations, is sometimes ignored until the patient is frankly disoriented and combative.

An acute brain syndrome seen in a general hospital usually indicates that the patient is seriously ill physically. Available evidence suggests that when the condition interferes with nursing care or treatment or when it disturbs other patients, the prognosis is poorer than is the case for patients with similar medical illnesses matched for age, sex, and race and who do not have an acute brain syndrome (18, 19).

Many patients with dementia may present with depressive symptoms or somatic complaints such as headache, abdominal pain, and constipation. Others are brought to physicians by relatives because of temper outbursts, socially embarrassing behavior, or suspiciousness. The brain syndrome may become evident as the patient's history is elicited

Depressed patients may complain of poor memory and some studies have revealed impairment of short-term memory in many. The memory difficulty improves with remission of the depression (38). Sometimes, however, it is important to distinguish between *complaints* of memory difficulty (pseudodementia) and *actual* impairment of memory. In some middle-aged and older patients suffering from depression, the complaint of memory impairment is disproportionately greater than the degree of memory impairment noted on systematic testing, and the perceived memory difficulty subsides as the depression improves (20, 25).

The most important point about dementia is that in some cases the underlying illness is treatable (20, 42). These cases should be recognized as early as possible because recovery may be related to the duration of the dementia. Drug intoxication (barbiturates and other sedatives), hypothyroidism, pernicious anemia, paresis, subdural hematomas, benign brain tumors, and normal pressure hydrocephalus are infrequent but recognizable causes of dementia (13, 16, 24, 27, 32, 37, 39, 40). Recurrent hypoglycemia due to insulin treatment of diabetes, pancreatic islet cell tumors, or the too rapid alimentary absorption of glucose in patients who have undergone subtotal gastric resection may also lead to severe dementia (3, 4, 8). All these disorders may be treated. Chronic alcohol abuse has been associated with dementia (6, 34) separate from the Wernicke-Korsakoff syndrome, but there is doubt about the etiologic significance of this association. The association raises the possibility that, if recognized early, the condition might be reversed by abstention from further drinking. Recent work has suggested that the dementia frequently associated with chronic renal dialysis may be caused by aluminum intoxication from the water used in such great quantities during dialysis (2, 29). While probably not readily reversible, this syndrome may now be preventable.

Most cases of dementia, however, are the result of senile brain disease or of arteriosclerotic changes in the blood vessels supplying the brain (42). Studies by Roth (35) suggest that in both groups of patients there is "a fairly strict quantitative relationship . . . between the amount of intellectual deterioration . . . and the amount of cerebral damage at postmortem. In each group of disorders there are . . . threshold effects, suggesting that up to a certain limit the destruction wrought by degenerative changes can be accommodated within the reserve capacity of the brain." In arteriosclerotic dementia, the intellectual deterioration is related to the volume of brain softening; in senile dementia, to the density of senile plaques.

Recent usage indicates a preference for the term multi-infarct dementia rather than arteriosclerotic dementia. This change reflects the recognition that the dementia results from loss of brain tissue, typically with a deterioration in intellectual function proportionate to the amount lost.

Other causes of dementia, still untreatable, are the presenile brain degenerations and traumatic injuries to the brain (17).

For many years a distinction has been made between Alzheimer's disease, a presenile dementia, and senile brain disease or dementia, despite the fact that the anatomical findings (senile plaques, neurofibrillary tangles, and granulovacuolar degenerative changes) in the two groups of patients are similar. In current practice the two conditions are viewed as probably identical (43).

Recent work has suggested that dementia of the Alzheimer's type, whether presenile or senile, may be associated with loss of central cholinergic neurons in the amygdala, hippocampus, and cortex (11, 14). Similarly, there is evidence that Huntington's chorea may be associated with the loss of gamma-aminobutyric-acid-synthesizing ability in the corpus striatum (15). These studies offer the promise that in time we will be able to treat many cases of dementia which are now hopeless.

Natural History

As noted, an acute brain syndrome may occur in the course of various medical illnesses. Often it is impossible to determine the most crucial factor in a patient with simultaneous heart failure, infection, fever, and dehydration who is also receiving a variety of medications. Generally, the brain syndrome subsides as the underlying abnormalities are corrected. Sometimes, when patients have been very sick and have had a prolonged brain syndrome, many days pass after medical abnormalities are controlled before the mental picture clears. Acute brain syndromes resulting from drug intoxication or drug withdrawal (e.g., alcohol or barbiturates) nearly always subside within a few days after discontinuing the drug.

Chronic brain syndromes usually develop insidiously. The early manifestations may be subtle and only in retrospect does their significance become evident. Fatigability, moodiness, distractibility, depression, irritability, and carelessness may be present long before memory difficulty, intellectual deterioration, and disorientation can be detected. Depending upon the underlying brain disease, the dementia may either progress to total incapacity and death or stabilize for long periods (20, 43).

Complications

Faulty judgment in important decisions, inability to care for oneself, accidents, and suicide are the principal complications of brain syndromes.

One of the more difficult decisions physicians must make concerns patients with chronic brain syndromes whose behavior raises questions about their mental competence. At some point in the course of many chronic brain syndromes, the patient's confusion, forgetfulness, temper outbursts, and questionable financial dealings will lead relatives and friends to question whether he is still "competent" to handle his affairs and care for himself properly. Losing or giving away large sums of money, writing bad checks, extreme carelessness of dress, unprecedented sexual behavior such as molesting children or displaying genitals, wandering away from home and getting lost, and unpredictable temper displays may require legal action to protect the patient from his own acts and to permit extended institutionalization.

Chronic brain syndrome, complicated by secondary depression, is one of the psychiatric disorders associated with suicide risk, though it accounts for only a small portion of suicides (33).

An infrequent but disturbing feature of some cases of delirium is the risk of death from accident or suicide. Often it is not possible to tell whether the patient jumped from a window with the intention of committing suicide or fell because of confusion and fear.

Family Studies

Investigations of the familial prevalence of organic brain syndromes have been concerned primarily with specific disorders that lead to dementia, such as Huntington's chorea and senile brain disease. The genetic basis of Huntington's chorea, which is carried by an autosomal dominant gene, is established (31), and senile dementia is apparently increased, perhaps fourfold, among the relatives of index cases (26). Similarly, the familial, and often genetic, basis of certain rare neurological disorders leading to dementia is clear (31). Yet there is no evidence of any general familial predisposition to brain syndromes.

Of considerable theoretical interest, however, is the recent observation that Alzheimer's disease, Down's syndrome, and myeloproliferative disorders cluster in the same families. Coupled with the finding that changes in the brain characteristic of Alzheimer's disease and associated with a dementing illness are seen in most persons with trisomy 21 who die as they approach middle age, this familial pattern has led to the suggestion that an important common denominator may be a genetically determined defect in neuronal microtubules (21, 22).

Recent evidence (7) suggests that individuals suffering from the Wernicke-Korsakoff syndrome may have a genetic predisposition to thiamine deficiency that becomes clinically significant when they are exposed to a poor diet, a possible explanation of why only some chronic alcoholics develop the syndrome.

Differential Diagnosis

Other psychiatric conditions may be mimicked by brain syndromes: patients' anxiety attacks may suggest anxiety neurosis; low mood and apathy, an affective disorder; hallucinations and delusions, schizophrenia. The crucial question in each case is whether the patient exhibits definite disorientation or memory impairment. These mental status abnormalities are pathognomonic of a brain syndrome; they are not manifestations of an uncomplicated, so-called "functional" disorder. If a patient with another psychiatric illness develops disorientation or memory impairment, one should suspect that something else has developed: a drug reaction or medical or neurologic illness.

When a patient is unable or unwilling to cooperate in the mental status examination, an acute brain syndrome may be suspected if there has been a sudden change in his behavior, speech, or manner and if the behavioral change develops in a clinical situation that frequently predisposes to an acute brain syndrome. A definitive diagnosis must await evidence of disorientation or memory impairment; these will usually become apparent as the patient is observed carefully.

Clinical Management

Correction of the underlying medical or neurological condition, whenever possible, is the principal aim of therapy in patients with brain syndromes. At the same time, certain measures often help in the management of the brain syndrome itself. Good nursing care is important. A calm, sympathetic, reassuring approach can turn a frightened, combative patient into a quiet, cooperative one. A patient with an acute brain syndrome often misinterprets stimuli and has unpredictable emotional responses. It is important, therefore, to provide a familiar, stable, unambiguous environment for such patients. Repeated simple explanations and frequent reassurances from familiar nurses, attendants, or relatives may be helpful. Patients do better with constant light; shadows or the dark easily frightens them.

Only the smallest effective doses of drugs acting on the central nervous system should be used, because patients with a brain syndrome are frequently sensitive to these agents. Brain syndromes are, in fact, often precipitated by sedatives or hypnotics and may subside when such drugs are discontinued. No drug is entirely safe. Careful attention to dosage and mental status are more important than the particular sedative or hypnotic used.

Some patients need to be kept from harming themselves. Usually, a relative, friend, or attendant who is able to be with the patient constantly—talking to him, explaining things, reassuring him —can calm him enough to permit appropriate care without restraints on a general hospital service. When this does not work or is not possible, rather than risk having a confused and frightened patient fall out of bed or jump out of a window, transfer to the psychiatric service or physical restraint may be necessary.

If a psychiatric unit is not available or if the patient's medical condition and treatment require bed rest, a body restraint may be necessary. Obviously, a restrained patient should be watched carefully, and the previously described measures should be continued with the hope of calming him quickly, making any period of restraint brief.

References

1. Adams, T. *Mystical Bedlam, The World of Mad-Men*. London, 1615.
2. Alfrey, A. C., LeGendre, G. R., and Kaehny, W. D. The dialysis encephalopathy syndrome. N.E.J.M. 294:184-188, 1976.

3. Bale, R. N. Brain damage in diabetes mellitus. Brit. J. Psychiat. 122: 337-342, 1973.
4. Banerji, N. K. and Hurwitz, L. J. Nervous system manifestations after gastric surgery. Acta Neurol. Scand. 47:485-513, 1971.
5. Bayle, A.L.J. *Recherches sur l'arachnitis chronique*. M.D. Thesis, Paris, 1822.
6. Berglund, M., Gustafson, L., Hagberg, B., Ingvar, D. H., Nilsson, L., Risberg, J., and Sonesson, B. Cerebral dysfunction in alcoholism and presenile dementia. Acta Psychiat. Scand. 55:391-398, 1977.
7. Blass, J. P. and Gibson, G. E. Abnormality of a thiamine-requiring enzyme in patients with Wernicke-Korsakoff syndrome. N.E.J.M. 297: 1367-1370, 1977.
8. Burton, R. A. and Raskin, N. H. Alimentary (post gastrectomy) hypoglycemia. Arch. Neurol. 23:14-17, 1970.
9. Calmeil, L. F. *De la paralysie considérée chez les aliénés*. Paris, 1826.
10. Corsellis, J.A.N. *Mental Illness in the Aging Brain*. London: Oxford University Press, 1962.
11. Davies, P. and Maloney, A. J. F. Selective loss of central cholinergic neurons in Alzheimer's disease. Lancet 2:1403, 1976.
12. de Alarcón, J. Social causes and social consequences of mental illness in Old Age. In *Recent Developments in Psychogeriatrics*, D.W.K. Kay and A. Walk (eds.). Ashford, Kent: Headley Brothers, 1971.
13. Easson, W. Myxedema with psychosis. Arch. Gen. Psychiat. 14:277-283, 1966.
14. Editorial. Cholinergic involvement in senile dementia. Lancet 1:408-409, 1977.
15. Enna, S. J., Bird, E. D., Bennett, J. P., Bylund, D. B., Yamamura, H. I., Iversen, L. L., and Snyder, S. H. Huntington's chorea: Changes in neurotransmitter receptors in the brain. N.E.J.M. 294:1305-1309, 1976.
16. Gjestland, T. The Oslo study of untreated syphilis. Acta Dermato-Venereologica, Supplement 34, 1955.
17. Gronwall, D. and Wrightson, P. Cumulative effect of concussion. Lancet 2:995-997, 1975.
18. Guze, S. B. and Cantwell, D. P. The prognosis in "organic brain" syndromes. Amer. J. Psychiat. 120:878-881, 1964.
19. Guze, S. B. and Daengsurisri, S. Organic brain syndromes. Prognostic significance in general medical patients. Arch. Gen. Psychiat. 17:365-366, 1967.
20. Hendrie, H. C., ed. *Brain Disorders: Clinical Diagnosis and Management*. The Psychiatric Clinics of North America, Vol. 1, April 1978.
21. Heston, L. L. and Mastri, A. R. The genetics of Alzheimer's disease. Arch. Gen. Psychiat. 34:976-981, 1977.
22. Heston, L. L. Alzheimer's disease, trisomy 21, and myeloproliferative disorders: Associations suggesting a genetic diathesis. Science 196:322-323, 1977.

23. Hunter, R. and Macalpine, I. *Three Hundred Years of Psychiatry. 1535-1860.* London: Oxford University Press, 1963.
24. Jacobs, L., Conti, D., Kinkel, W. R., and Manning, E. J. "Normal-pressure" hydrocephalus: Relationship of clinical and radiographic findings to improvement following shunt surgery. J.A.M.A. 235:510-512, 1976.
25. Kahn, R. L., Zarit, S. H., Hilbert, N. M., and Niederehe, G. Memory complaint and impairment in the aged. Arch. Gen. Psychiat. 32:1569-1573, 1975.
26. Larsson, T., Sjögren, T., and Jacobson, G. Senile dementia. Acta Psychiat., Suppl. 167, 1963.
27. Leading Article. Communicating hydrocephalus. Lancet 2:1011-1012, 1977.
28. Locke, B. Z., Kramer, M., and Pasamanick, B. Mental disorders of the senium at mid-century: first admissions to Ohio state public mental hospitals. Amer. J. Pub. Hlth. 50:998-1012, 1960.
29. McDermott, J. R., Smith, A. I., Ward, M. K., Parkinson, I. S., and Kerr, D. N. S. Brain-aluminium concentration in dialysis encephalopathy. Lancet 1:901-904, 1978.
30. Morgagni, G. B. *The Seats and Causes of Diseases Investigated by Anatomy.* Venice, 1761. Transl. by B. Alexander, London: Millar *et al.*, 1769.
31. Pratt, R.T.C. *The Genetics of Neurological Disorders.* New York: Oxford University Press, 1967.
32. Rice, E. and Gendelman, S. Psychiatric aspects of normal pressure hydrocephalus. J.A.M.A. 223:409-412, 1973.
33. Robins, E., Murphy, G. E., Wilkinson, R. H., Jr., Gassner, S., and Kayes, J. Some clinical considerations in the prevention of suicide based on a study of 134 successful suicides. Amer. J. Pub. Hlth. 49:888-899, 1959.
34. Ron, M. A. Brain damage in chronic alcoholism: A neuropathological, neuroradiological and psychological review. Psychol. Med. 7:103-112, 1977.
35. Roth, M. Classification and etiology in mental disorders of old age. In *Recent Developments in Psychogeriatrics,* D.W.K. Kay and A. Walk (eds.). Ashford, Kent: Headley Brothers, 1971.
36. Salmon, W. *Iatrica: Sen Praxis Medendi. The Practice of Curing Disease,* 3rd ed. London: Rolls, 1694.
37. Smith, C. K., Barish, J., Correa, J., and Williams, R. H. Psychiatric disturbance in endocrinologic disease. Psychosom. Med. 34:69-86, 1972.
38. Sternberg, D. E. and Jarvik, M. E. Memory functions in depression. Arch. Gen. Psychiat. 33:219-224, 1976.
39. Strachan, R. and Henderson, J. Psychiatric syndromes due to avitaminosis B_{12} with normal blood and marrow. Quart. J. Med. 34:303-317, 1965.

40. Trimble, M. R. and Reynolds, E. H. Anticonvulsant drugs and mental symptoms: A review. Psychol. Med. 6:169-178, 1976.
41. Victor, M., Adams, R. D., and Collins, G. H. *The Wernicke-Korsakoff Syndrome*. Philadelphia: F. A. Davis, 1971.
42. Victoratos, G. C., Lenman, J. A. R., and Herzberg, L. Neurological investigation of dementia. Brit. J. Psychiat. 130:131-133, 1977.
43. Wells, C. E. Chronic brain disease: An overview. Amer. J. Psychiat. 135:1-12, 1978.

11. Anorexia Nervosa

Definition

Anorexia nervosa is characterized by peculiar attitudes toward eating and weight that lead to obsessive refusal to eat, profound weight loss, and, when the disorder occurs among girls, persistent amenorrhea.

Historical Background

In 1689 Richard Morton published a monograph entitled "Phthisiologia or A Treatise of Consumptions." One of the early chapters in this monograph, called "Nervous Phthisis," contains case histories of the illness we recognize today as anorexia nervosa. A lengthy example follows:

> Mr Duke's Daughter in S. Mary Axe, in the Year 1684 and the Eighteenth Year of her Age, in the Month of July fell into a total Suppression of her Monthly Courses from a multitude of Cares and Passions of her Mind, but without any Symptoms of the Green-Sickness following upon it. From which time her Appetite began to abate, and her Digestion to be bad; her Flesh also began to be flaccid and loose, and her Looks pale, with other symptoms usual in Universal Consumption of the Habit of the Body and by the extreme and memorable cold weather which happened the Winter following, this Consumption did seem to be not a little improved; for that she was wont by her studying at Night, and continual poring upon Books, to expose herself both Day and Night to the Injuries of the Air, which was at that time extremely cold, not without some manifest Prejudice to the System of her Nerves. The Spring following, by the Prescription of some Empirik, she took a Vomit, and after that I know not what Steel Medicine, but without any Advantage. So from that time loathing all sorts of Medicaments, she wholly neglected the care of herself for two full Years, till at last being brought to the last degree of Marasmus, or

Consumption, and thereupon subject to frequent Fainting-Fitts, she apply'd herself to me for Advice.

I do not remember that I did ever in all my practice see one, that was conversant with the Living so much wasted with the greatest degree of Consumption, (like a Skeleton only clad with Skin) yet there was no Fever, but on the contrary a Coldness of the whole Body; no cough, or Difficulty of Breathing nor an appearance of any other distemper of the Lungs, or of any other Entrail; No Looseness, or any other sign of a Colliquation, or Preternatural Expence of the Nutritious Juices. Only her Appetite was diminished, and her Digestion uneasy, with Fainting-Fitts, which did frequently return upon her. Which symptoms I did endeavor to relieve by the outward Application of Aromatick Bags made to the Region of the Stomach, and by Stomach-Plaisters, as also by the internal use of bitter Medicines, Chalybeates, and Juleps made of Cephalick and Antihysterick Waters, sufficiently impregnated with Spirit of Salt Armoniack, and Tincture of Castor, and other things of that Nature. Upon the use of which she seemed to be much better; but being quickly tired with Medicines, she beg'd that the whole Affair might be committed again to Nature, whereupon, consuming every day more and more, she was after three Months taken with a Fainting-Fitt, and died.

Another vivid and accurate description was presented in 1908 by Dejerine and Gaukler (10).

It sometimes happens that a physician has patients—they are more apt to be women—whose appearance is truly shocking. Their eyes are brilliant. Their cheeks are hollow, and their cheek bones seem to protrude through the skin. Their withered breasts hang from the walls of their chest. Every rib stands out. Their shoulder blades appear to be loosened from their frame. Every vertebra shows through the skin. The abdominal wall sinks in below the floating ribs and forms a hollow like a basin. The thighs and the calves of their legs are reduced to a skeleton. One would say it was the picture of an immured nun, such as the old masters have portrayed. These women appear to be fifty or sixty years old. Sometimes they seem to be sustained by some unknown miracle of energy; their voices are strong and their steps firm. On the other hand, they often seem almost at the point of death, and ready to draw their last breath.

Are they tuberculous or cancerous patients, or muscular atrophies in the last stages, these women whom misery and hunger have reduced to this frightful gauntness? Nothing of the kind. Their lungs are healthy, there is no sign of any organic affection. Although they look so old they are young women, girls, sometimes children. They may belong to good families, and be surrounded by every care. These patients are what are known as mental anorexics, who, without having any physical lesions, but by the association of various troubles, all having a psychic origin, have lost a quarter, a third, and sometimes a half of their weight. The affection which has driven them to this point may have lasted months, sometimes years. Let it go on too long and death will occur, either from inanition or from secondary tuberculosis. However, it is a case of nothing but a purely psychic affection of which the mechanisms are of many kinds.

Gull and Lasègue described the syndrome independently in 1873 (11, 21). The English term for the illness has been "anorexia nervosa," the French *l'anorexie hystérique*, and the German *Pubertaetsmagersucht*. Of these, the last is probably most precise; its literal meaning is "adolescent pursuit of thinness." It is this relentless pursuit of thinness which especially distinguishes anorexia nervosa from other illnesses associated with loss of weight.

Older historical accounts of patients wasting to the point of death do not usually provide enough information to permit distinction between cases of anorexia nervosa, tuberculosis, or panhypopituitarism. Until relatively recently it was not possible to make the distinction with confidence. Some early photographs of alleged pituitary disease, illustrating markedly wasted patients, probably represent cases of anorexia nervosa (see section on differential diagnosis for further comment).

The cause of the illness is not known, though hypotheses involving endocrine, hypothalamic, and psychosocial factors abound (9, 24). One frequently invoked hypothesis is that the syndrome represents a rejection of adult sexuality with associated fears of oral impregnation.

Epidemiology

Anorexia nervosa is not a common illness. While no figures are available regarding its prevalence in the general population, on the basis of data from three separate community psychiatric case registers, in Scotland, England, and the United States, the average annual incidence appears to be low, in the range of one case per 100,000 population (8, 18). The Maudsley Hospital in London admitted 38 patients over a twenty-year period (17). Most large teaching hospitals admit several cases each year.

Anorexia nervosa occurs much more frequently in girls than in boys. Probably 90 percent of cases are girls. Obviously, if amenorrhea is required for the diagnosis, the disorder will be limited to females. Some authors believe anorexia nervosa is mainly an illness of middle-class and upper-class girls, but there are no controlled data to support this hypothesis. Anorexia nervosa appears to be rare in blacks.

Clinical Picture

The syndrome typically begins with concern about mild obesity, followed by negative attitudes toward eating. A disgust for food that is far stronger than hunger develops. As weight loss progresses, patients may lose their hunger. However thin, they still consider themselves fat and continue to lose weight. These patients may lose so much weight that they resemble survivors of concentration camps, but with several differences. Patients with anorexia nervosa are usually alert and cheerful. In addition, they may be hyperactive. They often engage in strenuous exercise, sometimes in an open effort to keep from gaining weight.

From the onset of the illness odd behavior relating to food may be seen. Patients may gorge themselves (bulimia), then induce vomiting voluntarily. While starving themselves, they may hoard food secretly or throw it away. To reduce weight, they may abuse laxatives, enemas, and diuretics.

Amenorrhea may begin before, with, or after the disturbance of appetite. It is present in most cases. A few patients develop anorexia nervosa after they have had the experience of motherhood, indicating that an undeveloped reproductive system is not always present. Other physical findings are bradycardia and lanugo (soft, downy, body hair).

Physiologic differences between patients with anorexia nervosa and others have been noted (23). Most investigators believe that starvation produces these abnormalities, which include an abnormal glucose tolerance curve, increased serum cholesterol, increased serum carotene levels, diminished urinary 17-ketosteroids, estrogens, and gonadotropins, and low basal metabolic rate (9). A striking "immaturity" in the pattern of luteinizing hormone secretion has been described in which the patients' hormone functioning resembles that of prepubertal girls, but returns to normal after remission of the anorexia nervosa (4, 16). Male anorexia nervosa patients are reported to have low testosterone levels (2).

Many reports suggest an association between anorexia nervosa and Turner's syndrome or other congenital gonadal dysgenesis (12, 20), but the data are still not conclusive (27).

Natural History

There has been disagreement about whether anorexia nervosa is a specific illness or a manifestation of other illnesses (17). However, if patients who have a preexisting psychiatric illness other than anorexia nervosa are separated from those whose history begins with the symptoms of anorexia nervosa, a pure group can be isolated (19).

The age of onset ranges from prepuberty to young adulthood, with the mean in the midteens (28). Premorbidly, patients with anorexia nervosa tend to be shy and introverted (9). A history of early feeding difficulties is common, as is a history of obsessional traits (9). The onset may be abrupt. There is one recorded case of an interval of six months from onset to the time of death (17). The illness may involve one lengthy episode lasting many months or years or it may be marked by remissions and exacerbations.

In one follow-up study, full recovery occurred in half the patients. Other patients had persistent difficulties, even when the problem of initial massive weight loss was resolved. These included menstrual dysfunction, sexual maladjustment, large weight fluctuations, and disturbed appetite (17). When full recovery occurs, it is usually within three years of the onset (9). Depressive symptoms may be common at follow-up (6), and occasional patients describe previous periods of anorexia nervosa so as to make them sound like episodes of depression.

Sometimes the illness is associated with possible "precipitating" events such as the death of a relative or a broken engagement (17). On the other hand, many patients (50 percent in one study) can give no reason for the onset of their dieting (9).

A better prognosis appears to be related to earlier age of onset and greater educational achievement. A poorer prognosis appears to be related to later age of onset, longer duration of illness, disturbed relationship with parents, vomiting and laxative abuse, and the severity of obsessionality and depressive symptoms (1, 13, 22, 26).

The extent of behavioral disturbance is not related to outcome. Thus, a patient who is adamant in her refusal to eat is no more likely to have a poor prognosis than one who cooperates (9).

Though the immediate response to treatment may be good, premature death occurs in up to 10 or 15 percent of cases hospitalized psychiatrically; sometimes patients die a few years after the onset of their illness. In one series, there was a 5 percent mortality within four years (22). Thus, anorexia nervosa should not be regarded lightly. When death occurs, the causes are starvation and its complications.

Complications

The most obvious complication of anorexia nervosa is death from starvation.

Patients with anorexia nervosa apparently develop psychoses no more often than do persons in the general population (9).

Family Studies

Some clinicians say that anorexia patients have dominating mothers and passive fathers (19), but others disagree, finding neither a single personality pattern among parents nor a single pattern of interaction among family members (9). Close relatives of patients with anorexia nervosa do not have an increased prevalence of schizophrenia (17), but the findings concerning familial affective disorders are contradictory (6, 17). There is evidence of increased parental "neurosis" (9, 17, 19), but anorexia nervosa is rare, though in one study (26) an increased prevalence among sisters was found. In another study (14), an increased familial prevalence of alcoholism was noted. At least three pairs of monozygotic twins have been reported: two concordant and one discordant (12).

Differential Diagnosis

Anorexia nervosa is characterized by unceasing pursuit of thinness and should not be confused with weight loss occurring in the course of illnesses such as depression or schizophrenia.

Starvation, when it has causes other than anorexia nervosa, is usually accompanied by apathy and inactivity rather than by the alertness and relative hyperactivity characteristic of anorexia nervosa.

Patients with anorexia nervosa and panhypopituitarism have low levels of urinary gonadotrophins, but they are not as consistently low in the former as in the latter (17). Hypopituitarism is seldom associated with the severe cachexia of anorexia nervosa or the strikingly high level of physical activity.

Clinical Management

Treatment of patients with anorexia nervosa is far from satisfactory, and there is no agreement about the best form. Some patients require constant observation on a locked psychiatric floor and tube feeding. Others have been successfully treated with phenothiazines (7). Quite recently, techniques of behavior modification have been used with reported success (3, 25). It is too early in the course of investigations of the treatment of anorexia nervosa by methods based on learning theory to evaluate their comparative usefulness.

References

1. Beumont, P. J. V., George, G. C. W., and Smart, D. E. "Dieters" and "vomiters and purgers" in anorexia nervosa. Psychol. Med. 6:617-622, 1976.
2. Beumont, P. J. V., Veardwood, C. J., and Russell, G. F. M. The occurrence of the syndrome of anorexia nervosa in male subjects. Psychol. Med. 2:216-231, 1972.
3. Blinder, B. J., Freeman, D. M. A., and Stunkard, A. J. Behavior therapy of anorexia nervosa: effectiveness of activity as a reinforcer of weight gain. Amer. J. Psychiat. *126*:1093-1099, 1970.
4. Boyar, R. M., Katz, J., Finklestein, J. W., Kapen, S., Wiener, H., Weitzman, E. D., and Hellman, L. Anorexia nervosa: immaturity of the 24-hour luteinizing hormone secretory pattern. N.E.J.M. *291*:861-865, 1974.
5. Bruch, H. Anorexia nervosa and its differential diagnosis. J. Nerv. Ment. Dis. *141*:555-566, 1965.
6. Cantwell, D. P., Sturzenberger, S., Burroughs, J., Salkin, B., and Green, J. K. Anorexia nervosa: an affective disorder? Arch. Gen. Psychiat. 34: 1087-1093, 1977.
7. Crisp, A. H. A treatment regimen for anorexia nervosa. Brit. J. Psychiat. *112*:505, 1966.
8. Crisp, A. H., Palmer, R. L., and Kalucy, R. S. How common is anorexia nervosa? A prevalence study. Brit. J. Psychiat. *128*:549-554, 1976.
9. Dally, P. *Anorexia Nervosa*. New York: Grune and Stratton, 1969.
10. Dejerine, J. and Gauckler, E. La réeducation des faux gastropathies. Presse méd. *16*:225, 1908.
11. Gull, W. W. Anorexia nervosa (apepsia hysterica). Brit. Med. J. 2:527, 1873.
12. Halmi, K. and Brodland, G. Monozygotic twins concordant and discordant for anorexia nervosa. Psychol. Med. 3:521-524, 1973.
13. Halmi, K., Brodland, G., and Loney, J. Prognosis in anorexia nervosa. An. Int. Med. 78:907-909, 1973.
14. Halmi, K. A. and Loney, J. Familial alcoholism in anorexia nervosa. Brit. J. Psychiat. *123*:53-54, 1973.
15. Halmi, K. A. and Rigas, C. Urogenital malformations associated with anorexia nervosa. Brit. J. Psychiat. *122*:79-81, 1973.
16. Kanis, J. A., Brown, P., Fitzpatrick, K., Hibbert, D. J., Horn, D. B.,

Nairn, I. M., Shirling, D., Strong, J. A., and Walton, H. J. Anorexia nervosa: a clinical, psychiatric, and laboratory study. Quart. J. Med. 43: 321-338, 1974.

17. Kay, D. W. and Leigh, D. The natural history, treatment and prognosis of anorexia nervosa based on a study of 38 patients. J. Ment. Sci. 100:411-431, 1954.
18. Kendell, R. E., Hall, D. J., Hailey, A., and Babigian, H. M. The epidemiology of anorexia nervosa. Psychol. Med. 3:200-203, 1973.
19. King, A. Primary and secondary anorexia nervosa syndromes. Brit. J. Psychiat. 109:470, 1963.
20. Kron, L., Katz, J. L., Gorznski, G., and Wiener, H. Anorexia nervosa and gonadal dysgenesis. Arch. Gen. Psychiat. 34:332-335, 1977.
21. Lasègue, E. C. De l'anorexia hystérique. Arch Gen. Med. 21:385, 1873.
22. Morgan, H. G. and Russell, G. F. M. Value of family background and clinical features as predictors of long-term outcome in anorexia nervosa: four year follow-up study of 41 patients. Psychol. Med. 5:355-371, 1975.
23. Pops, M. A. and Schwabe, A. D. Hypercarotenemia in anorexia nervosa. J.A.M.A. 205:533-534, 1968.
24. Russell, G. F. M. Metabolic aspects of anorexia nervosa. Proc. Roy. Soc. Med. 58:811-814, 1965.
25. Stunkard, A. New therapies for the eating disorders. Arch. Gen. Psychiat. 26:391-398, 1972.
26. Theander, S. Anorexia nervosa: a psychiatric investigation of 94 female patients. Acta Psychiat. Scand. Suppl. 214, 1970.
27. Wålinder, J. and Mellbin, G. Karyotyping of women with anorexia nervosa. Brit. J. Psychiat. 130:48-49, 1977.
28. Warren, W. A study of anorexia nervosa in young girls. J. Child Psychol. Psychiat. 9:27-40, 1968.
29. Ziegler, R. and Sours, J. A. A naturalistic study of patients with anorexia nervosa admitted to a university medical center. Compr. Psychiat: 9:644-651, 1968.

12. Sexual Problems

Introduction

Although medical interest in sexual problems dates at least to the time of Hippocrates, they were not always considered appropriate for scientific investigation. Concerning the literature on sex, Kinsey (20, 21) remarked, "From the dawn of human history . . . men have left a record of their sexual activities and their thinking about sex. The printed literature is tremendous, and the other material is inexhaustible. For bulk, the literature cannot be surpassed in many other fields; for scholarship, esthetic merit, or scientific validity it is of such mixed quality that it is difficult to separate the kernel from the chaff, and still more difficult to maintain any perspective during its perusal. It is, at once, an interesting reflection of man's absorbing interest in sex, and his astounding ignorance of it; his desire to know and his unwillingness to face the facts. . . ."

In recent years, there have been apparent changes in attitudes toward sex, and probably in sexual behavior as well. Concerning the limits of normalcy and the issues of what is deviant there is less consensus than there once was (8, 10). Nonetheless, physicians still find that patients bring sexual problems to medical attention. *Patients as well as physicians* define these problems as appropriate for the attention of doctors.

Physicians are confronted with patients who have many sexual problems: impotence, frigidity, fetishism, pedophilia, exhibitionism, homosexuality, transsexualism (26, 27). Only two, homosexuality and transsexualism, are included here. They have been studied extensively and illustrate the application of follow-up and family studies to such conditions.

Homosexuality

Homosexuality involves sexual preference for and sexual activity with members of the same sex.

While homosexuality is known to have existed in ancient civilizations, it is not clear how prevalent it was. Nor is it known now how widespread it may be in other societies.

The Kinsey epidemiological studies of the late 1940's indicated that homosexual experience is a common, passing concomitant of adolescence in men, and also, less frequently, in women. The Kinsey data also provide one of the few estimates of the prevalence of exclusive homosexuality among adults. About 5 percent of adult men and a smaller percentage of adult women reportedly were homosexual.

Homosexual behavior is similar in many ways to heterosexual behavior. Kissing, fondling, mutual masturbation, oral-genital play, and (among men) anal intercourse may occur. Both male and female homosexuals usually report that mutual masturbation was their first form of homosexual behavior (33). Older homosexual men engage chiefly in oral-genital and anal intercourse, while homosexual women tend to continue to prefer mutual masturbation with oral-genital behavior next most common. Most homosexual men and women alternate in "active" and "passive" roles. These terms are ambiguous, but, in general, active indicates taking an aggressive role to initiate sexual acts; passive implies a submissive role (24, 29, 30).

Many studies of homosexuality (usually of males) have involved special groups of subjects, such as prisoners—an obvious source of bias (13). Recently, studies of members of homophile organizations have appeared. These are among the most extensive and complete studies available. They have been criticized as not representing homosexuality in "typical" form; however, such studies give us at least a partial view of the natural history of homosexuality (19, 29, 30, 31, 32, 33).

Both homosexual men and women often show a childhood preference for play that most adults would consider typical for the opposite sex. This "effeminacy" in boys and "tomboyishness" in girls is frequently transitory—present in childhood but not in adulthood. Effeminacy in adult male homosexuals and masculinity in adult female homosexuals may be somewhat more common than among heterosexuals, but many homosexuals are not inappropriately masculine or effeminate (33).

Most homosexuals report homosexual fantasies, attachments, and sexual experiences early in adolescence—roughly parallel to the development of heterosexual fantasies, attachments, and experiences among other adolescents. Boys generally engage in homosexual behavior at a somewhat earlier age than girls (29, 30).

Most homosexual men and women have had heterosexual psychologic responses, but not persistently. These responses are transient fantasies, dreams, or experiences occurring during adolescence, not consolidating as a dominant pattern of sexual behavior. Homosexual men and women often date persons of the opposite sex during adolescence and their early twenties, even experimenting with heterosexual intercourse. This is apparently a time of role testing, often associated with psychological turmoil (28, 29, 30, 33). Subsequently, most homosexual men and women settle into patterns of predominant or exclusive homosexuality (33). Such predominant or exclusive homosexuality would be rated as 5 or 6 on the Kinsey scale of the continuum of heterosexual-homosexual adjustment (Table 1).

The pattern of homosexual behavior which develops in men and women is different. Homosexual women are likely to have prolonged relationships and relatively few partners (19, 24, 29). Homosexual men are more likely to report many partners and many casual "one-night stands," frequently the result of pick-ups in streets, bars, lavatories, or other public places (30).

In terms of social variables, homosexuals and heterosexuals differ minimally (16, 29, 30, 33). There is no evidence that homosexuals differ from the general population in terms of educational or occu-

Table 1. Heterosexual-Homosexual Rating Scale

0. Exclusively heterosexual. No homosexual.
1. Predominantly heterosexual. Incidentally homosexual.
2. Predominantly heterosexual. More than incidentally homosexual.
3. Equally heterosexual and homosexual.
4. Predominantly homosexual. More than incidentally heterosexual.
5. Predominantly homosexual. Incidentally heterosexual.
6. Exclusively homosexual. No heterosexual.

From Kinsey *et al.* (20, 21).

pational achievement. Some authors suggest that homosexuals are equally as well "adjusted" in our society as heterosexuals (16, 34). However, there is evidence that both homosexual men and women are at relatively higher risk for depression, suicide attempts, and alcohol or drug abuse (31, 32).

While most homosexuals are never psychiatrically hospitalized, psychiatrists do see homosexuals (28, 33). Depression may be the most common reason that homosexuals seek psychiatric attention. Some homosexuals seek medical attention with the hope of achieving a change of sexual orientation, but most come for other reasons (24, 28, 33).

The families of homosexuals have been studied extensively, usually indirectly through patients' retrospective reports. Hostile and negative relationships with the parent of the same sex are frequently reported. Such relationships could be the result, rather than cause of homosexuality. There is little substantial evidence that any particular family structure is responsible for producing homosexuality (18, 33).

Evidence of hormonal differences between homosexuals and controls has been presented (6, 9, 22, 23), but contradictory findings have also been reported (3, 17). It is fair to say that although much effort has been expended in studying endocrine function in sexuality, our understanding of the relationship between hormones and human sexual behavior is still unsatisfactory (2).

The differential diagnosis of homosexuality is usually not a problem, though some effeminate homosexuals who cross-dress (usually men wearing women's clothes) may be confused with transvestites or transsexuals.

Transvestites are usually heterosexual men. They achieve sexual arousal from dressing partially or completely as women, often with masturbation. Many transvestites cross-dress only in private.

Effeminate homosexuals who cross-dress often do so in public. Here, the act of cross-dressing itself is not as much the source of arousal as the masquerade is, sometimes with subsequent homosexual encounter.

Transsexuals (see below) do not seek arousal in cross-dressing; instead they seek the role of a woman (in the case of male transsexuals). The object of the male transsexual is to *be* a woman, rather than *act* like a woman.

The treatment of homosexuality depends on the presenting problem. If the patient does not wish to change his homosexual orientation, and most do not, it is probably not wise to attempt such change (19, 33). Even if the patient does wish to change his sexual orientation, no one therapeutic measure has proved consistently effective. Reports of success in changing sexual orientation by means of psychotherapy come from small, highly selected, and highly motivated groups of patients (33). There have been some reports of greater than usual success by means of aversion therapy (negative reinforcement), but these reports are preliminary and have not been reproduced on a large scale (25).

The treatment of homosexuality is usually supportive, often directed at the presenting complaints of depression or of problems with alcohol or other drugs.

Transsexualism

The term transsexualism was introduced by Cauldwell to refer to persons desiring to be actual members of the opposite sex (4). Several features distinguish transsexualism as a syndrome. Transsexuals have a sense of belonging to the sex opposite to that of their anatomy, even feeling they were born into the wrong sex. They may find their sexual organs repugnant and may have a persistent desire for transformation to the opposite sex by hormonal or surgical treatment. They desire to live as permanent members of the opposite sex (38).

The prevalence of transsexualism is not known precisely. The gender identity clinic at Johns Hopkins University estimated the prevalence among men to be one per 100,000; among women, one per 400,000 (15). Walinder, gathering data from Swedish physicians, estimated that one in 40,000 men and one in 100,000 women in Sweden was transsexual (38). Hoenig and Kenna estimated that in England and Wales the prevalence was similar to that in Sweden (12).

Some transsexuals, after hormonal and surgical change, live undiscovered as members of the opposite sex. Some male transsexuals have reported relatively successful sexual adjustment, but the meaning of such reports is not entirely clear. The majority of transsexuals wish to have a permanent change of sex by whatever means available. Not all are able to achieve that goal; in fact, most are not. Even transsexuals who have not undergone hormonal or surgical change may choose to live as members of the sex opposite to that in which they were born. Some do so quietly, sometimes even holding a job successfully. The majority of such persons do not marry, and those who do rarely have a successful marriage (14).

The cross-gender identification and behavior of transsexuals usually begin in early childhood. Transsexuals and their family members can often remember that the patient acted as a member of the other sex and wished to be considered as such by age three or four (11). The transsexual's sense of certainty about being of the wrong sex is puzzling to relatives and friends. Transsexuals themselves are often at a loss to explain it (15). They may persist in asserting that they are of the wrong sex despite harsh responses from relatives (11). Male transsexuals, compared to heterosexual controls, seem to be more ignorant concerning sexual matters, have had fewer sexual experiences of all kinds, and report more adverse psychological symptoms and dysphoric affect (5).

One of the complications of transsexualism derives from such harsh responses of relatives and peers. Though transsexuals may seem impervious to criticism, they often do not lead well-adjusted lives. Cultural pressures make such a life difficult at best. It is reported that suicide attempts and attempts at self-mutilation (sometimes of the genitals) are common (15). Antisocial behavior is also frequent (14).

No single family pattern that distinguishes the families of transsexuals has been identified (11, 15).

A patient with a severe psychiatric disorder in addition to transsexualism should not be surgically transformed. Transvestites and effeminate homosexuals should not be transformed. Only carefully studied transsexuals who have lived as members of the opposite sex for months or years should come to surgery (35, 39).

Attempts to treat transsexuals with psychotherapy so that the desire to be a member of the opposite sex is removed or attenuated have not been successful (11, 15, 36). A patient judged to be transsexual should be referred to a specialized gender clinic for evaluation by experienced physicians.

The first surgical sexual transformation is attributed to Abraham (1). Surgical sexual transformation became publicized in the 1950's and gender identity clinics began to appear in the 1960's. At present, surgical transformation of the female transsexual is a relatively primitive and unsuccessful procedure; however, surgical techniques for male transsexuals have become more sophisticated and comparatively successful (7). An artificial vagina can be constructed between normally existing fascial planes. The male genitals can be amputated and an artificial vulva created with transposition of the urethra to a position approximating that of women. The most common postoperative complications are recurrent bladder infections associated with construction of a new urethral meatus, and scarring, shrinking, and stenosis of the artificially created vagina (35).

In the absence of long-term follow-up studies of transsexuals who have been surgically transformed, the effects of transformation remain controversial (37).

References

1. Abraham, F. Z. Sexualwiss. *18*:223, 1931-32.
2. Bancroft, J. Hormones and Sexual Behavior. Editorial. Psychol. Med. 7: 553-556, 1977.
3. Brodie, H. K. H., Gartrell, N., Doering, C., and Rhue, T. Plasma testosterone levels in heterosexual and homosexual men. Amer. J. Psychiat. *131*:82-83, 1974.
4. Cauldwell, D. O. Psychopathia transsexualis. Sexology *16*:274, 1949.
5. Derogatis, L. R., Meyer, J. K., and Vazquez, N. A psychological profile of the transsexual. I. The male. J. Nerv. Ment. Dis. *166*:234-254, 1978.
6. Doerr, P., Pirke, K. M., Kockott, G., and Dittmar, F. Further studies on sex hormones in male homosexuals. Arch. Gen. Psychiat. 33:611-614, 1976.
7. Edgerton, M. T. and Bull, J. Surgical construction of the vagina and labia in male transsexuals. Plastic and Reconstructive Surgery *46*:529-539, 1973.
8. Gadpaille, W. J. Research into the physiology of maleness and femaleness: Its contributions to the etiology and psychodynamics of homosexuality. Arch. Gen. Psychiat. *26*:193-206, 1972.
9. Gartrell, N. K., Loriaux, D. L., and Chase, T. N. Plasma testosterone in homosexual and heterosexual women. Amer. J. Psychiat. *134*:1117-1118, 1977.
10. Green, R. Homosexuality as a mental illness. Int. J. Psychiat. *10*:77-128, 1972.
11. Green, R. Childhood cross-gender identification. J. Nerv. Ment. Dis. *147*:500-509, 1968.
12. Hoenig, J. and Kenna, J. C. The prevalence of transsexualism in England and Wales. Brit. J. Psychiat. *124*:181-190, 1974.
13. Hemphill, R. E., Leitch, A., and Stuart, J. R. A factual study of male homosexuality. Brit. Med. J. *1*:1317-1323, 1958.
14. Hoenig, J., Kenna, J., and Yond, A. Social and economic aspects of transsexualism. Brit. J. Psychiat. *117*:163-172, 1970.
15. Hoopes, J. E., Knorr, N. J., and Wolff, S. R. Transsexualism: considerations regarding sexual reassignment. J. Nerv. Ment. Dis. *147*:510-516, 1968.
16. Hopkins, J. The lesbian personality. Brit. J. Psychiat. *115*:1433-1436, 1969.
17. James, S., Carter, R. A., and Orwin, A. Significance of androgen levels

in the aetiology and treatment of homosexuality. Psychol. Med. 7:427-429, 1977.
18. Kaye, H. E., Berl, S., Clare, J., et al. Homosexuality in women. Arch. Gen. Psychiat. 17:626-634, 1969.
19. Kenyon, F. E. Studies in female homosexuality. IV. Social and psychiatric aspects. V. Sexual development, attitudes and experience. Brit. J. Psychiat. 114:1343-1350, 1968.
20. Kinsey, A., Pomeroy, W., and Martin, C. Sexual behavior in the human male. Philadelphia: W. B. Saunders, 1948.
21. Kinsey, A., Pomeroy, W., Martin, C., and Gebhard, P. Sexual behavior in the human female. Philadelphia and London: W. B. Saunders, 1948.
22. Kolodny, R. C., Master, W. H., Hendryx, J., and Toro, G. Plasma testosterone and semen analysis in male homosexuals. N.E.J.M. 285:1170-1174, 1971.
23. Kolodny, R. C., Masters, W. H., Jacobs, L. S., Toro, G., and Daughaday, W. H. Plasma gonadotrophins and prolactin in male homosexuals. Lancet 2:18-29, 1972.
24. Loney, J. Background factors, sexual experiences, and attitudes toward treatment in two "normal" homosexual samples. J. Consult. Clin. Psychol. 38:57-65, 1972.
25. MacCulloch, M. J. and Feldman, M. P. Aversion therapy in management of 43 homosexuals. Brit. Med. J. 2:594-597, 1967.
26. Masters, W. H. and Johnson, V. E. *Human Sexual Inadequacy*. Boston: Little, Brown, 1970.
27. Mohr, J. W., Turner, R. E., and Jerry, M. B. *Pedophilia and Exhibitionism*. University of Toronto Press, 1964.
28. Roesler, T. and Deisher, R. W. Youthful male homosexuality. J.A.M.A. 219:1018-1023, 1972.
29. Saghir, M. and Robins, E. Homosexuality. I. Sexual behavior of the female homosexual. Arch. Gen. Psychiat. 20:192-201, 1969.
30. Saghir, M., Robins, E., and Walbran, B. Homosexuality. II. Sexual behavior of the male homosexual. Arch. Gen. Psychiat. 21:219-229, 1969.
31. Saghir, M. T., Robins, E., Walbran, B., and Gentry, K. Homosexuality. III. Psychiatric disorders and disability in the male homosexual. Amer. J. Psychiat. 126:1079-1086, 1970.
32. Saghir, M. T., Robins, E., Walbran, B., and Gentry, K. Homosexuality. IV. Psychiatric disorders and disability in the female homosexual. Amer. J. Psychiat. 127:147-154, 1970.
33. Saghir, M. and Robins, E. Male and female homosexuality: natural history. Compr. Psychiat. 12:503-510, 1971.
34. Siegelman, M. Adjustment of homosexual and heterosexual women. Brit. J. Psychiat. 120:477-481, 1972.
35. Stoller, R. J. A biased view of "transsexformation operations." J. Nerv. Ment. Dis. 149:312-317, 1968.
36. Stoller, R. J. The term "transvestism." Arch. Gen. Psychiat. 24:230-237, 1971.

37. Stoller, R. J. Male transsexualism: uneasiness. Amer. J. Psychiat. 130: 536-539, 1973.
38. Walinder, J. Transsexualism: Definition, prevalence and sex distribution. Acta Psychiat. Scand. Suppl. 203:255-257, 1968.
39. Wålinder, J., Lundström, B., and Thuwe, I. Prognostic factors in the assessment of male transsexuals for sex reassignment. Brit. J. Psychiat. 132:16-20, 1978.

Appendices

Preface

Psychiatrists have a medical degree, but many wonder why. They do not set bones, wield a scalpel, deliver babies. Mainly they listen. They give pills, but often without enthusiasm. Within the field and without, the attacks are frequent and avid. Psychiatrists, it is said, do not deal with diseases, but with problems in living (as if cirrhosis, for example, is not a problem in living). Every psychiatric patient is unique and should not be branded with a label (every liver also is unique). The "medical model" in psychiatry is mechanistic, dehumanizing, and should be abandoned—some say.

As may be obvious by now, we do not share this view. Because the view is popular, however, a defense of the medical model is presented in Appendix A.

The second appendix is for clinical investigators and others interested in precise diagnostic criteria. The need for standardized clinical criteria is obvious. The problem is: *which* criteria? Many investigators invent their own. The result is diagnostic anarchy, with conflicting results as logically attributable to definitional differences as to differences in the material.

In the first edition of this book, the diagnostic criteria in Appendix B had been developed at Washington University in St. Louis through follow-up studies. Their application, we felt, permitted some basis for prognosis. In this, they differed from definitions born in committees where consensus was reached by fiat, without reference to studies. A prime example then was the American Psychiatric Association Diagnostic and Statistical Manual of Mental Disorders (DSM-II), in which diagnosis was based on the "best clinical judgement and experience" of a committee and its consultants.

Since our first edition, a heartening development has occurred in psychiatry. Under the leadership of Dr. Robert Spitzer, the APA Task Force on Nomenclature and Statistics adopted an approach to classification different in one critical respect from earlier approaches. While still "born in committees," the nosologic categories were based as much as possible on systematic clinical studies, preferably of large groups, preferably longitudinal. Also, diagnostic criteria were introduced—criteria often strikingly similar to those used at Washington University.

Unlike former DSM's with their relatively vague definitions laden with causal inferences, DSM-III bypasses theory (if for no other reason, because there are so many theories) and presents, for *reporting and research purposes,* a descriptive approach to classification.

For this, the authors can only say *amen!* and high time! Appendix B now contains, not Washington University criteria, but APA criteria developed by many of America's most able clinicians and investigators.

Nevertheless—as in the first edition—the following must be said: some arbitrariness is inevitable in any classification; DSM-III is no exception. Particularly difficult is the problem of selecting cutoff points separating who "has" a disease from who has not. Diagnosis is seldom difficult when the condition is "four-plus." In all of medicine, however, the mild or atypical case produces controversy and indecision.

The criteria, finally, are for research purposes. The clinician, struggling to discover what his patient has and what can be done, should view them as guidelines, not gospel.

Appendix A
Disease in Medicine and Psychiatry

Any condition associated with discomfort, pain, disability, death, or an increased liability to these states, *regarded by physicians and the public as properly the responsibility of the medical profession*, may be considered a disease. Whether a condition is regarded as a disease is a function of many factors: social, economic, biological, etc. As a society becomes better educated and more secular, disabilities often cease to be regarded as moral or theological problems and become medical ones. Many illnesses have passed through such a transition: epilepsy, mania, various psychoses. Similar shifts may currently be taking place for alcoholism and sociopathy.

Diseases may be thought of as representing either qualitative changes from the normal or quantitative deviations from the average, though, perhaps in some ultimate philosophical sense, such differentiation may be difficult to sustain completely. Often similar conditions may appear to be the result of quantitative change in some patients and qualitative change in others. For example, many cases of mental deficiency seem to be simply those people at the low end of a normal distribution curve. Individuals with these quantitative deviations generally come from families with similar intelligence scores. Such individuals do not have recognized anatomical or biochemical abnormalities.

There are other individuals whose mental deficiency appears to represent qualitative differences from the average. Included are patients with phenylketonuria, Down's syndrome, brain damage resulting from infection or trauma, etc. In general, the intelligence among the relatives is not different from that in the general popu-

(Modified from Guze, S. B., The Need for Toughmindedness in Psychiatric Thinking, Southern Medical Journal 63:662-671, 1970.)

lation, *unless* the relatives have anatomical or biochemical deviations associated with a particular genetically transmitted disorder.

High blood pressure is another condition in which questions of quantitative versus qualitative variation arise. Some cases result from changes in kidney or endocrine function. But the cause of most hypertension is unknown and it may represent normal quantitative variation, like height, weight, or intelligence. According to this view, what is called high blood pressure refers only to the drawing of an arbitrary line at a particular point on the normal distribution curve for blood pressure. Regardless of viewpoint, however, no one doubts the medical importance of the condition.

Similar discussions are possible for conditions such as anxiety neurosis or depression. Each may be approached as manifestations of either quantitative or qualitative variation. It may turn out that some cases will be examples of the former, others examples of the latter. Evidence for an hereditary basis has been offered for both disorders though, as yet, only for depression is the evidence extensive.

The point is that whether a condition seems the result of a qualitative abnormality or represents normal quantitative variation suggests little about cause. Biological factors may be etiologically important in each, and disability or death may be increased in both. Thus, while the quantitative-qualitative variation dichotomy may be useful for dividing illnesses into categories for research or treatment purposes, its use in defining what is or is not a disease is usually inconsistent and confusing.

A hurdle to accepting the disease model in conditions such as alcoholism or sociopathy is that "voluntary" behavior is involved. This raises questions of "free will" and personal responsibility, issues which may be avoided if it is recognized that disease is a convention, and may be defined independent of cause or mechanism.

Cause

A cause may be defined as any event (A) that increases the likelihood of another event (B). Specifically, in the context of disease, anything that increases the likelihood of an illness is a cause of that illness.

Causes may be divided into three kinds: 1) necessary and sufficient, 2) necessary but not sufficient, and 3) facilitating or predisposing that are neither necessary nor sufficient.

The first kind of cause—one that is necessary and sufficient—is not frequent. Examples are those rare or unusual genes that produce disorders such as phenylketonuria, sickle cell anemia, red-green color blindness, and alkaptonuria. When the genes are present, the individual has the disease; when the genes are absent, the disease is not seen.

Infectious agents such as bacteria or viruses are examples of causes that are necessary but not sufficient. For example, the tubercle bacillus is necessary to produce tuberculosis, but exposure to the tubercle bacillus is not sufficient to cause the disease. In fact, only a small proportion of people exposed to the tubercle bacillus, as manifested by a positive tuberculin test, ever show clinical evidence of tuberculosis. Other factors that modify the virulence of the bacillus or the resistance of the host are crucial. Among these are malnutrition, alcohol abuse, perhaps genetic predisposition.

Another example of a cause that is necessary but not sufficient is alcohol. By definition, alcoholism is "caused" by the ingestion of alcohol, but not everyone who drinks becomes an alcoholic. Other factors must be operating—cultural, familial, genetic, etc.

These other factors—malnutrition, heredity, sex, race, age, other illnesses—shown to influence the likelihood of developing an infection or of becoming an alcoholic are examples of modifying or facilitating causes. They are not necessary causes because the illness is possible in their absence, and they are not sufficient causes because they cannot produce the disease in the absence of the necessary cause. Recognizing the importance of these factors may permit effective prevention or treatment even though the necessary cause is not touched. For example, improved nutrition reduces the risk of tuberculosis even if nothing is done about reducing the exposure to the tubercle bacillus.

Recognizing that only a few diseases are the result of single necessary and sufficient causes has resulted in the concept of multicausality. Sometimes this is mistaken for omnicausality, i.e., the belief that anything can cause anything. To demonstrate the interaction between several causes is difficult, and requires sophisticated study with careful controls. To demonstrate the causal role of malnutrition in the etiology of tuberculosis, it is not enough to take into consideration the effect of nutrition alone; similar exposure to the tubercle bacillus must also be assured. A minimum of four groups of subjects must be studied: one malnourished and exposed to the infectious agent, one malnourished but not exposed to the agent, one well-nourished and exposed, and the last well-nourished but not exposed. Omnicausality, however, requires no such controls. It seemingly proceeds on the premise that any plausible assumption based upon any apparent association between events is the same as demonstrating a causal connection. It leads naturally to the belief, not always made explicit, that the causal factors are different for each individual case of a given illness. Thus, if in studying one patient with schizophrenia, a cold and rejecting mother, no father at home, and a younger sibling with whom the patient is in rivalry are found, these factors are viewed as causal, even though in studying the next patient, it may be learned that he is the youngest of four children, whose mother is overprotective, and whose friendly father is a successful lawyer. In studying still another patient, it may be found that the parents are normal and that the patient is an only child, hence requiring still a different causal hypothesis.

There is, in fact, no logical necessity for insisting that there must be a necessary cause for each illness. There may be illnesses that can be produced by such a variety of causes, that no two cases result from the same causal pattern. In such a situation, however, it would be impossible to prove the causal connections in any given case.

Cause and the Experimental Approach

An association between two events A and B may be the result of 1) A causing B, 2) B causing A, 3) another event C causing both A and B, or 4) A and B being associated with other events C, D, . . . which, in turn, are caused by Z. In order to show that an association is, in fact, a causal one, experiments are necessary: nature's or man's. The essence of the experimental approach is that one of the associated events is varied to study its effect on the other events. In the planned experiment, whether in the laboratory or in the field, such variation is controlled, usually easily defined, and relatively uncomplicated. Unfortunately, such deliberate experimentation is often not possible, particularly when dealing with man. Instead of such man-made experimentation, it is necessary to look for nature's experiments. Those situations in which the appropriate variation occurs naturally must be identified so that the effects of the variation may be measured. These natural experiments are not likely to be as precise, as well controlled, or as clear-cut as planned experiments. Yet for the solution of many problems, the study of nature's experiment is the first step.

For some problems, such experiments of nature may be the best available despite their shortcomings. For example, it is not possible to carry out a deliberate experiment in man to study the effect of cigarette smoking on the development of lung cancer or coronary heart disease. The control needed to maintain the necessary variation in smoking over a long enough time is not feasible. Instead it is necessary to study the effects of spontaneously occurring variations in cigarette smoking. This is not as satisfactory, but it is the best that can be done, except for studying the effects of cigarette smoke and other cigarette products upon animal tissues. The increase in lung cancer associated with cigarette smoking can be confirmed indirectly by studying the effect of reducing, through education, the amount of cigarette smoking.

Similar problems exist in psychiatry: for example, attempts to study the effects of childhood deprivation on adult personality and mental health. No one would propose a deliberate experiment even though it is important to know the results of such experiences. Instead it is necessary to make comparisons between people who have had a particular childhood experience and people who have not. In such studies, all other variation must be controlled for; i.e., the "experimental" and control groups must be selected so as to match as closely as possible on all other variables that might influence adult personality and mental health. Thus, as an illustration, they should be matched as to sex, race, age, education, ethnic background, economic status, family history of illness, etc. In other words, the groups should be selected so that the only known difference between them is the particular childhood experience. To do this is obviously very difficult, and that is why so little good work has been done along these lines. But without such controlled evaluations of nature's experiments, and in the continued absence of planned experiments, questions about causality, the effects of treatment, or prognosis *cannot* be answered.

Family-Genetic Studies

One of the most important and controversial questions about psychiatric disorders is whether they are hereditary. Nearly every study of the common psychiatric conditions, including schizophrenia, depression, mania, anxiety neurosis, hysteria, alcoholism, sociopathy, and mental deficiency, indicates that each of these conditions runs in families. Such familial patterns can be the result of similar environments, similar genetic predispositions, or both.

The study of identical and fraternal twins is the classical method for measuring the relative roles of heredity and environment. Identical twins have identical assortments of genes while fraternal twins share identical genes only to the same extent as other same-sexed siblings. Comparisons of concordance rates between identical twins, same-sexed fraternal twins, and non-twin same-sexed siblings can make possible an estimate of the influence of heredity on a given trait or condition, *if* it is assumed that the environment is the same for all the individuals. The environment, however, is never exactly the same. If it is known which environmental factors are important, it should be possible to know whether they were the same for all the individuals being studied. When it is not known which environmental factors are important, and when the total environmental influence is being considered, complete conviction about identical environments is not possible. The size of the difference in concordance rates between identical and fraternal twins, the difference in concordance rates between fraternal twins and ordinary same-sexed siblings, and the apparent similarity of the environments need to be weighed in deciding on the conclusions to be drawn from the studies. So, for example, if the concordance rates for identical twins are much greater than for fraternal twins, and if the concordance rates for fraternal twins and ordinary siblings are the same, and if there are no known gross environmental differences, most investigators will conclude that hereditary influences are significant.

What are the facts from twin studies in schizophrenia? There are at least eleven published reports from eight different countries of series of cases (3). In all except one the concordance rate for identical twins is significantly higher than the concordance rate for non-identical twins, though the absolute percentages vary from study to study. The concordance rates for identical twins varies between about three and five times the concordance rates for fraternal twins. Furthermore, the concordance rates for same-sexed fraternal twins are not significantly different from the concordance rates for ordinary same-sexed siblings. Finally, there is no evidence that schizophrenia is more common among twins than among non-twins. Thus, most investigators have concluded that twin studies provide evidence for an hereditary predisposition in schizophrenia.

The ideal study is easy to specify: a comparison of concordance rates between identical twins reared together and reared apart. No one has reported a series of such cases. There are a few case reports, however, suggesting that the concordance rate for identical twins reared apart is not significantly lower than that for identical twins reared together (6). Because of the possibly increased likelihood of identifying and reporting concordant cases, conclusions from isolated case reports must be regarded with caution.

There have been several studies of adopted children that may provide answers nearly as satisfactory as those obtainable from studies of twins reared apart. The first was a study by Heston (4) of the grown children of women hospitalized because of schizophrenia. These children were separated from their mothers within a few days of birth, because of the mother's illness and need for hospitalization. In order to eliminate any environmental familial factor possibly associated with the development of the mother's illness, only children raised without any contact with any member of the mother's family were selected for the study. These children were compared with another group of children, also separated at birth from their mothers, also without any further contact with the maternal family, but whose mothers did not suffer from schizophrenia. At follow-up, the 97 children (47 from schizophrenic mothers and 50 from control mothers) were evaluated systematically. Five of the 97 children were found to be suffering from schizophrenia as adults, and all five were children of women with schizophrenia. This finding supports the hypothesis that there is an hereditary predisposition to schizophrenia.

Other work in which adopted children were studied has been carried out in Copenhagen under the auspices, and with the financial support, of the National Institute of Mental Health. This work has been reported only in preliminary form thus far, but the results seem to indicate again that there is an hereditary predisposition to schizophrenia, since the children of schizophrenic parents, despite being raised by non-schizophrenic adoptive parents, were still likely to develop schizophrenic illnesses (5).

Sociology and Psychopathology

That psychiatric disturbances result from the effects of the social environment is so plausible that it is often difficult to get the idea critically examined. It is evident that much indeed is influenced by the environment: language, customs, religion, politics, and ethics derive from environment. Culture so profoundly influences ideas, attitudes, and behavior that it must shape personality and temperament. Yet to say this is not very useful, it is necessary to know *which* social factors, under *which* circumstances, predispose to *which* personality traits. In other words, specific associations need to be proven before causal connections between social environment and psychopathology may be asserted. It must be shown that a given psychiatric condition results from either more or less of a given environmental influence, or that it results from a particular kind of environmental influence. This again calls for controlled observations—usually of nature's experiments.

It has been shown that the proportion of patients suffering from schizophrenia who are of low socioeconomic status is greater than would be expected if social class and schizophrenia were not related. This increased prevalence of low socioeconomic status has been taken to indicate that there is something in the culture of this class of people that predisposes to schizophrenia. If this is true (see below), it is an important conclusion, because it suggests that schizophrenia may be prevented by improving the socioeconomic status of the population.

A problem in studying social class and schizophrenia is that conventional measures of social class, such as education, occupation, place of residence, and income, are themselves influenced by the schizophrenic disorder. Schizophrenia typically begins in late adolescence and early adulthood. It apparently reaches its full clinical flowering in the late twenties and early thirties; this is the average age of first hospitalization. Thus schizophrenia begins and flourishes at the time in life when advanced education and the beginnings of a career are usually taking place. The illness itself may account for at least some of the low socioeconomic status. That this is probably true may be concluded from the results of recent studies comparing the socioeconomic status of the parents of schizophrenic patients with the general population (1, 2). These two reports, one from England and the other from the United States, indicate that the socioeconomic status of the patients' parents is the same as that of the general population, showing, therefore, that schizophrenic patients are not more likely to come from lower socioeconomic homes than would be expected by chance, and that the low socioeconomic status of schizophrenic patients *is* very likely the consequence of the illness itself.

Recent work on the association between sociocultural influences and suicide is also relevant. There are striking differences in suicide rates between countries, and between different cities within countries. Such observations have led to considerable speculation about the cultural and socioeconomic context of suicide. Alleged differences in national personality and character or in the local culture of various communities have been suggested to explain the different suicide rates.

However, there are alternative explanations. For example, different cities and countries use different criteria for defining a suicide death, and comparisons must take this into account. In some communities, autopsies are infrequent, toxicologic analyses of tissues are rare, and all but the most obvious cases of suicide are termed accidental or natural deaths. In other communities with a good medical examiner system, autopsies are usual, toxicologic analyses are the rule, and all leads are pursued to determine whether or not suicide occurred. Obviously, the reported suicide rates for such different communities will not be similar. This is not to say that there are no important sociocultural differences in suicide rates; on the contrary, there probably are such differences, but they cannot be identified with certainty yet.

Treatment

The "natural history" of disease bears directly on the evaluation of treatment. Knowledge about the natural history of disease (mode and time of onset, characteristic features, course without treatment or with only symptomatic treatment) is one of the most important goals in medicine; it is essential for scientific therapeutics. Because studies of the natural history of a disorder will reveal patient characteristics (sex, age of onset, etc.) that will be associated with different clinical courses, such studies are concerned intimately with the selection of comparison groups.

Similarity of treatment and control groups can be accomplished in one of two ways. One is to assign patients so that each group contains the same number of people with each of the features known to be associated with differences in outcome. This is sometimes called a stratified sample. Each group will have the same number of women and men, the same range and average age, the same socioeconomic distribution, the same proportion with a positive family history of psychiatric illness, etc. In other words, it is necessary to set up controls for every factor known to be, or considered likely to be, associated with the outcome of a particular illness.

Another way to obtain a matched control group is to assign patients randomly in large enough numbers so that, by chance alone, there will be an equal distribution of all factors related to outcome. This method, however, while less demanding in execution, is not as likely to result in well-matched groups.

After the groups are selected, outcome criteria need to be defined. Groups may be compared in terms of cure, improvement, social adjustment, hospitalization, suicide, or persistence in treatment. Explicit standards are needed for defining these results. Bias or prejudice of the investigator must be minimized, whether for or against a particular treatment. Often a "double-blind" technique must be used. Hospitalization rates and suicide rates are relatively easy to define. Clinical improvement and social adjustment are not. In addition, methodologic considerations are made more complex by the demands of medical ethics. Under what circumstances is it permissible to treat some patients with placebos? Since systematic therapeutic studies now require the informed consent of the patients, how will this "volunteer" status affect the results? Can experimental designs be devised to compensate?

Scientifically valid therapeutic investigations are difficult to carry out. Very few published reports of treatment experiments in general medicine as well as in psychiatry are free of serious methodologic defects. As of today, there are no *proven* curative or preventive treatments for the common psychiatric disorders. The results of treatment—whether by psychotropic drugs, electroshock, psychotherapy, or psychoanalysis—are still hard to evaluate. The available treatments make possible some relief of symptoms, they provide psychological support and guidance for distressed patients and their families, and they *may* significantly modify the course of some illnesses. There is still much disagreement about the indication for particular forms of treatment, and there is no basis whatsoever for doctrinaire claims that certain forms of treatment are inherently superior to others. Assertions without supporting data derived from systematic studies should be greeted skeptically.

Tough-mindedness

It is argued that because it is difficult to measure psychological phenomena and to characterize psychiatric disturbances, tolerance is called for in assessing the validity of theories concerning etiology and claims about the effectiveness of treatment. One hears that this is a difficult field and too much should not be expected. There is no disagreement about the difficulties and the slow progress. Nevertheless, just because it is hard to make valid observations and accurate measurements, because objectivity is so elusive, because unintended error is so easy, it is necessary to be even more careful than would be necessary in a more developed field. Knowing that it is easy to form erroneous opinions when dealing with psychological phenomena, knowing that it is more difficult to eliminate or reduce observer bias in studies of psychological processes, we should demand more rather than less in the way of repeatedly demonstrated, systematic, controlled evidence.

Paradoxically, such tough-mindedness is sometimes attacked in the name of humanitarianism. It is asserted, or implied, that a critic who demands "data," who asks about controls, who insists that the burden of proof is on the affirmative, reveals thereby that he is not interested in people. The observation that the effectiveness of a particular treatment is still in doubt leads to the reply that the skeptic is antitherapeutic and hence subversive. It is even suggested that the too vigorous teaching of the skeptical viewpoint is harmful to medical students and psychiatric residents because it weakens their self-confidence and faith in what they are doing. This, in turn, is said to impair their therapeutic effectiveness. If the latter did occur, it would be unfortunate, but there is *no* evidence that this happens.

Scientific skepticism is in no way incompatible with compassion for the sick or disabled. In fact, it is the desire to help patients that causes one to be frustrated by the lack of definite knowledge about what really helps and what does not. There are few things more humanitarian than the effective use of knowledge to relieve suffering. The men who discover or develop an effective treatment for schizophrenia will further humanitarian goals far more than those who may want to help but, because they are limited by impotent methods, must fail.

The need for effective methods of treatment in psychiatry is clear. Between 10 and 15 percent of the population suffers from a clinically significant psychiatric disorder, frequently associated with great discomfort and disability, and often of long duration. Many others experience milder or more transient disturbances. The importance of the field far outstrips the available knowledge. Despite statements to the contrary, no one yet knows how to prevent schizophrenia, mania, depression, alcoholism, or hysteria; nor can one be sure just what the long-term results of treatment are. Only a great deal of careful, sophisticated, tough-minded research is likely to improve the situation.

References

1. Dunham, H. W. *Community and Schizophrenia.* Detroit: Wayne State University Press, 1965.
2. Goldberg, E. M. and Morrison, S. L. Schizophrenia and social class. Brit. J. Psychiat. 109:785-802, 1963 (Dec.).
3. Gottesman, I. I. and Shields, J. Contributions of twin studies to the perspectives on schizophrenia. In *Progress in Experimental Personality Research,* Vol. 3. New York: Academic Press, 1966.
4. Heston, L. Psychiatric disorders in foster home reared children of schizophrenic mothers. Brit. J. Psychiat. 112:819-825, 1966 (Aug.).
5. Rosenthal, D., Wender, P. H., Kety, S., Schulsinger, F., Welner, J., and Østergaard, Lisa. Schizophrenics' offspring reared in adoptive homes. J. Psychiat. Res. Suppl. 1, 1968.
6. Shields, J. *Monozygotic Twins.* London: Oxford University Press, 1962.

Appendix B
Diagnostic Criteria for Use in Psychiatric Research*

Depression

A. Dysphoric mood or loss of interest or pleasure in all or almost all usual activities and pastimes. The dysphoric mood is characterized by symptoms such as the following: depressed, sad, blue, hopeless, low, down in the dumps, irritable, worried. The disturbance must be prominent and relatively persistent but not necessarily the most dominant symptom. It does not include momentary shifts from one dysphoric mood to another dysphoric mood, e.g., anxiety to depression to anger, such as are seen in states of acute psychotic turmoil.

B. At least four of the following symptoms:
   (1) Poor appetite or weight loss or increased appetite or weight gain (change of one lb. a week or ten lbs. a year when not dieting).
   (2) Sleep difficulty or sleeping too much.
   (3) Loss of energy, fatigability, or tiredness.
   (4) Psychomotor agitation or retardation (but not mere subjective feelings of restlessness or being slowed down).
   (5) Loss of interest or pleasure in usual activities, or decrease in sexual drive (do not include if limited to a period when delusional or hallucinating).
   (6) Feelings of self-reproach or excessive or inappropriate guilt (either may be delusional).

* Adapted from the American Psychiatric Association Diagnostic and Statistical Manual of Mental Disorders, Third Edition, Draft III. Only those categories described in our book are included. The criteria in the final version of DSM-III, scheduled to appear in 1979 or 1980, should not differ substantially from those appearing here.

(7) Complaints or evidence of diminished ability to think or concentrate such as slow thinking, or indecisiveness (do not include if associated with obvious formal thought disorder).

(8) Recurrent thoughts of death or suicide, or any suicidal behavior, including thoughts of wishing to be dead.

C. A period of illness of at least one week's duration from the time of the first noticeable change in the individual's usual condition.

D. None of the following which suggests Schizophrenia is present.

(1) Delusions of being controlled or thought broadcasting, insertion, or withdrawal.

(2) Hallucinations of any type throughout the day for several days or intermittently throughout a one-week period unless all of the content is clearly related to depression or elation.

(3) Auditory hallucinations in which either a voice keeps up a running commentary on the individual's behaviors or thoughts as they occur, or two or more voices converse with each other.

(4) Delusions or hallucinations for more than one month in the absence of prominent affective (manic or depressive) symptoms (although typical depressive delusions, such as delusions of guilt, sin, poverty, nihilism, or self-deprecation or hallucinations of similar content are permitted).

(5) Preoccupation with a delusion or hallucination to the relative exclusion of other symptoms or concerns (other than delusions of guilt, sin, poverty, nihilism, or self-deprecation, or hallucinations with similar content).

(6) Marked formal thought disorder if accompanied by either blunted or inappropriate affect, delusions or hallucinations of any type, or grossly disorganized behavior.

E. Not due to any Organic Mental Disorder.

F. Not superimposed on Schizophrenia, residual subtype.

G. Excludes Simple Bereavement following loss of a loved one if all of the features are commonly seen in members of the individual's subcultural group in similar circumstances.

Mania

A. One or more distinct periods with a predominantly elevated, expansive, or irritable mood. The elevated or irritable mood must be a prominent part of the illness and relatively persistent although it may alternate with depressive mood. Do not include if mood change is apparently due to alcohol or drug intoxication.

B. If mood is elevated or expansive, at least four of the following symptom categories must be definitely present to a significant degree (five if mood is only irritable).

   (1) More active than usual—either socially, at work, sexually, or physically restless.
   (2) More talkative than usual or feels a pressure to keep talking.
   (3) Flight of ideas or subjective experience that thoughts are racing.
   (4) Inflated self-esteem (grandiosity, which may be delusional).
   (5) Decreased need for sleep.
   (6) Distractibility, i.e., attention is too easily drawn to unimportant or irrelevant external stimuli.
   (7) Excessive involvement in activities without recognizing the high potential for painful consequences, e.g., buying sprees, sexual indiscretions, foolish business investments, reckless driving.

C. The period of illness is clearly distinguished from usual functioning and the affective disturbance is sustained for at least one week (or any duration if hospitalized).

D. Has none of the following schizophrenic-like symptoms.

(Note: Because a single symptom is given such diagnostic significance, its presence should be clearly established.)

Symptoms from criterion A for Schizophrenia, which are indicative of Schizoaffective Disorder in the context of an affective syndrome:

(1) Delusions of control: Experiences his thoughts, actions, or feelings as imposed on him by some external force.

(2) Thought broadcasting: Experiences his thoughts, as they occur, as being broadcast from his head into the external world so that others can hear them.

(3) Thought insertion: Experiences thoughts, which are not his own, being inserted into his mind.

(4) Thought withdrawal: Belief that thoughts have been removed from his head, resulting in a diminished number of thoughts remaining.

(5) Auditory hallucinations in which either a voice keeps up a running commentary on the individual's behavior or thoughts as they occur, or two or more voices converse with each other.

(6) Auditory hallucinations on several occasions with content having no apparent relation to depression or elation, and not limited to one or two words.

Other symptoms that indicate Schizoaffective Disorder in the context of an affective syndrome:

(7) Preoccupation with a delusion or hallucination to the relative exclusion of other symptoms or concerns (other than delusions of guilt, sin, poverty, nihilism, or self-deprecation, or hallucinations with similar content).

(8) Delusions (or hallucinations) which were concurrent with the affective syndrome, persisting for at least one month after the complete resolution of the affective disturbance.

E. Not due to any Organic Mental Disorder.

F. Not superimposed on Schizophrenia.

Schizophrenia

A. At least one symptom from any of the following 10 symptoms must be present during an active phase of the illness (because a single symptom is given such diagnostic significance, its presence should be clearly established).

Characteristic delusions

(1) Delusions of being controlled: Experiences his thoughts, actions, or feelings as imposed on him by some external force.

(2) Thought broadcasting: Experiences his thoughts, as they occur, as being broadcast from his head into the external world so that others can hear them.

(3) Thought insertion: Experiences thoughts, which are not his own, being inserted into his mind (other than by God).

(4) Thought withdrawal: Belief that thoughts have been removed from his head, resulting in a diminished number of thoughts remaining.

(5) Other bizarre delusions (patently absurd, fantastic, or implausible).

(6) Somatic, grandiose, religious, nihilistic, or other delusions without persecutory or jealous content.

(7) Delusions of any type if accompanied by hallucinations of any type.

Characteristic hallucinations

(8) Auditory hallucinations in which either a voice keeps up a running commentary on the individual's behaviors or thoughts as they occur, or two or more voices converse with each other.

(9) Auditory hallucinations on several occasions with content having no apparent relation to depression or elation, and not limited to one or two words.

Other characteristic symptoms

(10) Either incoherence, derailment (loosening of associations), marked illogicality, or marked poverty of content of speech—if accompanied by either blunted, flat, or inappropriate affect; delusions or hallucinations; or behavior that is grossly disorganized or catatonic.

B. During the active phase of the illness, the symptoms in A must have been associated with significant impairment in two or more areas of routine daily functioning: work, social relations, self-care.

C. Chronicity: Signs of the illness must have lasted continuously for at least six months at some time during the person's life and the individual must now have some signs of the illness. The six-month period must include an active phase during which there were symptoms from A with or without a prodromal or residual phase, as defined below.

Prodromal phase: A clear deterioration in functioning not due to a primary disturbance in mood or to substance abuse, and involving at least *two* of the symptoms noted below.

Residual phase: Following the active phase of the illness, at least *two* of the symptoms noted below, not due to a primary disturbance in mood or to substance abuse.

Prodromal or Residual Symptoms: (a) social isolation or withdrawal; (b) marked impairment in role functioning as wage-earner, student, homemaker; (c) markedly eccentric, odd, or peculiar behavior (e.g., collecting garbage, talking to self in corn field or subway, hoarding food); (d) impairment in personal hygiene and grooming; (e) blunted, flat, or inappropriate affect; (f) speech that is tangential, digressive, vague, overelaborate, circumstantial, or metaphorical; (g) odd or bizarre ideation, or magical thinking, e.g., superstitiousness, clairvoyance, telepathy, "sixth sense," "others can feel my feelings," overvalued ideas, ideas of reference, or suspected delusions; (h) unusual perceptual experiences, e.g., recurrent illusions, sensing the presence of a force or person not actually present, suspected hallucinations.

D. The full depressive or manic syndrome (criteria A and B of Depressive or Manic Episode) is either not present, or if present, developed after other psychotic symptoms.
E. Not due to Organic Mental Disorder.

Panic Disorder (Anxiety Neurosis)

A. At least three panic attacks, occurring within a three-week period and occurring at times other than during marked physical exertion or a life-threatening situation, and in the absence of a physical disorder that could account for the symptoms of the anxiety. Further, these attacks do not occur only upon exposure to a circumscribed phobic stimulus.
B. The panic attacks are manifested by discrete periods of apprehension or fearfulness, with at least four of the following symptoms present during the majority of attacks:
   (1) Dyspnea
   (2) Palpitations
   (3) Chest pain or discomfort
   (4) Choking or smothering sensations
   (5) Dizziness, vertigo, or unsteady feelings
   (6) Feelings of unreality
   (7) Paresthesias

Somatization Disorder (Hysteria)

A. A dramatic, vague, and complicated medical history, in the judgment of the clinician, with some symptoms of physical sickness beginning prior to the age of 25. (This should be easily elicited by obtaining the present and past medical history by patient interview.)
B. A minimum of at least one reported manifestation in at least five of the following six groups for women and four for men.

The symptoms need to have been severe enough that the individual took medicine (other than aspirin), altered his life pattern, or saw a physician for them. The mere report of a symptom by the individual is not enough in most cases to consider it present, and physical symptoms that in the judgment of the clinician are explained by physical illness are not considered positive. On the other hand, the clinician need not obtain confirmatory evidence that the symptom was actually present, e.g., vomiting spells. Report of the symptom by the individual is sufficient if it has in some way altered his or her everyday life pattern.

Group 1: Individual believes that he or she has been sickly for most or a good part of his or her life.

Group 2: Loss of sensation, aphonia, trouble walking, any other pseudoneurologic conversion symptom (e.g., paralysis, blindness, convulsions, deafness, diplopia), or dissociative reaction (e.g., amnesia, loss of consciousness).

Group 3: Abdominal pain, vomiting spells.

Group 4: Judged by the individual as occurring more frequently or severely than in most women: dysmenorrhea, menstrual irregularity including amenorrhea and excessive bleeding.

Group 5: For the major part of the individual's life after opportunities for sexual activity: sexual indifference, uninterested in having sex, lack of pleasure during intercourse, or pain during intercourse.

Group 6: Back pain, joint pain, pain in extremities, or more headaches than most people.

Obsessional Neurosis

A. Obsessions and/or compulsions. Obsessions are recurrent, persistent ideas, thoughts, images, or impulses which are ego-alien. Compulsions are behaviors that are not experienced as the outcome of the individual's own volition, but are accompanied by a sense of subjective compulsion and a desire to resist (at least initially).

B. The individual recognizes the senselessness of the behavior.

C. The obsessions or compulsions are a significant source of distress to the individual or interfere with social or role functioning.

D. The obsessions or compulsions are not symptomatic of other psychiatric disorders.

Phobic Neurosis

A. Avoidance of the irrationally feared object or situation. If there is any element of danger in these objects or situations, it is reacted to out of proportion to reality.

B. Avoidance behavior (actual avoidance or compelling desire to avoid phobic stimulus) is a significant source of distress to the individual or interferes with social or role functioning.

C. The individual recognizes the irrational nature of his fear.

D. The phobic symptoms are not symptomatic of another mental disorder, such as Obsessional neurosis or Schizophrenia.

Alcoholism

A. Continuous or episodic use of alcohol for at least one month.

B. Social complications of alcohol use: Impairment in social or occupational functioning (e.g., arguments or difficulties with family or friends over excessive alcohol use, violent while intoxicated, missed work, fired), or legal difficulties (e.g., arrest for intoxicated behavior, traffic accidents while intoxicated).

C. Either (1) or (2):

(1) Psychological dependence: Compelling desire to use alcohol; inability to cut down or stop drinking; repeated efforts to control or reduce excess drinking by "going on

the wagon" (periods of temporary abstinence) or restriction of drinking to certain times of the day.

(2) Pathological pattern of use: Drinks nonbeverage alcohol; goes on binges (remains intoxicated throughout the day for at least 2 days); occasionally drinks a fifth of spirits (or its equivalent in wine or beer); has had two or more blackouts (amnesic periods for events occurring while intoxicated).

D. Either (1) or (2):

(1) Tolerance: Increasing amounts of alcohol required to achieve desired effect, or diminished effect with regular use of same dose.

(2) Withdrawal: Development of Alcohol Withdrawal (e.g., morning "shakes" and malaise relieved by drinking) after cessation or reduction of drinking.

Drug Dependence

A. Continuous or episodic use of drug or drugs for nonmedicinal purposes for at least one month.

B. Social complications of substance use: Impairment in social or occupational functioning (e.g., fights, loss of friends, missed work) or legal difficulties (other than due to possession, purchase, or sale of an illegal substance).

C. Either (1) or (2):

(1) Psychological dependence: Compelling desire to use drug, inability to cut down or stop use; repeated efforts to control use through periods of temporary abstinence or restriction of use to certain times of the day.

(2) Pathological pattern of use: Remains intoxicated throughout the day.

D. Either (1) or (2):

(1) Tolerance: Increasing amounts of the substance required to achieve desired effect, or diminished effect with regular use of same dose.

(2) Withdrawal: Development of withdrawal symptoms after cessation or reduction of substance use.

Antisocial Personality Disorder (Sociopathy)

A. Current age at least eighteen and a history of continuous and chronic antisocial behavior in which the rights of others are violated.

B. Onset before age fifteen as indicated by a history of two or more of the following:

(1) Truancy (positive if at least five days per year for at least two years, not including the last year of school).
(2) Expulsion from school.
(3) Delinquency (arrested or referred to juvenile court because of behavior).
(4) Running away from home overnight at least twice while living in parental or parental surrogate home.
(5) Persistent lying.
(6) Unusually early or aggressive sexual behavior.
(7) Unusually early drinking to excess, or substance abuse.
(8) Thefts.
(9) Vandalism.
(10) Required to repeat school grades or grades markedly below what would be expected on basis of estimated or known IQ.
(11) Chronic violations of rules at home and/or at school (other than truancy).

C. At least three of the following since age fifteen:

(1) Poor occupational performance over several years as shown by either (a) frequent job changes (three or more jobs in five years not accounted for by nature of job or economic or seasonal fluctuation), (b) significant unemployment (six months or more in 10 years when expected to work), (c) serious absenteeism from work (average three days or more per month—late or

absent). Note: Poor academic performance for the last few years of school may substitute for this criterion in individuals who by reason of their age or circumstance have not had an opportunity to demonstrate occupational adjustment.

(2) Three or more nontraffic arrests, or a felony conviction.

(3) Two or more divorces and/or separations (whether married or not).

(4) Repeated physical fights or assault (not required by one's job or to defend someone or oneself).

(5) Repeated thefts, whether or not caught.

(6) Illegal occupation (e.g., prostitution, pimping, selling drugs).

(7) Repeated defaulting on debts or other major financial responsibilities, such as child support.

(8) Traveling from place to place without a prearranged job or clear goal for the period of travel or clear idea when the travel would terminate.

D. No period of five years or more without antisocial behavior between age fifteen and the onset of adult antisocial behavior, when the individual was not bedridden, confined in hospital or penal institution, or under treatment.

E. Antisocial behavior is not symptomatic of either severe Mental Retardation or another psychiatric disorder.

Acute Brain Syndrome With Delirium

A. Disturbance of attention, as manifested by either:

(1) Impairment in ability to sustain attention to environmental stimuli

(2) Impairment in ability to sustain goal-directed thinking

(3) Impairment in ability to sustain goal-directed behavior

B. Disordered memory and orientation, if testing not interfered with by attention disturbance.

C. At least two of the following:

(1) Reduced wakefulness or insomnia
(2) Perceptual disturbance: simple misinterpretations, illusions, or hallucinations
(3) Increased or decreased psychomotor activity

D. Clinical features develop over a short period of time and fluctuate rapidly.

E. There is evidence from either physical examination, medical laboratory tests, or the history, of a specific organic factor that is judged to be etiologically related to the disturbance.

Dementia (Chronic Brain Syndrome)

A. A deterioration of previously acquired intellectual abilities of sufficient severity to interfere with social or occupational functioning.

B. Memory impairment.

C. At least one of the following:
(1) Impairment of abstract thinking as manifested by reduced capacity for generalizing, synthesizing, differentiating, logical reasoning, and concept formation.
(2) Impairment in judgment or impulse control.
(3) Personality change.

D. Patient does not meet the criteria for Acute Brain Syndrome, although these may be superimposed.

E. Either (1) or (2):
(1) There is evidence from either physical examination, medical laboratory tests, or the history, of a specific organic factor that is judged to be etiologically related to the disturbance.
(2) In the absence of such evidence, an organic factor necessary for the development of the syndrome can be presumed.

Anorexia Nervosa

A Refusal to maintain body weight over a minimal normal weight for age and height.

B. Weight loss of at least 25 percent of original body weight, or if under eighteen years of age, weight loss from original body weight plus projected weight gain expected on pediatric growth charts may be combined to comprise the 25 percent.

C. Disturbance of body image with inability to accurately perceive body size.

D. Intense fear of becoming obese. This fear does not diminish as weight loss progresses.

E. No known medical or psychiatric illness that would account for loss.

F. Amenorrhea (in females).

Homosexuality

A. A persistent pattern of absent or weak heterosexual arousal significantly interferes with initiating or maintaining wanted heterosexual relationships.

B. There is a sustained pattern of homosexual arousal. (According to DSM-III, the diagnosis is only applicable when the individual complains that the homosexual arousal is unwanted or a source of distress.)

Transsexualism

A. Persistent sense of discomfort and inappropriateness about one's anatomic sex.

B. Persistent wish to be rid of one's own genitals and to live as a member of the other sex.

C. The disturbance has been continuous (not limited to periods of stress) for at least two years.
D. Absence of physical intersex or genetic abnormality.
E. The disturbance is not symptomatic of another mental disorder, such as Schizophrenia.

Index